Germaine de Staël

Germaine de Staël

A POLITICAL PORTRAIT

Biancamaria Fontana

PRINCETON UNIVERSITY PRESS
PRINCETON AND OXFORD

Library of Congress Cataloging-in-Publication Data

Names: Fontana, Biancamaria, author.
Title: Germaine de Staël : a political portrait / Biancamaria Fontana.
Description: Princeton : Princeton University Press, 2016. | Includes
bibliographical references and index.
Identifiers: LCCN 2015028539 | ISBN 9780691169040
(hardback : acid-free paper)
Subjects: LCSH:, Staël Madame de (Anne-Louise-Germaine), 1766-1817. |
Staël, Madame de (Anne-Louise-Germaine), 1766-1817—Political and social
views. | Women intellectuals—France—Biography. | Intellectuals—France—
Biography. | Women political scientists—France—Biography. | Women
authors, French—18th century—Biography. | Authors, French—18th century—
Biography. | France—History—Revolution, 1789-1799. | France—Politics and
government—1789-1815. | BISAC: HISTORY / Europe / France. | POLITICAL
SCIENCE / History & Theory. | PHILOSOPHY / Political.
Classification: LCC DC146.S7 F58 2016 | DDC 944.04092—dc23
LC record available at http://lccn.loc.gov/2015028539

British Library Cataloging-in-Publication Data is available

Contents

Acknowledgments

THIS BOOK has been too long in the making, and through the years several friends and colleagues have offered me help and advice, or simply listened patiently as I rambled on about Germaine de Staël and her pressing political problems. I wish to thank Bronislaw Baczko for his encouragement at the beginning of my research, John Dunn and Bernard Manin for their continuing support, Ruth Scurr and Sylvana Tomaselli for their helpful comments on the text. I am grateful to Thierry Bornand, Antoine Chollet, Francesca Dal Degan, Ran Halévi, the late Istvan Hont, Caroline Humphrey, Béla Kapossy, Silvia Kimmeier, Rahel Kunz, Patrizia Lombardo, Michael Sonenscher, Gareth Stedman Jones, and David Womersley. I wish to thank Léonard Burnand (for the Institut Benjamin Constant) and Stéphanie Genand (for the Société des études staëliennes); finally Benjamin Tate at Princeton University Press for adopting the project and Lauren Lepow for her skillful editing.

This book is dedicated to my fellow researchers and conversationalists at the Centre Walras Pareto of the University of Lausanne.

B. F.
Lausanne, July 2015

Germaine de Staël

A Passion for Politics

"L'AVENIR N'A POINT DE PRÉCURSEURS"

Two centuries after her death in 1817, Anne-Louise-Germaine Necker de Staël-Holstein is by no means a forgotten or even a neglected author. Indeed, her personal history is such a good one that her contemporaries, and later her biographers, have narrated it over and over again, now in gossipy, now in admiring tones, insisting on the most salient—dramatic, scandalous, adventurous—anecdotes. It is the story of the banker's daughter who became one of Europe's best-connected intellectuals, or, if you prefer, that of an exceptionally talented woman, born to great wealth and privilege, who achieved a degree of public influence to which not even her social advantages would normally have entitled her. At times of great political turmoil, when the lives of so many around her were wrecked or destroyed, she succeeded in carving out an independent path for herself and in making her views heard, first by the powerful men around her, and later by the European public at large.

The story has a very distinguished cast of kings, queens, and emperors, famous generals, politicians, and ministers, as well as great writers and intellectuals. It has elegant settings, with a good selection of *hôtels particuliers*, castles, and royal palaces in Paris, Geneva, Versailles, and, further away, in London, Vienna, Stockholm, and Saint Petersburg. It offers such political intrigue, tangled love affairs, and spectacular reversals of fortune as the

French Revolution and the Napoleonic Empire managed to produce in the span of two decades. The narrative varies slightly according to the preferences and prejudices of whoever is telling it, but on the whole—short of some sensational archival discovery—it is not going to change significantly.[1]

So why return to it once again? The main reason is that the reputation Staël enjoys today as a novelist and literary critic, as the archetypal independent writer battling against despotism, is very high; on the other hand, the dimension of her life she cared most about, politics—the theory and practice of the exercise of power—has been set aside by historians as being, if not exactly irrelevant, possibly exhausted as a topic of research and a source of inspiration. Significantly, the bulk of her political writings, some of which were originally published in England as well as in France, are no longer available in English translation.

This decline of interest rests essentially on two grounds. The first is the belief that Staël's political activities were always dictated by personal and emotional motives, and therefore should be treated as a feature of her biography, a dimension in a broader life narrative. Even those historians who are prepared to credit her with genuine political vision tend to fall back on psychological stereotypes as the explanation of her actions: her devotion to her father, her ambitions for her husband or for her lovers, her loyalty to her friends. Naturally personal elements are always relevant in political life: family and professional relations, local affinities or chance encounters, individual sympathies or dislikes—all may play a role. Indeed, now that women have gained access to high office, marriage and love affairs have once again come to the forefront of public attention. But as a rule these private and relational factors are regarded as contingent, rather than essential, to political alliances and strategies, while in Staël's case they are offered as primary causes.

The second reason is the widespread view that Staël's contribution to political theory was on the whole unoriginal, as it was part of an established liberal tradition, and a mere complement to the doctrines of the men she was closest to, in particular her father, Jacques Necker, and her lover and friend Benjamin Constant. Thus, if she has been granted a (secondary) place in the pantheon of liberal thinkers, this is because she supported and promoted the same principles as her male associates: moderation, representative government, the separation of powers, and the defense of civil liberties against arbitrary rule.[2]

Clearly gender has been a crucial factor in determining both how Staël experienced politics, and the manner in which her contemporaries and posterity have judged her. Because she was a woman, she could act only by proxy, delegating her political initiatives to some male agent. This dependence she seems to have taken in her stride: if in her writings she denounced the vulnerable position of women in society, she never actually complained, publicly or privately, about being unable to stand for office, and, unlike a few of her contemporaries, she did not advocate women's suffrage. Again, because she was a woman, her political enemies added to the usual personal attacks a great many fanciful sexual allegations. Conscious of that, although she lived as freely as circumstances allowed her, she was always very careful to preserve appearances and to protect herself from scandal (she even avoided divorce, though in postrevolutionary France this had become possible and, to some extent, socially acceptable). Concern for respectability also dictated the destruction of an important part of her private papers, in particular the bulk of the correspondence with Benjamin Constant, though in this case the responsibility rests not with her but with her immediate family.[3]

As to her posthumous reputation, historians have often ridiculed her political ambitions and assumed she was always led by her "infatuation" with some more or less deserving male personality. They have also diminished her political role, downgrading her backstage canvassing to feminine intrigue, and reducing her contribution to that of a somewhat overambitious and hyperactive salon hostess.[4] The fact that she was a moderate, rather than a revolutionary militant, has not helped, since she could not be cast in the role of victim or challenger of a male-dominated system, except of course in her opposition to Bonaparte (and there too it has been suggested that her motivation was personal—the emperor's lack of admiration for herself—rather than political).[5] On the whole, while gender is obviously relevant to the shaping of Staël's career and reputation, the way in which she lived her limitations was so peculiar, so deliberately self-fashioned, that it does not lend itself to any stereotyped classification and must therefore be taken on its own terms.[6]

The main purpose of this book, then, is to provide an account of Staël's approach to politics that brings out the independence and originality of her contribution. Its main focus is the evolution of her views in the years 1789 to 1800, when she had the opportunity to take part (albeit intermittently) in French political life, and to set forth projects and strategies connected with it. It also considers her later assessments of the impact of the Revolution and of its long-term consequences. It is not intended as an exhaustive presentation of Staël's oeuvre, and touches only marginally on her best-known—and more widely studied—fictional and literary works, though naturally these do also have some political relevance.[7] Asserting the originality of Staël's contribution does not mean denying that she was close to or influenced by other thinkers who shared a set of common values; rather, it means recognizing the distinctive mark of her approach to politics, the intimate relation she established between theory and practice, her unwillingness to separate principles from their application.

It has been suggested that the protracted exile into which she was forced during the empire was at the origin of Staël's major literary achievements, as it provided her with both the opportunity and the incentive to develop her true potential as a writer.[8] But before this distinguished second life as proscribed romantic novelist and European literary celebrity, Staël lived another existence, marked by frantic activity, great hopes, and confused aspirations, an existence informed by her passionate commitment to politics.

The romantic writer Alphonse de Lamartine may have been exaggerating a little when he claimed, in his *Histoire des Girondins* (History of the Girondins), that Staël had been "breathing politics since the moment she was born."[9] It is true, however, that her introduction into the world of politics—apart from her precocious readings of classical authors on the subject—was provided very early on by the progress of her father's public career. She was only eleven in 1777 when Necker—until then a private banker with some intellectual ambitions—was appointed by Louis XVI to the newly created post of director general of finance; by the time he left this position, four years later, she had learned enough to write him an anonymous letter commenting on and praising his *Compte Rendu au Roy* (Account to the king)[10]—the provocative book unveiling the situation of the French state budget that was at the origin of his resignation. When Necker returned to the same ministerial post in 1788, Staël, at twenty-two, was already a married woman with a public status of her own: in 1786 she had become the wife of a Swedish aristocrat, Erik-Magnus de Staël-Holstein, who was granted the post of ambassador to the French court as part of the marriage settlement.[11] Yet, in spite of her many social obligations at the Swedish embassy in Paris, she would often linger on in Versailles at the end of the day, hoping for a few minutes of confidential exchange with her father. As well as being influenced by his opinions and writings, she followed very closely the ups and downs of his popularity, the attitudes of the various cabals that gravitated around the court, and the reactions of the general public. The difficult context of Necker's second ministry, his sudden dismissal and his recall by the king after the events of 14 July, gave her ample opportunity to observe the obstacles and traps that stood in the path of successful government and enduring consensus.[12]

While Staël felt passionately about her father's reputation, and never ceased to idealize him as a great, if underestimated, statesman, once the Estates-General had metamorphosed into the Constituent Assembly in the summer of 1789, the focus of her interest began to shift toward this new political environment. Accustomed to the rules of backstage court politics, Necker found it difficult to relate to the new institution he had unwittingly called into being by urging the summoning of the Estates-General and the doubling of the deputies of the Third Estate.[13] Whatever his views on the merits of parliamentary politics, the actual dynamics of a large representative assembly—with its factions, its popular speakers, its complex allegiances and voting procedures—was still an alien landscape. His inability or unwillingness to agree on a common strategy with some of the moderate leaders of the assembly—an attitude that had disastrous consequences for all concerned—was a clear indication of this unease.

On the other hand, his daughter, once faced with the assembly, found herself fully in her element: from the gallery, where she was admitted as the wife of a diplomat, she followed the debates, transmitted information and instructions, and canvassed on behalf of the different groups of moderate deputies loosely associated with the "patriot party" of reformers. Thus she not only detached herself gradually from Necker's views— by becoming reconciled to the idea of a less elitist, nonhereditary form of government—but actually developed an independent understanding of the new political forces that were taking shape under her eyes at a surprising speed.

In 1798, when the French army occupied Switzerland, Necker destroyed his daughter's letters, for fear they might be seized and used against her; other parts of their almost daily correspondence have simply been lost, and the surviving letters tell us more about their domestic affairs than about any political or intellectual issues. There is, however, sufficient evidence to suggest that once Necker retired from politics in 1790, Staël found his company, in the seclusion of the château of Coppet, increasingly depressing and tedious, especially after Mme Necker's death in 1794. "I adore my father," she once confessed; "it is a cult, but one yawns in church."[14] It was a rather natural evolution in their relationship; however, she repressed it while he was alive by displaying unfailing filial devotion, and after his death in 1804 by taking all possible opportunities to extol his memory.

The three years that elapsed from the summer of 1789 to the beginning of the Terror with the massacres of September 1792 (when she was finally forced to leave Paris for the safety of Switzerland) were probably the most exciting and intense of Staël's entire life, for the radical changes and the new perspectives they seemed to open. At the same time they marked the failure of the revolutionary project in which she had believed so passionately: the establishment in France of a constitutional monarchy modeled on the English example of 1688. It was a debacle from which she never fully recovered, so dramatic was the fall from the high hopes and empowerment of the early months of 1789 into the nightmarish scenario played out in the streets of Paris, where she searched frantically for the bodies of her friends three years later. The unexpected wreckage of a project that, in theory, was bound to succeed, combined with the horrors of persecution and violence, left an indelible mark on her subsequent understanding of the risks and limits of political action.

The mechanisms of power observed from the inside, the difficulty of stabilizing popular favor, and the opacity of public responses were all formative experiences that Staël did not share with the other influential man in her life, the Swiss writer Benjamin Constant. Constant had spent the years of the Revolution pursuing an obscure literary career away from France and its troubles. If he was ready to condemn the Jacobin dictatorship, he had no direct experience of what it had actually meant in practice, nor had he lived through the bitter disappointments of the Revolution's earlier phases.[15] His encounter with Staël in Lausanne in 1794 (their families shared a common Swiss provincial background) resulted in fifteen years or so of intellectual and political partnership, until they were finally separated by temperamental differences and by stormy emotional conflicts.[16] Together they lived through a second phase of great political hopes and expectations by becoming involved in the directorial republic of 1795–99 and in the consular one established by Bonaparte in 1800, until they were pushed into political opposition and, finally, into exile by the authoritarian character of the new regime. During this period they worked together on the architecture of the modern republic, the form of representative government best suited to the needs of large commercial nations such as postrevolutionary France; they also gave shape to the ideal of modern liberty, the aspiration of individuals to personal happiness and independence in a context where the traditional values of citizenship were increasingly undermined.

While they both contributed to the definition of what we have come to regard as the fundamental principles of modern liberalism, they did so from somewhat different perspectives. Like Staël, Constant believed that representative government was necessary to rule a particular type of society, one characterized (like modern commercial states) by an expanding economy and upward social mobility. Yet his idea of the relation between the two dimensions—socioeconomic circumstances, on the one hand, and political institutions on the other—was rather mechanical: if existing institutions failed to conform to the needs of society, history would eventually take care of them, making them dysfunctional and obsolete. He knew of course that in practice things were not so simple, that historical contexts did not fit neatly into predetermined molds; but he still preferred to concentrate on those issues that political theory was best equipped to address—constitutional models, principles, rules—rather than on the gray areas around them.[17] Significantly his ambitious attempt to venture into the analysis of social beliefs, the monumental *De la religion* (History of religion),[18] was never brought to completion. Staël for her part had seen too many "imperfect" adjustments in politics—transitions, discontinuities, frictions, exceptions, short-cuts—not to wish to understand what was behind them, even if this implied straying outside the field of political theory into the unexplored territories of mentalities, emotions, and social identities. In this respect the shift from her earlier political writings to the later essays on the history of literature followed a quite logical progression in the adjustment of her intellectual interests.

The difference in the two writers' approaches is best highlighted by their respective analysis of the nebulous sphere of popular consensus, what in the course of the eighteenth century had come to be described as "public opinion."[19] Constant believed that the existence of free public opinion was an essential condition for the success of representative government, but he treated it as an extra-constitutional dimension, upon which politics had ultimately very little control. He expressed concern about its possible evolution—arguing for example that a growing indifference to civic values could make modern societies vulnerable to new forms of despotism; but he did not carry his analysis much further, concentrating on issues such as the responsibility of rulers, and the means of control of the action of government by the citizens.[20]

Staël, on the other hand, was fascinated by and obsessed with the nature of opinion, a trait that probably represented Necker's most enduring legacy to her. From him she had acquired the belief that at the heart of any viable political regime in the modern world was the interdependence of public credit, trust, and popular consensus. Governments were tested on their capacity to satisfy the interests and expectations of the people; but their ability to do so depended to a large extent on the trust they were able to inspire both in economic and financial actors and in the public at large. At the same time the need to secure public credit compelled governments to act transparently and reliably in the people's best interest. Thus credit and trust were the pivot around which any free and stable government must turn.[21] It was an approach that placed enormous emphasis on the bond of confidence between rulers and subjects, in ways that transcended the institutional mechanisms of representation.

The elusive nature of this bond, and its mutations in the light of the revolutionary upheavals, constituted the puzzle that Staël relentlessly dismantled in her writings. This involved looking very closely at a wide range of factors: from the evolution of social aspirations and popular sentiments to the fashioning of national cultures, the impact of ideologies, and religious traditions. She also studied the evolution of political language, focusing on the popularization of political discourse, the role of deliberation in representative assemblies, the control and circulation of information, and the use of propaganda. Seen through the opaque filter of opinion, the legitimation by the people of political regimes seemed far more complex than the simple endorsement or rejection of rulers by the popular vote.

Naturally Staël's vision of politics was deeply embedded within the history of the French Revolution and the particular circumstances associated with it. However, this history contained significant, if fragmentary, anticipations of the future that has become our present: phenomena such as the shifting nature of social and national identities, the popularization of culture, the intensified scrutiny of the media, the personalization of politics, the emergence of celebrity as a dimension of leadership—all made their ghostly appearance at the time, in a way very few observers were able to recognize. It is in fact Staël's attention to these "liquid" elements in representative regimes—those factors that cannot be captured or contained within constitutional frameworks—that brings her reflection so close to our own concerns with the evolution of contemporary democracies.

CHAPTER I

Interpreting the Opinion of the Majority of the Nation (1789–91)

THE ARTICLE "A quels signes peut-on connoître quelle est l'opinion de la majorité de la nation?" (From what signs can we tell which is the opinion of the majority of the nation?)[1] appeared in the *Journal des indépendants*—a short-lived periodical edited by Jean-Baptiste Suard and Pierre Louis Lacretelle—on 16 August 1791. This was, as far as we know, Staël's first published intervention in the revolutionary debate. She may of course have published other articles at the time that have not been identified, and she did on various occasions help to draft the writings and speeches of some of her political friends, though the extent of these interventions remains conjectural.[2] "From What Signs" is, however, the only text from that period to be included in the posthumous edition of her collected works published by her son Auguste de Staël in 1820–21, the only one therefore to be acknowledged as her own.

Seen from the vantage point of the author's later writings, the article seems a very sketchy, tentative contribution to political analysis, and as such it is generally referred to only en passant (if at all) by commentators. Yet, set against the views expressed by Staël since the beginning of the Revolution, the article shows how far the twenty-five-year-old ambassadress had traveled, politically speaking, in the two years that elapsed between the opening of the Estates-General, in May 1789, and the death of the charismatic leader of the constitutional monarchists, the marquis de Mirabeau, in April 1791. In between she had witnessed a bewildering sequence of events: from Necker's triumphant return to power after 14 July to the struggle in the assembly over the royal veto in September that broke up the moderates' camp into rival groups; from the people's march on Versailles on 5–6 October to the increasing deterioration of royal authority and of Necker's own position within the government.[3]

"From What Signs" did not address any of the major constitutional issues that feature prominently in Staël's later writings. Instead it focused upon a question of immediate practical relevance: after two years of profound political upheaval, what did French public opinion really want? What were the expectations of the majority of the nation? It was a question with far-reaching implications, since it pointed at the fragmentation of the revolutionary project into rival and opposed strategies; it also exposed the growing gap between the sentiments of large sections of the French population and those political factions that claimed to speak for them, both inside and outside the Constituent Assembly.[4]

Staël had returned to Paris early in January 1791, after an absence of a few months. Early in September 1790 Necker had finally resigned his ministerial post—marking his disagreement over French government's issue of a new type of paper money, the assignats—and obtained the assembly's permission to retire to Switzerland. Though much concerned for her father's state of mind, Staël had not accompanied her parents, as she was still recovering from the birth of Auguste, the first of the two sons born of her relationship with Louis, comte de Narbonne-Lara, a grand aristocrat from her political entourage.[5] When she finally joined them in October, she found the atmosphere at the château of Coppet—a place she disliked at the best of times—unbearably gloomy, while the social events she duly attended in Geneva and Lausanne proved a poor compensation for the loss of her Parisian friends and activities, spurring her to return to the French capital. She remained in Paris only four months before further complications in her personal circumstances—this time connected with her husband's diplomatic position—forced her to return to Switzerland at the beginning of May. "From What Signs" was probably written during this period of residence in Paris: the article evokes in dramatic terms the sudden disappearance of Mirabeau—who died on 2 April—but makes no reference to the critical turning point represented by the royal family's flight to Varennes on 20–21 June.[6]

On her return to Paris Staël had found a murky and unstable situation, marked by growing unrest in the provinces and by increasingly volatile, ever-shifting political allegiances. She had also rapidly become the object of vicious attacks in the press, emanating principally, at this stage, from royalist circles: in Necker's absence the attacks focused upon her association with some prominent constitutional monarchists, in particular Charles-Maurice de Talleyrand-Périgord who, as a former bishop, attracted special blame for promoting the civil constitution of the clergy.[7] While the loss of her father's position deprived Staël of some political clout, she was free at last to act independently of him, and to develop her own position.[8] The article reflects the preoccupations that dominated this particular phase in her public engagement: the ambition to persuade the scattered constitutional monarchists to pursue a single, coherent policy; the aspiration to see the same divided, quarrelsome factions turn into something resembling an organized party; the search for a credible leadership, capable of overruling personal rivalries and of expressing the position of the moderate majority in the assembly.

THE ECLIPSE OF PUBLIC OPINION

The title of the article, with the interrogation it raises about "signs," is the first indication that something had changed very drastically in the author's perception of the nature of public opinion. Before the Revolution, Staël's scattered references to the subject echoed a set of commonplace views widely shared by eighteenth-century writers, regardless of their political or philosophical differences: while popular passions were naturally unstable, public opinion was the expression of the true interests and aspirations of the majority of the people; taken over a reasonably long period of time, it proved both clear and reliable in assessing public issues and in judging the conduct of governments. Wise, enlightened rulers should encourage and guide, rather than repress, the development of an independent opinion within the nation.[9]

This positive notion of popular judgment appeared in an enhanced form in Necker's own writings, where opinion was described as an irresistible force, a power comparable to royal authority, indeed invested with near-sovereign prerogatives. If the former minister's use of terms like "public opinion," "public spirit," or "public voice" was not always very consistent and rigorous, his practical attitude toward what he regarded as a novel phenomenon of paramount importance was clear enough. While in power, since his early experiences in government in the late 1770s, he had placed opinion at the center of his political strategy, giving a maximum of publicity to his initiatives, and adjusting his policies to popular responses. Predictably, this keen attention to public expectations and reactions—more common among today's politicians than under the Old Regime—was readily stigmatized by his critics as mere opportunism, the product of an obsessive quest for popularity.[10] For Staël it was of course the proof of her father's superior dedication to the general will and the public good: from him she had learned to regard opinion as the true source of political legitimacy, as the inspiration and the driving force behind any process of political change. In her *Lettres sur les écrits et le caractère de J.-J. Rousseau* (Letters on the writings and character of Jean-Jacques Rousseau), published for the benefit of a small circle of family and friends in 1788, she explained how, with the opening of the Estates-General that had just been summoned, France was about to obtain "by the mere progress of enlightenment" the kind of advantages that nations generally gain only "by floods of blood," that is to say, through civil violence.[11] But now, less than three years later, the leading light of opinion, guiding the nation toward progress, had turned into an opaque, uncertain force, to be watched and interpreted by its mysterious "signs," like a menacing oracle.

In the opening paragraph of "From What Signs" Staël outlined the difficulties that, in the particular context of contemporary France, stood in the way of an adequate understanding of opinion: the question of what was the opinion of the majority of the nation

> in quiet times would be easy to answer; but during an insurrection, which seems to show the emergence of a dominant opinion, things need to be considered with particular attention. It is in fact necessary to distinguish between what belongs to the moment, and what will last; what is dictated by fear, and what is inspired by reason; finally what stems from hatred of the Old Regime, and what comes from attachment to the new.[12]

In pointing at the differences between long-term and short-term reactions, Staël identified as a major obstacle to any reliable analysis the unprecedented acceleration of the process of political change. Before the Revolution, those writers who addressed the question of public opinion—Necker among them—had generally stressed the necessity of distinguishing between the durable beliefs and aspirations of society, and the immediate reactions of the public in particular circumstances. While the values and expectations of any society were bound to prove relatively stable through time, or at least to change very slowly, popular responses to particular, noteworthy events would often be extreme and passionate, while proving ephemeral and inconsequential.

The few years Staël herself had spent at the French court, after her marriage to the Swedish ambassador in 1786, had offered her ample evidence of how readily the public voice might embrace a particular cause, only to abandon it the next day, how rapidly it could make, or destroy, someone's reputation. In one of the long missives she regularly addressed to the king of Sweden Gustav III, reporting the incidents and gossip that occupied French society, she observed, "What is really cruel in this country is the fact that opinion serves only for a short time; it supports you in a fight, provided it lasts only twenty-four hours, but it deserts you, if you should need it for longer."[13] Victims of miscarriages of justice newly liberated from the Bastille, protagonists of society scandals, authors of controversial works, disgraced ministers—all suffered the same quick transition from fame to oblivion. In principle such fitful responses of the "public voice" should not be confused with the steady trend of opinion; but in practice, since the beginning of the Revolution, everything "belonged to the moment," and the only relevant time span was the short term. In another letter to Gustav III, written shortly after the events of 14 July, the young ambassadress described how "a thousand years" seemed to have gone by in the course of few weeks.[14] On another occasion, she confided despairingly to her husband that living in such uncertain and troubled times felt like "walking on quicksand."[15] Inevitably public life came to be dominated by the impressions and emotions of the moment: how could people be expected to form considered, rational judgments about anything, when every day confronted them with new upheaval and turmoil? The rapid succession of events, and the constant shifting of circumstances, turned the very notion of a united and stable "public opinion" into an ever-vanishing mirage.

The instability of French opinion was not, however, merely the consequence of the accelerated process of change, a change long overdue, and now realized too hastily; it was above all the product of widespread conflicts within French society, of divisions as deep as they were opaque and difficult to define. As

Jacques Necker had explained in 1784 in his *De l'Administration des finances de la France* (On the administration of finances of France), at times of civil discord and conflict (for example, during the religious wars) public opinion, in the proper sense of the term, did not exist, since it could not come into being. Public opinion was transparent and infallible only insofar as it represented a broad consensus, uniting the nation under its "peaceful standards."[16] For all his professed admiration for the English constitution, Necker did not think that the existence of opposed parties, characteristic of the English political system, could ever be compatible with French traditions and French temperament. In France the role of opinion must be confined to stimulating and correcting the action of the monarchy, but only on those issues that already constituted the object of a large popular consensus. Any situation where public opinion gave voice to rival political ideologies or interests could only result in disorder and instability.

However influenced by her father's views she might originally have been, by the beginning of 1789 Staël had clearly set aside any illusion of a consensual opinion. Writing to the Swedish diplomat Nils von Rosenstein in January 1789, a few months before the opening of the Estates-General, she expressed her skepticism and anxiety about the French expectation that the nation, divided as it was into a multitude of particular interests, could naturally achieve, by some unknown process, a unity of sentiment and intent: "As to the French, they are in a state of great agitation. They think public spirit can be created out of a thousand particular interests. They believe that a constitution will emerge from the shock of opposed parties. I do wish it could be so, but I tremble for the pilot [Necker], who is expected to guide them in navigating so many obstacles."[17] In such difficult circumstances, imagining opinion as a harmonious agreement could only reduce the chances of interpreting it. Bringing to light the exact nature of the divisions within the nation, acknowledging the differences that separated beliefs and interests, began to appear as the only means of identifying a viable political strategy for the future.

OUR PARTY

Having moved on from this notion of "consensual" public opinion, Staël was inclined to adopt the view that the revolutionary transformation of French society resulted from the confrontation of two main parties: "those who are for what exists already, and those who desire what would be best." The idea of two "natural" parties, supporting, respectively, stability and innovation, conservation and improvement, had its roots in those eighteenth-century moral doctrines that identified "rest" and "movement" as the two main springs of human happiness. Reacting against the classical Stoic ideal of happiness as dispassionate quietude, French writers such as Montaigne, Diderot, D'Holbach, Mably, Voltaire, and Montesquieu had variously argued that, given the instability of human passions, tranquillity and excitement were equally necessary to personal fulfillment. Human happiness derived less from the persistence of a particular emotional state than from the contrast and alternation of different ones.[18]

The original context of those arguments had been the prescription of moral and existential guidelines for individual conduct. However, as the pioneering analysis of Michel de Montaigne's *Essais* demonstrated, the perception of man's passions as fluid and unstable had obvious implications for the understanding of collective movements at times of political unrest. The stability of regimes was bound to be directly affected by "waves" of favor or hatred, enthusiasm or indifference, tranquillity or fear, that reflected, on a large scale, the impact of changing individual emotions.[19] In the *Esprit des lois* Montesquieu offered a direct application of this condition of emotional fluctuation to political analysis. In a chapter of book 19 entitled "Comment les lois peuvent contribuer à former les moeurs, les manières et le caractère d'une nation" (How laws can contribute to forming the mores, manners and character of a nation), where he returned to the model of free government set forth in book 6, he argued that the experience of political liberty was bound to unleash and excite all popular passions. Without these a free state would be "like a man who, laid low by disease, has no passions because he has no strength." Normally these unbridled passions may result in a state of confused and permanent agitation; luckily, however, people were led by their interest to attach themselves either to the executive power (if they hoped for favor and advancement) or to the legislative (if the government in place had nothing to offer them). Even though such allegiances were seldom stable through time, the convergence of passions on two main forces ensured a certain balance, as each party would naturally react against the excessive influence of the other. It is true that the people's representatives—the legislative body—were prone to excite popular passions (for example, by spreading fears of what the executive might do) whenever they thought it expedient; but as they were more enlightened than the mass of the people and enjoyed their confidence, they were able, if necessary, to dispel the people's anxieties and "to calm their movements."[20]

A few years later Staël was to outline her own version of the dynamics of popular passions in relation to representative government, reviewing and updating Montesquieu's insights in light of the revolutionary experience.[21] "From What Signs" inaugurated this line of reflection by indicating the general principle that could explain the conflicts within French society. This principle was the natural tension between men's aspiration to a static condition, on the one hand, and their craving for movement and change on the other—contrasting desires that Staël, like Montesquieu, identified with the opposed aspirations to stability and freedom: "Two all-powerful forces are present both in the moral and in the physical nature of man: the tendency to quietude (*repos*), and the impulsion toward liberty; one or other of these is bound to prevail in turn; but it is from the combination of both that the permanent and general will of men derives."[22] The project of a "combination of both" was clearly inscribed within the ideal of balance and moderation. But what, more precisely, was the relation between these rather vague notions about the alternation of emotional states and the dynamics of revolutionary events? In the heat of the early political clashes, first at the Estates-General, and then in the Constituent Assembly, Staël readily adopted a perspective of partisan confrontation. In her correspondence—which documents her daily monitoring of debates in the assembly—she was soon speaking in terms of "us" and "them." On the one hand, there was "our party" and "our friends," the patriots and lovers of liberty, who wished to transform the French monarchy into a constitutional regime. On the other, there was the court, with its different cliques, supported by those members of the Estates-General who had originally refused to join the assembly, united in the effort to preserve the privileges and abuses of the Old Regime.

At first Staël was under the illusion that this confrontation between the *parti de la court* and the *parti populaire* (as she called them, echoing the English terms "court" and "country") must necessarily end with the victory of the latter; in other words, that the aspirations of the majority of the nation must necessarily prevail against the resistance of a minority of privileged individuals. Yet soon enough, as the assembly progressed in its initiatives, this simple picture of two opposed forces was replaced in her mind by a far more confused and uncertain perception of the various groups' alignment, and of their strategies. It was soon apparent that "our friends"—the constitutional monarchists who represented the large majority of the Constituent Assembly— were often in disagreement, pursuing separate agendas, and falling prey to personal rivalries, at times when their concerted action was essential to secure some major common objective.

The realization that "our party" was in fact nothing of the kind seems to have crystallized in September 1789, at the time of the debate over the royal veto, the so-called royal sanction. The two-week discussion on whether the king should be able to stop altogether, or to suspend pro tempore, the laws voted by the Legislative Assembly turned out to be one of the most dense and controversial passages in the discussion of the new constitution, finally adopted in 1791. Though in practice the issue was probably less relevant than others addressed by the assembly at the same time (such as the question of bicameralism), the veto became the focus of profound disagreements over the nature of limited government and the separation of powers; it also came to represent, in the popular imagination, the very symbol of royal authority and all it stood for, exciting passionate, if confused and ill-informed, popular reactions.[23]

The debate saw the assembly divided, for the first time, into at least three distinct positions. One group of deputies, on the right and center-right, supported the option of an absolute royal veto, inspired by the model of the English constitution (though by then English monarchs had ceased to exercise it). They believed that the power of arresting the deliberations of the legislative was indispensable, if the executive, in the person of the king, was to enjoy the necessary strength and authority; they also saw it as a necessary precaution against the possible abuses of the legislative. Without the absolute veto—claimed one of its most eloquent partisans, Mirabeau—the people's representatives in the legislative body could easily extend their own privileges and prerogatives, turning themselves into an elective aristocracy, unopposed and unchecked by any other power.[24]

On the left of the assembly, a second group resorted to the same principle of the separation of powers to oppose the institution of any kind of royal veto. As the leading exponent of this view, Emmanuel Joseph Sieyès, argued, the king's right to oppose the laws would constitute, in practice, a form of participation of the executive in the legislative function, since blocking a law was as relevant to the legislative process as introducing it. In recalling the principles of representative government, Sieyès also stressed that, with the royal veto, the will of a single individual, the king, would count as much as the will of the twenty-five million people who were represented by the legislative body; in other words, giving the king the right of veto was equivalent to stating that the nation could be adequately represented by a single individual.[25]

Between these two extremes, various deputies of the center and center-Left favored the solution of compromise represented by some form of temporary veto. Their argument was that a temporary suspension by the king of the laws voted by the Legislative Assembly (some deputies spoke of two or three legislatures; others evoked the possibility of one legislature, followed by a referendum) would be sufficient to control the legislative, and to ensure the desirable balance of powers. This option would be preferable to the absolute veto, as the latter, without being more effective, was bound to generate suspicion and controversy among the people. As Jacques-Guillaume Thouret pointed out in his speech of 5 September, the very idea of an unlimited veto in the hands of the king might easily lead to a frontal opposition between the monarch and public opinion, thus damaging the credibility of the crown. In spite of a certain confusion as to the specific form that a temporary veto might take, it was this solution of compromise—temporary veto for two legislatures—that finally prevailed, gaining a large majority of 673 votes against an opposition of 325. This victory was achieved, however, only after those who had originally opposed any veto switched their support to the option of the temporary veto.[26]

Staël's reaction to the ongoing battle over the veto is well documented by her correspondence. From Versailles, where the assembly was still meeting at the time, she wrote daily to her husband in Paris, commenting on the progress of the debates. There is no doubt that, at first, she was in favor of the absolute veto—unsurprisingly, given the views she would later develop on the need to preserve the balance of powers by upholding the prerogatives of the executive. Writing to Erik-Magnus—who complained about her continuing absence from Paris—she explained that she had spent the previous evening in the company of "M.

[Alexandre] de Lameth, to talk to him about the deliberation voted yesterday (1 September), and to prevent him from publishing a text in support of the temporary (*suspensif*) veto."[27] On the morning of 4 September, she announced another strategy she was attempting in favor of the absolute veto, this time through the intermediary of her friend (and admirer) Stanislas de Clermont-Tonnerre, though apparently without feeling confident about the outcome: "It is settled that I shall return [to Paris] tomorrow, after losing—or not—my trial (*procès*) on the veto. I have been reduced to an amendment, that my speaker Tonnerre will support."[28]

There was in fact no amendment: Clermont-Tonnerre made a speech to support both the project of a legislative consisting of two chambers and the absolute veto. On 9 September he was elected president of the assembly, whereupon he could no longer take part in the debates.[29] Clearly, Staël's pessimism about the chances of the absolute veto was justified: when Necker decided that it would be expedient to support the option of a temporary veto extended to two legislatures, she rallied to this position, and canvassed with the usual energy to promote it, as is suggested by the following note, addressed by Antoine Barnave to her, rather than to Necker himself:

> For the success of tomorrow's initiative, it is very important to specify in the [Necker's] letter that will be read [to the assembly], that the king does not intend to use his temporary veto on the decisions of the present assembly, but only on the laws that may be proposed by the subsequent assemblies.[30]

On 10 September, Staël described the state of play to her husband in the following terms: "My father will send tomorrow to the National Assembly a report addressed to the King's Council, informing the king that the temporary veto, valid for two legislatures, suits him better than the absolute veto, and . . . that the temporary veto for a single legislature would be very bad. I have great hopes from this resolution: it will make the king popular without humiliating him, and he will be seen as making a gracious sacrifice rather than being a victim. It is good, it is necessary, but it is dangerous."[31]

Having accepted the temporary veto as the only viable option, and in spite of her "great hopes," she obviously retained serious reservations concerning the outcome. In fact, under the lighthearted, arch tone she often employed when communicating with her husband, her correspondence betrays her mounting frustration, and even fury, in the face of the deputies' specious arguments and deliberately divisive strategies. The letters to Erik-Magnus written during those weeks are peppered with expressions such as "that wicked assembly," "those infamous aristocrats" (prompted by the uncooperative attitude of the faction led by Jean-Joseph Mounier),[32] and even "your charming assembly," in the accusing tone one parent uses to speak to another about a delinquent child. The experience of the veto confronted her for the first time with a reality she would repeatedly encounter in the years to come: that of a political class ready to sink a major policy objective, and even to jeopardize their own survival, rather than overcoming their ideological prejudices and personal rivalries.

LEARNING FROM THE ENEMY

By the beginning of 1791, the differences that had emerged in the debate on the veto had broken up the front of the constitutional monarchists, crystallizing the formation of several distinct factions. In her later writings Staël provided a map of these factions, and of their leaders, during the Constituent Assembly's last months of life. She described how two "extreme" parties occupied the Right and Left of the assembly. On the right, the "aristocrats" were in fact those members of the Estates-General (including thirty deputies from the Third Estate) who had originally refused to join the assembly, and who still rejected all its deliberations and only followed the debates "out of prudence," to keep an eye on things. Staël expressed strong disapproval of this group, as they pursued a sort of *politique du pire*, refusing to join forces with the moderates, even when such an alliance would have been in the monarchy's best interest. The other "extreme" party, on the left, was represented by the "democrats," or "Jacobins," whose power and influence, both inside and outside the assembly, were alarmingly on the increase. Between these two blocs, moving from the Right to the Left, we find the moderates of the Plain (Gérard de Lally-Tollendal, Mounier, Pierre-Victor Malouet), while what remained of the "popular party" was now divided into four or five separate factions, grouped around as many would-be leaders, namely, La Fayette, Mirabeau, Duport, Barnave, and Sieyès. In her retrospective assessment Staël stated very clearly that these factions were separated less by any objective political and ideological differences than by the ambition and vanity of their chiefs, all of whom aspired to a leading role in the revolutionary process, whatever the collective cost of their personal rivalries. The fact that some of the men in question were capable, intelligent, and even admirable individuals could not mitigate the self-destructiveness of their divisive political attitude.[33]

For obvious reasons, the picture of the alignments in the assembly set forth in "From What Signs"—at a time when Staël was still hoping that the factions might be persuaded to unite—did not include any damning judgment on their leaders. What the article did stress, however, was the disproportionate influence of the two minority parties—"aristocrats" and "Jacobins"—over the political agenda of the assembly, and the corresponding weakness of the moderate majority. The text also emphasized the growing influence of the Jacobins, not just in the assembly, but over the network of political clubs and societies, in Paris as in the provinces. The first aspect, the power of organized minorities in the assembly, was easy enough to explain: the divisions within the moderate center allowed Right and Left to exercise a decisive influence over the vote by forming tactical alliances, by abstaining, or even simply by deserting the proceedings (a form of obstructionism often adopted by the Right). The question of the Jacobins' influence in the country at large was more problematic: why was the majority of public opinion, which by its very nature should have favored moderate views and moderate policies, so captivated and enthralled by a relatively small, radical faction?

The main reason offered in the article was the overwhelming fear of counterrevolution, a fear that the ranting declarations of the émigrés—with their threats of war and revenge—could only feed. The large majority of the people did not want to go back to the past and were ready to rally around any political force that seemed to guarantee protection against a return to the Old Regime, a return most likely to be imposed by violent means. Staël judged this kind of sentiment perfectly understandable: during her recent stay in Switzerland, she had encountered the views and attitudes of the French émigré community, and had been appalled by their lack of understanding of their predicament. The local aristocracy seemed to her equally blind to the dangerous consequences of counterrevolution, in particular the destabilization of the economy: "They are aristocrats—she commented—and will hold to their position unless I make them understand that bankruptcy and counterrevolution are inseparable. All the difficulty of this business is, after all, the public debt."[34]

All things considered, given the choice between counterrevolutionaries and Jacobins, at this stage she confessed to her friend the comte de Gouvernet (the future marquis de la Tour du Pin) that she still preferred the Jacobins.[35] In the article, however, she explained that the popular hatred for the abuses of the past must not be confused with a well-considered, committed support of Jacobin ideology and Jacobin policies. Public opinion was biding its time, as the nation was not sufficiently assured of its enemies' defeat to risk making a choice between its friends. The problem was that the people must be offered an alternative to Jacobinism, in the form of a large, united moderate party. Fear of counter-revolution was not in fact the only factor in the Jacobins' success, a success that, in Staël's view, depended crucially on their superior capacity for organization and propaganda. At what stage and to what extent (if at all) the Jacobins did actually become an organized party in the modern sense of the term remains an open and controversial question for historians of the Revolution. During the twentieth century the issue has become inextricably bound with disputes over Marxist interpretations of the Revolution, and over the Leninist doctrine of the revolutionary party. Present historiography is still divided between readings that favor a sociological approach to the study of party organization and membership and interpretations that focus upon Jacobinism as a political ideology.[36]

At the time the only contemporary example was that of English parliamentary parties, a model Staël deeply admired, but that was clearly very distant from the phenomenon of Jacobinism and of little heuristic relevance in the circumstances. Yet at this stage one hardly needed a sophisticated understanding of the nature of parties to realize that the Jacobins were performing better, as an organized group, both in the assembly and in the clubs, than the squabbling, unruly cohort of "our friends." Staël had clearly given much thought, for some time, to Jacobin tactics. From Coppet, in the last months of 1790, she bombarded her friends in Paris with advice on how these should be countered. In another letter to Gouvernet she argued that it was essential (as she had "already explained in detail to the bishop," i.e., Talleyrand) to force the Jacobins to take up government posts in person, rather than allocating them to men they could control. Only in this way would they become responsible for the conduct of affairs and be deprived of the moral advantage of being always in opposition. Thus one could "take away that mask of disinterestedness of which they make such good use."[37] A month later, she summarized her attitude toward the Jacobins' strategy in the following terms:

Fidelity, constancy, and fierce partisanship are excellent qualities of our adversaries. We do not need to be told that we
change incessantly, and without losing time to stigmatize the
defects of our friends (since we cannot change them), we
should profit from those qualities . . . let us learn from the Jacobins the art of fighting against them.[38]

In the article she returned to the question of the "hypocrisy" of
the Jacobins, comparing them to the Puritans, whose influence
during the English Revolution had rested upon "the appearance
of all virtues." This idea of the moral duplicity of the revolutionary leadership was to resurface in Staël's later analysis of the
nature of partisanship.

THE INVISIBLE LEADERSHIP

In "From What Signs" Staël repressed her doubts about the political performance of the supporters of constitutional monarchy,
addressing them instead with a passionate appeal to unity. The
position of a moderate party during a revolution—she argued—
was especially difficult, since it involved fighting simultaneously
on two fronts, withstanding the attacks of both Left and Right.
Yet the support that such a party could hope to attract was potentially very large: the majority of the people were undoubtedly
anxious to secure the conquests of the Revolution, but they
wished to enjoy them under a stable and orderly government.
Constitutional monarchy was, in the circumstances, the only regime that could reconcile this dual aspiration to freedom and
stability:

I believe the majority of the nation wants, and will always
want, equality and liberty; but it also desires order and be-
lieves that, to secure it, the legal authority and legitimate force
of a monarch is necessary.[39]

What the moderate party should do was to abandon all ambiguous and defensive attitudes, and to declare itself openly to the

"numerous army" of potential supporters, who waited only for a sign on their part. It also needed a forceful personality to lead it: unfortunately, while the cause of moderation attracted many followers, it seemed to produce few chiefs, possibly because the task of leading a center party promised lesser personal glory than what would accrue to the guide of more extreme formations. It was a role that demanded a certain amount of self-denial, as the leader in question should be prepared to renounce "the acclamations he might hope to attract en route," to look only at the final result of his efforts. The issue of leadership, or rather lack of it, was central to Staël's preoccupations at this stage of her political reflection. In her later works she often returned to the idea that the French Revolution had been characterized by a surprising absence of eminent personalities. Rather than by men, it had been led by the "invisible leadership" of abstract notions and principles; those who had enacted it were a crowd of mediocre and colorless individuals, who could take one another's place without noticeable consequences. The only possible exception was Robespierre: but when Robespierre had tried to set himself against the assembly, he had been destroyed.[40]

Some Jacobin writers had seen the "dictatorship without dictator" of the Convention as a positive feature of the revolutionary regime, the establishment of a power that made no concession to individual characteristics and personal ambitions. Staël's explanation of the phenomenon, on the other hand, was that the French were too deeply attached to the traditional image of the great monarch to wish to see any ordinary individual in a position of excessive power or influence. Thus they preferred to submit to the anonymous rule of committees, assemblies, public offices, and institutions, rather than to the authority of prominent military or civil leaders. It was not until Napoleon rose to power that this tendency was dramatically reversed, and personal rule returned with a vengeance.

While in retrospect the absence of a visible and personalized leadership could be explained to some extent as a distinctive trait of the French political tradition, in 1791 the lack of an inspiring and unifying guide of the revolutionary movement represented an immediate practical problem. The absence of a recognized leadership—at this stage common to all factions—could only accentuate the divisions and rivalries both within the assembly and in the many political associations across the country. This difficulty was dramatically brought home by Mirabeau's sudden death: Staël (who probably helped to draft the speech Talleyrand delivered at the funeral)[41] rightly interpreted the strong emotion occasioned by this event as a sign of great political disorientation and uncertainty, on the part both of the public and of the political class.

Mirabeau had not been one of Staël's political friends, though there was in fact considerable proximity between their respective views on the role and prospects of constitutional monarchy. Mirabeau's declared (and reciprocated) hostility toward Necker had prevented any collaboration between them: while Staël was prepared to overlook the marquis's reputation for immorality, she could not forgive his repeated attacks against her father in the press, nor his constant intrigues to undermine Necker's position, in order to take his place as "principal minister" of the crown. Yet at the moment of his death she was struck, like other observers, by a sense of major and irreplaceable loss. Mirabeau appeared in retrospect as the only man who had the necessary charisma, energy, and prestige to keep the revolutionary movement on the path of constitutional reform.

That man, who often defied public opinion, but always supported the general will, had become for a time the leader of the aspirations of the greatest number . . . The terror that had seized all spirits in learning of his loss . . . is the unquestionable sign of the wish of the majority of the nation. Such regrets are for the man who, like a true friend of liberty, believed that the existence of a king, armed with the constitution, and with sufficient strength to execute the laws, was necessary to France, and . . . who seemed ready to dedicate himself to the defense of such truth.[42]

One could plausibly argue that, on the eve of his untimely death, Mirabeau had already failed in the task of rallying the moderates. The recollections of his secretary, the Genevan expatriate Etienne Dumont,[43] document the marquis's poor attendance of committees, his disregard of voting, and above all his inability to control his own arrogance and personal ambition to form useful alliances: the famous episode of his disastrous interview with Necker in 1789 (at a time when an agreement between the two might have changed the course of events)[44] offers a convincing illustration of his temperamental incapacity to function as a mediator between the monarchy and the assembly, and as a party leader.

In his study of the Constituent Assembly the Italian historian Roberto Martucci recalls these elements, arguing that Mirabeau's impressive speeches and forceful personality were not sufficient to secure a parliamentary majority, and therefore do not justify the relevance attributed to him in the revolutionary process by historians like François Furet and Guy Chaussinand-Nogaret.[45] Staël herself was far from blind to Mirabeau's "terrible faults";[46] the characteristics she attributed in her article to the ideal leader of the moderates—courage but also modesty and a spirit of sacrifice—clearly excluded some of the marquis's most flamboyant traits. At the same time she saw no other politician who could embody in the same way, with the same vigor and charisma, the cause of constitutional monarchy.

The problem of leadership was not, in fact, just a matter of personalities, but also one of identification between the potential leaders and the cause they claimed to represent. Though in France factions fought one another furiously and even viciously, they were generally reluctant to announce their true colors. Each party—Staël argued—claimed hypocritically to speak for the entire nation, and this fiction of unity prevented any serious political confrontation between them. The legitimate grounds for disagreement were not made explicit but remained concealed, and thus they could not be discussed and resolved. There was in fact an objective opposition between those who rejected monarchical government in any form and those who wished to preserve it. Both positions—republican and monarchical—were legitimate and could be justified; since royalty was no longer regarded as a sacred entity, but merely as a political regime like any other, arguments could be produced for and against it. But all political groups must be honest and open about what it was that they stood for:

> Once this question is clarified, we shall be left with two parties: they will fight, but at least they will stop deceiving one another . . . Whoever desires a monarchy is not necessarily a slave; and whoever wants a republic is not necessarily seditious. The only ones who deserve to be called slaves and seditious are the hypocrites.[47]

The article's concluding paragraph made it clear that the accusation of hypocrisy was chiefly directed against the republicans, who were unwilling to declare their opposition to the king, and who pretended to be loyal to a monarchical constitution while constantly undermining it. The fault of the royalists, on the other hand, was nothing less than their cowardice: they should have said clearly that a republic in a large state was possible only in the form of a federation (*république fédérative*); they should have forcefully defended monarchical institutions—instead they remained silent, fearful of alienating a restless and confused public opinion. Moderation was not a cause that could be promoted by "feeble and timid" partisans; on the contrary, more than any other political actor, the moderates needed real courage "to brave all suspicions and dangers." The opinions of moderates may be reasonable and wise, but their character must be audacious.

NOT REELIGIBLE

While she was publicly fustigating "our friends," urging them to be brave and to rally around the crown, Staël was privately convinced that the Constituent Assembly was politically spent and possibly best brought to an end. In her correspondence she expressed hopes for the new legislature, which was due to begin on 1 October 1791, as an opportunity to start afresh, and to stop the rapid deterioration of the political context. In her more optimistic moments she even saw the application to the new assembly's election of the rule of "active citizenship" (restricting the suffrage on a property basis) as a chance to promote a moderate electorate. While in her later writings she stigmatized the decree of nonreeligibility as a disastrous political choice, claiming that the constituents might have saved France had they been reelected as members of the new Legislative Assembly, at the time her position was not so clear-cut, as she still hoped that some benefits might come from a simplification of political alignments.[48] Obviously the automatic exclusion of the members of the old assembly meant that the benefit of having her own personal contacts would be lost, as she was not likely to be equally close to any of the new deputies. In a letter addressed to her husband from the "silence and infernal peace" of Coppet, she commented ironically: "Since I won't know anybody in this new legislature, I absolutely resign from my political career; I too am not reeligible. Fine arts and letters will occupy my leisure."[49]

Needless to say, this resignation was not to take effect immediately. In spite of her reservations about the revised constitution of 1791, which failed to guarantee an adequate separation and articulation of powers, Staël believed that constitutional monarchy continued to be a viable option for France, a card that could still be played. Writing to Nils von Rosenstein in September 1791, a few days after Louis XVI had reluctantly signed the constitution, she alerted him to the dangers of a move against France on the part of the European powers, in a style reminiscent of her favorite writer, Montesquieu: "Whatever folly France might commit, while there are large associations of men, the monarchy will subsist. It is in the nature of things, and nothing can prevent a return to it; but if the political balance of Europe is overturned, it will be a long time before it settles again. I believe, moreover, that this revolution is directed against the aristocracy far more than against royalty. In the struggle between aristocracy and democracy, the monarchy can still easily *tirer son épingle du jeux*."[50]

The optimistic statement about the prospects of monarchical government in France may have been somewhat exaggerated, designed to discourage von Rosenstein's master, Gustav III, from pursuing his ambition of leading an anti-French European coalition (an ambition brought to an end by his assassination a few months later). In fact it soon became clear that the Legislative Assembly was heading for the same kind of difficulties that had undermined the activity of the Constituent. Only a month after her letter to Rosenstein, commenting on the apparent goodwill of Louis XVI in applying the constitution, she confided to Gouvernet: "All is favorable, the disposition of the king and those of foreign powers, all except this infamous legislative, which deteriorates every day, the majority of which disappears in front of a hundred factious men, and that the Abbé Sieyès influences secretly, with diabolical success."[51] Although the ambassadress battled on for several months after writing these lines, trying to build bridges among the rival groups in the new assembly, as well as canvassing to obtain a ministerial post for Narbonne, she soon realized that the fate of the Legislative Assembly was going to be a more spasmodic replay of that of the Constituent. The Constituent Assembly, she wrote in the *Considerations*, had aged in its two years of life as much as Louis XIV had in forty. After so many years, she added, she still felt the same "vivid pain" when considering what opportunity had been lost with it.[52]

Over the last two decades, several historians of the Revolution have provided a variety of explanations to account for the rapid disintegration of what had started as a most promising political enterprise. Some have stressed the profound ideological rift that separated the constituents: the party of equality against that of delegated power; patriotism versus liberalism; Rousseau versus Montesquieu; republic versus monarchy.[53] Others have explored the sociological profile of deputies, detailing their various regional provenance, their heterogeneous careers, and their consequent diverging interests.[54] They have also stressed the deputies' lack of experience, pointing out that even those who had previously served in the local administrations or in the *parlements* were unprepared for the functioning of a large parliamentary assembly. This inexperience manifested itself in a poor mastering of voting procedures, a lack of coordination, a certain rigidity in the defense of abstract principles, and a general inability to mediate and compromise.

All of these difficulties would have been familiar to Staël. By 1791 she had obviously come to recognize the fundamental division between republicans and monarchists as inevitable in the circumstances, a latent conflict to be faced, rather than concealed or ignored. Her diligent attendance at the sessions of the assembly had also made her aware of all that was dysfunctional in its proceedings: the poor discipline of debates, with minority speakers often unheard or silenced; the absence of organized parliamentary groups and the consequent confusion in voting procedures; and the pressure of popular mobilization on the deputies.[55]

Yet in her eyes none of these factors, however relevant, could absolve from their responsibility those men who, having been entrusted with the course of the Revolution, had failed to steer it in the right direction. She believed that the constitutional monarchists, who formed the large majority of the Constituent Assembly, were there to represent the durable interests of the bulk of the nation, interests that would be best served, in the long run, by a moderate constitution. Their inability to create, out of their differences, stable institutions and a viable political regime was to a large extent the product of their own personal vices: ambition, envy, vanity, cowardice. But it was also the result of an ingrained blindness to what politics was really about. Through their failure, the issue of political agency was brought, once and for all, to the forefront of Staël's political thinking.

CHAPTER 2

The View from the Executive (1792)

THE EIGHT months or so that elapsed between the end of December 1791 and the beginning of September 1792—most of the lifetime of the Legislative Assembly[1]—are ill documented by Staël's own writings. For a variety of reasons, nearly all her correspondence for this period is lost, and, as far as we know, no published or unpublished texts have survived—although, given her compulsive writing habits, it seems unlikely she did not produce any. This interruption in the stream of evidence about the writer's own perception of events is especially frustrating, as it coincides with a politically crucial episode in her life. At the beginning of December 1791 the promotion of Narbonne to the post of minister of war—an appointment largely brought about by her own relentless efforts—placed Staël at the center of the political stage and gave her once again access to the highest levels of power. No doubt the allegations set forth by a hostile press and by her political enemies—that, through her lover, the young ambassadress was de facto governing France, dictating foreign policy, controlling the army, or ruling the cabinet—were malicious exaggerations; but they did contain an element of truth.[2]

For a few months Necker's daughter found herself at the heart of the new government run by the group of constitutional monarchists known as Feuillants (from the name of their club),[3] in a more independent position than when she had been at her father's side at the beginning of the Revolution. If she did not rule

France, she took part in the discussions and confrontations within the cabinet, helped to draft speeches and reports, kept diplomatic contacts abroad, and generally worked hard to secure wider political support for the new minister of war, both in the assembly and among the general public.

In the belated reconstruction of those months presented in the *Considerations* she was notably reticent about the episode of Narbonne's ministry, no doubt because of the fanciful, and often damaging, allegations about her own role. Thus chapter 5 of part 3 ("Of the First War between France and Europe") offers only the briefest of accounts of Narbonne's appointment, his zealous service, and his swift dismissal at the beginning of March 1792, without the embellishment of any personal remarks or recollections. A reference to the former minister's death in the aftermath of the Battle of Leipzig, oddly placed at the beginning of this short narrative, contributes to marking the author's distance from the whole episode:

> The war department was entrusted, in the end of 1791, to M. de Narbonne, who afterwards lost his life at the siege of Torgau.[4]

As Narbonne did not die until 1813, when he was serving the empire as governor of Saxony, this deliberate obliteration of more than twenty years of his life turns the brief passage into a chilling epitaph. While Staël's reluctance to recall an episode charged with personal implications is understandable, it is reasonable to assume that those months spent in close proximity to the tottering monarchical executive did leave a durable impression.

"OUR COUNCIL"

For a short while, toward the end of 1790, Staël had shared the hopes of the leaders of the Feuillants (the so-called triumvirs: Adrien Duport, Antoine Barnave, and Alexandre de Lameth)

that the election of a new assembly, with a more restricted fran-
chise than that adopted for the Estates-General, might contribute
to stabilizing the political situation, increasing the weight of
moderate opinion, and giving some breathing space to the new
constitutional monarchy. Urging the comte de Gouvernet to reg-
ister as "active citizen" in Paris, she explained: "There are two
important things: to end this assembly, before it is entirely used
up . . . ; and to make sure that the present electors will not elect
the next legislature."[5] The revised constitution presented to the
assembly on 5 August 1791 altered the conditions of electoral
suffrage, with the intention—made explicit by its authors—of
ending unrest and restoring order by enhancing the influence of
the moderate electorate represented by property owners.[6] There
were, Barnave explained in a speech of 11 August 1791, three
conditions to ensure a free and responsible electorate: a sufficient
degree of enlightenment, a commitment to public affairs, and an
independent fortune. The privileged classes had the education
and the economic independence, but were not necessarily committed to the public good, as they possessed separate interests of
their own; the common people, because they lacked both the
education and the necessary independence, were too exposed to
manipulation and corruption; as only the "middle class" could
offer guarantees on all three fronts, the bulk of the electorate
must be taken from that class alone.[7]

The restriction of voting rights was facilitated by the fact
that—given the large size of the population involved—the constitution of 1791 established elections in two degrees (a practice
that survived until the Restoration). The conditions for "active
citizenship"—the right to take part in "primary assemblies," that
is, in first-degree elections—were fixed at the low property conditions originally adopted in 1789 for the Estates-General (three
days' wages), confirming a potential electorate of about four million men. On the other hand, the requirements for the "electors"—those who took part in "electoral assemblies" or second-
degree elections—were sufficiently restrictive (from 150 to 200

days' wages or their equivalent, according to the localities) to bring down the number to about fifty thousand[8]—an asymmetry designed to widen the social distance between the mass of the electors, on the one hand, and those who actually chose the deputies and the local administrators on the other.

The halfhearted hope of a significant change in the nature and disposition of the electorate—in Staël's case more wishful thinking than serious expectation—was not confirmed by the outcome of the elections; in any case the very low popular participation registered in the summer of 1791 minimized any possible impact of the new rules. As to the deputies who were elected, historians of the Legislative Assembly agree in describing them as, on average, younger and more militant in their support of the Revolution than the members of the Constituent, often formed by some experience in local administration, and generally less prosperous than their predecessors (if not exactly poor). As a friend of Staël—the comte de La Marck—observed, the large majority of the new members "had no better carriage than their galoshes and their umbrellas."[9] As to their political disposition, the large majority were still favorable to the constitutional monarchy, but with a marked democratic orientation. In addition, as the assembly set to work, the practice of voting by nominal appeal (voice vote) had the immediate effect of exposing moderate deputies to the pressures and threats of the Jacobin militants ever present in the galleries, a situation that favored the approval of more radical measures and pushed the majority toward the left.

Thus the only expectation expressed by Staël at the time to be confirmed by the events was that her personal contacts within the new assembly would be seriously diminished. She had indeed very few acquaintances among the new members, and in any case several of her former political allies, discouraged by the experience of the Constituent Assembly, had retired to their provinces or estates, while others had already chosen to emigrate. Though she continued to follow the debates of the Legislative, the ambassadress now found herself in the position of a passive—if well-informed and opinionated—bystander. This loss of connections was not, however, the only consequence of the altered political setting. The king's acceptance of the constitution in September 1791 soon led to a laborious ministerial reshuffle, opening some interesting new perspectives for those members of "our party" who had not yet abandoned political life and the cause of constitutional monarchy. In the circumstances Staël was ready to shift her attention away from the unpromising battlefield of the new assembly to the familiar ground of court patronage and the backstage negotiations around government positions. In the playful language she sometimes adopted in her correspondence, "our party" was replaced by "our council," the ministerial department around which her aspirations now revolved.[10]

A NOT-SO-CASUAL VACANCY

The first piece to be moved on the chessboard of ministerial appointments was the post of the minister of foreign affairs, then held by the comte de Montmorin. A prominent member of government since 1787, well-liked and trusted by the king, Montmorin was showing increasing signs of discouragement and disaffection: his inability to handle the pressure created by the émigrés' belligerent appeals led to the widespread feeling that his resignation was long overdue. Staël thought him incompetent and feeble and, in one of several censorious remarks about him, observed that he had "the genius of inaction." Her judgment was clearly shared by Barnave, who in a letter to the queen described the minister (who was still hoping to be asked to form a new government) as "absolutely not up to the circumstances," indeed "incapable of judging them," concluding that, by his inertia, he was leading the king to his ruin.[11]

In his diary the American ambassador to Paris, Gouverneur Morris, recalled two "coalition dinners" organized by Staël on 15 and 25 October, claiming that their purpose was to prepare Montmorin's succession.[12] Though Morris, in his eagerness to appear always well informed, is often inaccurate or malicious in his accounts of events, it is true that by mid-October Staël was mentioning in her letters the possible vacancy of Montmorin's post. The resignation of the minister of foreign affairs—when he was finally persuaded to go—led to new appointments in other departments, namely, the Department of the Navy (Montmorin also held the navy portfolio), that of the Interior, and that of War.[13] Filling these vacancies was far from easy, since those candidates who aspired to the positions were generally distrusted by the king or vetoed by his entourage; while those the king was prepared to appoint were reluctant to serve and were sometimes discouraged from accepting by the aggressive attitude that the Legislative Assembly displayed toward the executive. In an atmosphere of growing distrust between the two powers, the routine reports ministers were expected to present to the assembly were turning increasingly into grueling interrogations. The assembly also took the initiative of summoning ministers to unscheduled meetings to answer all manner of questions about their conduct, in a climate—it was claimed—reminiscent of the tribunals of the Inquisition. Staël reported, for example, that the assembly's treatment of the minister of war, Louis Duportail, had discouraged Louis-Philippe de Ségur from accepting the Department of Foreign Affairs the king was offering him.

A series of letters addressed by Staël to Gouvernet, who had just been appointed to a diplomatic post at La Haye, document the ups and downs of the various candidacies, and the obvious difficulties of finding a satisfactory solution through the maze of patronage claims, personal incompatibilities, cross vetoes, and refusals.[14] Staël regarded Narbonne as a natural candidate for a prominent position in the new government: on the one hand, he had a powerful sponsor at the court, in the person of his godmother (possibly natural mother) Mme Adélaide, the king's aunt. At the same time his reputation as a patriot would make him acceptable to the assembly, where he could at least count on the approval of what she called "the democratic party" (meaning in fact the left wing of the Feuillants, rather than the Jacobins). Her ambitions for him focused from the start upon Montmorin's post, partly because the Ministry of Foreign Affairs was the most prestigious position in the government, but also because of her own familiarity with the diplomatic milieu, where she was confident of finding the necessary support. However, Narbonne's name, when it was proposed by Duport, did not elicit a very enthusiastic response from the king and queen. The official reason given for the rejection of his candidacy was that he occupied the post of commander of the Garde soldée (the professional regiments of the Garde nationale stationed in Paris), a post he must not relinquish since the king relied on him for his own security in the event of an insurrection.[15]

It is difficult to assess precisely the different factors that led the royal couple to distrust Narbonne. The main one was no doubt the open support he had given to the Revolution and the fact that they obviously identified him with the cohort of those grand aristocrats who had "betrayed" the cause of the monarchy. His close friendship with the marquis de La Fayette and his very public liaison with Staël (generally hated by the court as Necker's daughter) were no doubt also against him, though, as Barnave explained to the queen in their secret correspondence, his association with such persons was a good reason for keeping him on their side. After expressing the view that Staël had been absolutely shameless in promoting Narbonne's candidacy, he added: "No matter how unsuited M. de Narbonne might seem for the position he covets, the queen will of course realize that this affair must be conducted in such a way as not to offend him; it is necessary, as far as possible, to avoid causing any resentment among the people close to him (*sa société*); in other circumstances, it would not matter very much; but at times of crisis it is important to keep on one's side all those who might have some influence upon public opinion (*le mouvement public*)."[16]

Staël herself was ready to admit that her support had probably disserved Narbonne with the court, though it might have helped him with the ministers.[17] In the end the coveted Department of Foreign Affairs went to Claude-Antoine de Lessart, while Narbonne, after much hesitation, was persuaded to replace Louis Duportail at the Ministry of War. Historians have described Narbonne's appointment as the crowning of his belligerent ambitions, portraying him as an impetuous young man (he was in fact in his mid-thirties, a mature age for the time), anxious to attain glory by leading France into war.[18] According to Staël his acceptance of the post was a second-best choice, mainly dictated by his considerable financial difficulties, consequent to the loss of his wife's "colonial" fortune in the slave uprisings at Santo Domingo. This is how she described to Gouvernet the circumstances of the appointment: "Will you believe that the minister of foreign affairs has not yet been appointed? They are now talking of giving it to de Lessart, the interior to our friend Garnier, and the war to Narbonne. This department would suit him far less than that of foreign affairs; but given the diminished state of his fortune, and with the hope of being the main influence on the *Conseil*, he should perhaps accept."[19] In a letter to Axel von Fersen, Marie-Antoinette related the event with a famously poisonous comment on Staël: "The comte de Narbonne is finally, since yesterday, the minister of war. What glory for Mme de Staël, and what pleasure to have the whole army at her disposal. [Here a line has been carefully crossed out.] He may be useful, if he wants, since he is sufficiently spirited to rally the Constitutionnels and he can find the right tone to address the army of today."[20]

In the context of what she described as a distribution of ministries at a discount (*au rabais*)[21] the ambassadress was in fact far from enthusiastic about having anything to do with the French army. She was convinced that the minister responsible for that department would face considerable difficulties in the event of a war against the European monarchies, for which she thought France was totally unprepared.[22] The only thing she valued about the position at this stage was, as she naively confessed to her correspondent, the opportunity it might offer to influence, and possibly even lead, the government. The design that now took shape in her mind was that the ground the moderates were losing inside the assembly might perhaps be regained through the influence of a charismatic presence in the cabinet, that the leadership "our party" had failed to exercise thus far within the legislative might come instead from the executive.

A DETESTABLE CONSTITUTION

The question of the role of executive power is inseparable from the broader issue of the merits and demerits of the constitution of 1791. Staël's awareness of this text's defects oriented her later works on the subject of constitutional theory. Unfortunately, the "few reflections" written on the subject at the time, mentioned in a letter to Nils von Rosenstein on 16 September 1791, have not resurfaced thus far from the archives.[23] But by the time the constitution was accepted by a reluctant Louis XVI in September 1791, Staël was privately more than clear about its shortcomings, even if her public position conformed to the official Feuillant line of unconditional support.

Before the episode of Varennes, there had been hopes among the moderates of improving the constitution's design, reinforcing royal authority and the power of the executive. But after the royal family's flight and forced return to a virtual imprisonment in Paris, such hopes were reduced to formal adjustments (such as the definition of the king as "representative" of the nation), while the only path open to the partisans of constitutional monarchy was to stand by the charter as it was. As Staël explained to Gouvernet, inviting him, somewhat ironically, to write from La Haye "highly patriotic" dispatches: "It would be mad today to have any other hope than the one expressed by the epigram of the Feuillants: *la Constitution, toute la Constitution, rien que la Constitution.*"[24] But what precisely were Staël's objections to a constitution she did not hesitate to qualify as "detestable"? In her view the main flaw in its design had been apparent from the start, from the moment bicameralism had been rejected in favor of a single chamber: this choice created, in fact, a fundamental imbalance between legislative and executive power. As she explained to Rosenstein: "[The constitution] fails to establish any equilibrium. If the king has the majority in the only existing chamber, he is all-powerful; if he does not, he has no power at all. The design of the English constitution is far more ingenious!"[25] In the same letter she stigmatized the French attitude that consisted in pursuing novelty and invention at the expense of solid experience, as if a constitution—"like an epic poem"—should shine for its originality. Indeed, the unanimous rejection of the model of the English constitution had seen the king, the nobility, and the "democrats" united in a common display of absurd national vanity.[26] This judgment about the widespread hostility to any form of bicameralism is confirmed by the way in which the tentative efforts, made by the Feuillants in the summer of 1791, to put some sort of second chamber back on the constitutional agenda were received by all concerned; not only the Left of the assembly, but the king's entourage as well, were clearly opposed to the suggestion, which sunk without trace.[27]

Staël understood that the rejection of bicameralism was dictated by a fervent opposition to the prospect of a hereditary body—indeed, that the hostility of revolutionary opinion was directed against aristocratic privilege far more than against royalty. She also shared the view, frequently expressed by the moderates in this period, that a single legislative assembly, unchecked by some other institution, might prove as "aristocratic" as any hereditary assembly (indeed, might easily decide to turn itself into one). The project set forth by the Feuillants, though rather hazy on the composition of a second chamber, did not envisage it as a hereditary institution (which is probably why the king did not support the project). It is reasonable to assume that Staël herself also favored discarding heredity in this context, though she expressed herself clearly on this point only after the end of the Revolution.

Directly connected with the question of bicameralism was the ambiguous role reserved to royal authority. In theory, the constitution attributed to the king considerable prerogatives as head of the executive; in practice, however, he was prevented from exercising them by the relentless pressure that the assembly exerted both upon his own initiatives and upon those of his agents, namely, the ministers. Long before his attempted escape to Varennes, the king's difficult position had been repeatedly pointed out and represented a major concern for the supporters of constitutional monarchy, from Mirabeau to Barnave. The enthusiasm Staël manifested when Louis XVI finally resolved to use his right of veto, by suspending the decree of 9 November on the émigrés, showed how anxiously the Feuillants were watching for any signs of resilience on the part of royal power.[28]

Just as the monarch's weak position resulted from a combination of poor constitutional design and mistrust of the royal function, the ministers' situation suffered from a mixture of diffidence toward their role (as agents of the king) and a faulty understanding of the articulation of functions between the legislative and the executive. On this particular issue Staël could rely on the analysis provided by Necker in his illuminating work *Du pouvoir exécutif dans les grands états* (On executive power in large states), published in April 1792, and written precisely during the short-lived Feuillant government. The book summarized the experience accumulated by the author, during his entire ministerial career, with regard to the general difficulties associated with the execution and enforcement of legislation. It detailed at the same time the specific factors that hindered the action of ministers in the constitution of 1791.[29] Appointed by the king, and regarded with suspicion as "agents of royalty," ministers were—Necker observed—completely excluded from legislative activity: they could speak only at the invitation of the assembly and were prevented from taking active part in its debates. Consequently much legislation was passed without any understanding of the means that would be necessary to enforce it. The ministers were then held responsible for failing to apply the decisions of the legislative, thus creating further tensions and conflicts. This lack of cooperation and harmony between the legislative and executive bodies inevitably resulted in a general incapacity to enforce the law, paralyzing the action of the cabinet, and making the country simply ungovernable. As the new Legislative Assembly set to work, this fracture between the two powers, unintentionally created by the constitution, had deepened even further, as the action of ministerial departments was increasingly controlled and dictated by more than twenty special committees, appointed by the assembly, who rapidly took over the tasks and prerogatives of the executive.[30]

Ever ready to admire and promote her father's writings, Staël would have been more than familiar with his analysis. On the other hand, what the surviving evidence fails to show is to what extent her own observations from the War Department may have seeped back into her father's work: judging from the usual frequency of their correspondence, she must have reported back to him almost every day, but unfortunately the letters are lost. No doubt the difficulty of recruiting new ministers ready to face the displeasure of the Legislative Assembly, which emerged at the time of Montmorin's resignation, came to confirm Necker's most pessimistic anticipations about the absence of a viable working relation between the different powers of the state.

THE "ENGLISH MINISTRY"

In his reflections on the executive Necker did not address a question that preoccupied his daughter during the months of Narbonne's ministry, namely, the problem of the coordination among the different ministerial departments. In France ministers were appointed individually by the king, and although some departments carried more weight than others, no minister occupied in principle the position of head of government. This was not very different from what happened in England: in both constitutional models there was no premier, as it was assumed that the head of the executive was the king himself, even if sovereigns were not invariably active in this role. In England, however, a practice apparently initiated by Walpole's government in the 1720s, and gradually stabilized over the following decades, attributed to one of the ministers (originally the first lord of the treasury) the role of leader of the cabinet.

In his book on executive power, Necker discussed in detail the issue of the penal and political responsibility of ministers, comparing the French constitution, which recognized only the principle of penal responsibility, to the English one, which in his view acknowledged a degree of political responsibility.[31] He did not, however, raise the question of the collective responsibility of the executive, a notion that had apparently gained some credit among the Feuillants and attracted Staël's interest. Rivalries and conflicts between the ministers, who individually sought the support of the king and the approval of the assembly, often at the expense of their colleagues, dominated the brief experience of Narbonne at the War Department—leading to his forced resignation and to the premature dissolution of the cabinet. More generally, over its duration of less than a year, the Legislative Assembly saw an unprecedented turnover of ministers (six ministers of the interior, six of foreign affairs, and seven ministers of war).

The matter was discussed in an article entitled "Observations sur le ministère anglais" (Observations on the English ministry), published anonymously a few days after Narbonne's dismissal, and probably emanating from Staël's entourage (if not actually written by her).[32] The article unfavorably compared the French constitution to the English one, stressing how, in order to be effective, the action of ministers must follow a single directive and conform to a single policy. In England, the article explained, the king reigns through his ministers, who carry the responsibility of government on his behalf, not as separate individuals, but as a collective body:

> Executive power has real strength in [the ministers'] hands, because they form a perfectly united body that deliberates jointly and always follows the position of the majority, with no single member acting against it. The same thing cannot be said of France. Thus executive power will always lack strength—quite apart from all other causes—until the ministers will all follow the same principles, forming a united body acting in concert.[33]

Only by adopting the principle of collective responsibility could French governments hope to act with the necessary authority. The text referred specifically to Narbonne's recent dismissal, arguing that he had been excluded for two reasons:

> because he openly attacked those ministers who did not follow, like him, the constitutional line, and because he insisted, with energy, on the necessity of composing a cabinet in which all members had the same principles, deliberated in common, and acted in concert.[34]

The article then refuted the view, suggested to the king by Narbonne's enemies, that a cabinet so composed would have, "like the English one," great strength and would make itself "independent of the king," having on its side the majority of the National Assembly and public opinion. It is unclear whether England was really taken as a model in this particular case, or whether the English example was merely introduced for polemical purposes. Shortly after the publication of the article, in May 1792, William Pitt obtained from King George III the dismissal of the chancellor of the exchequer Lord Thurlow, who had openly criticized in the House of Lords his government's financial policy, invoking the principle of collective responsibility. The episode can be read as an indication that the notion of collective responsibility was gaining ground, or, alternatively, as proof of the desire on Pitt's part to impose his own authority because he felt it was being threatened.[35] In France the dismissal of the Feuillant ministers, and their replacement by an executive formed by the Girondins (a more radical group within the assembly, one committed to republican ideals), soon put a stop to any further discussion on the subject of the premiership, as apparently the Girondins had no interest in the matter.[36]

For Staël, however, the creation of a strong executive power required conditions other than a cabinet united under a "principal minister" or "English minister." The real problem for her was that—in order to be effective—executive power must possess a recognizable personal identity, a distinct image, capable of capturing popular imagination and of inspiring trust. The importance of the personal dimension of political representation had always been a favorite topic of Necker: in his writings he explained how electors would naturally place greater trust in local candidates than in outsiders, or prefer men from established families, however mediocre, to brilliant newcomers. His belief in the advantages of a ruling class of notables, and his preference for a federal, over a centralized, political system, were both connected with these considerations. In his view, this personal rapport between electors and rulers was especially important for the members of the executive, since they had the difficult task of enforcing the law, that is to say, of being obeyed. It was also crucial in all circumstances where a government attempted to introduce new measures, or to promote reforms, that might disrupt popular habits and expectations.

Staël shared Necker's views on the general merits of proximity and personal recognition in political representation: later on—during her visit to England in 1793, for example—she was very impressed by the way in which English members of Parliament came in direct personal contact with their electors, listening to their grievances or explaining their policies. But in the context of the Revolution, "personalized" representation could perform a more essential symbolic role: given the lackluster performance of Louis XVI, the presence of a highly representative figure at the head of the executive seemed a necessary condition for the preservation of consensus and the legitimacy of authority. In his daughter's view Necker, at the height of his popularity, had provided precisely this emblematic connection between the king and the nation; since his departure, no one had been quite able to take his place. She had already discussed this subject in her essay "Eloge de M. de Guibert," written as an apologia for the famous military theorist in 1789, and left unpublished, possibly because of its limited interest for the general public.[37] In the early years of her marriage Staël had befriended the comte de Guibert, who was an old acquaintance of her parents, showing toward him a vivid admiration that had elicited some jealous responses from her husband.

Her text was mainly a defense of Guibert's controversial views on the reform of the French army, and a vindication of his short-lived experience as minister of war on the eve of the Revolution. It also briefly presented Guibert's literary works, among them his *Eloge de l'Hôpital*, a celebration of the chancellor who had served the Valois monarchy in the difficult years of the religious wars, written for a competition set by the Académie française. Given his own personal experience, Staël argued, Guibert was better placed than most men of letters to understand "the talents of a minister who had to struggle both against his own times, and against the court." She then proceeded to paint a portrait of de l'Hôpital—"the greatest personality before our century"—filled with transparent references to Necker; in particular the definition of de l'Hôpital as "minister and citizen" was, along with "patriot minister," among her favorite formulas to describe her own father:

> minister and citizen, negotiator between the nation and the throne; forced to be silent about the obstacles that were opposed to his action . . . forced by his conscience to remain in a position where the best he could do was to prevent the great-

est evil, when shining glory belongs only to those who secure the greatest good.[38]

Possibly Staël's fond image of Necker performing the unique function of mediator between the nation and the crown betrayed a naive, exaggerated belief in the former minister's importance, while her hope that Narbonne might acquire a dominant influence over French government was just an instance of wishful thinking. Yet, setting aside the question of her own personal bias, in advocating an authoritative head of government, Staël was making a substantial point. She believed the French had lived for too long under the spell of a powerful royal image to identify with a fading constitutional monarch, even less with the impersonal institutions of a republic. She insisted in particular on the incapacity of the revolutionary movement to bring forth a leader with a distinct personal identity. Thus in her view the future prospects of representative government in France depended, to a large extent, on a capacity to fill the imaginative void left by the legacy of the old monarchy, which the sequence of new regimes and new leaderships had not yet been able to occupy.[39]

WORKING A MIRACLE

Staël's ambition to secure for Narbonne a position in government, and the circumstances of his service as minister of war between December 1791 and March 1792, shortly before the outbreak of the revolutionary wars, have led some early commentators and historians to assume that she was a partisan, even a promoter, of France's attack against the other European monarchies. The implausible image of Staël plotting the war with the Girondins in order to propel Narbonne into high office—originally set forth by royalist and Jacobin propaganda—has thus found its way into the influential narratives of Jules Michelet, Alphonse de Lamartine, Jean Jaurès and Edgar Quinet, and has left lasting traces in modern historiography.[40] The scarcity of reliable information about Staël's contacts and activities during this period has left ample scope for unsubstantiated rumors and allegations. It has fed all manner of conspiracy theories, suggesting (not for the last time) her involvement in various unspecified plots aiming at driving France to war, overturning the monarchy, and establishing a military dictatorship. Although in her edition of Staël's correspondence, published in the 1960s, Béatrice Jasinski has provided a well-documented refutation of such allegations, her patient scholarly work has not entirely succeeded in dispelling the legend, a legend that fits well into the tenacious picture of the ambassadress's salon as a hotbed of warmongering intrigues.[41]

In reality Staël's position on the prospect of a war, at the time of Narbonne's appointment, was very much in line with that of other moderate observers of France's position. She believed France was unprepared to sustain a military confrontation with the other European powers for a variety of reasons: the critical situation of the nation's finances, the poor condition of fortifications and armaments, the scarcity of reliable troops after a series of mutinies, and the wave of officers' desertions that followed Varennes. She also thought that the war would serve the cause of those who wished to prolong and radicalize the Revolution, destroying the newly established constitutional monarchy. She was especially anxious about the inability, on the part of the court and of the government, to respond to the provocations of the émigrés, sensing that the mood of the country, and especially that of the Parisian crowds, was mounting into a militant patriotic response that would soon prove impossible to control. Finally, Staël's many diplomatic contacts, and her familiarity with the international situation, made her especially aware of the risks involved in a destabilization of the European balance of powers, the consequences of which were bound to prove far-reaching and deeply disruptive.

In September 1791, in the same letter in which she expressed her reservations about the new constitution, she put Nils von

Rosenstein on guard against the dangers of a concerted military intervention against France. The message was really intended for Rosenstein's master, the king of Sweden Gustav III, whose attitude toward the ambassadress and her husband had considerably cooled since the beginning of the Revolution, as he considered them politically too radical. Gustav III was very hostile to the constitutional developments in France and was planning to lead a military coalition to restore Louis XVI to his full powers as absolute monarch. A disastrous campaign against Russia in 1788—in which Sweden had suffered a crushing defeat—had left him with an unsatisfied appetite for military triumphs; he was also concerned about the loss of the substantial subsidies that the Swedish crown had been receiving from the king of France since his own accession to the throne in 1771.[42]

In her letter, Staël stressed the risks involved in overturning the European international order and questioned the belief that revolutionary France could be simply written out of the system of the balance of powers. She also warned Rosenstein against the illusion that Sweden, like other small European states (such as the German principalities), had anything to gain from an alliance of the great powers that, united against France, would still be free to pursue their own separate ambitions.

> Whatever they say, France will be again a power to be reckoned with; it is perhaps not wise to fail to take it into account in the balance of the European political system. The German princes will not profit from the alliance with the king of Prussia and the emperor, and I doubt Sweden will gain from the union of the powers of Russia and England without any counterweight. I must confess these interests have always seemed to me superior to what they call "the cause of kings" . . . once the political balance of Europe is overturned, it will be a long time before it is settled again.[43]

The ambassadress's warnings went unheard: Gustav III persisted in his unrealistic bellicose plans, apparently unaware that his failure in the recent Russian campaign was unlikely to recommend him as a possible leader for an anti-French military coalition. His determination to engage his country in the support of the counterrevolutionary cause probably contributed to his assassination, by a conspiracy of Swedish aristocrats, in March 1792.[44] Erik-Magnus de Staël, who had been recalled to Sweden but delayed by stormy weather, managed to reach the country only after his death. Concern and anxiety about the possible effects of a foreign military intervention are apparent in Staël's reaction to Jacques-Pierre Brissot's famous speech of 20 October, in which he denounced to the assembly a vast international conspiracy against France and claimed that the nation could achieve an easy military triumph over her enemies. She had been present when the speech was delivered and had been shocked to see that Montmorin, at the time still minister of foreign affairs, had not taken the trouble to turn up and to react in some way. In a letter to Gouvernet she expressed her dismay at the foreseeable international consequences of Brissot's declarations and irritation at the minister's irresponsible negligence: "Brissot has made an incendiary speech; what will be retained of it, I believe, is a violent attack against the princes. If M. de Montmorin did his job, he should have been present and should have prevented the publication of a speech so insulting for the powers; but the ministers are there, it seems, to prevent the king from acting."[45]

Two months later, when Narbonne finally resolved to accept the War Department, she was fully aware of the fact that he was placing himself in an impossible position. On the one hand, taking up the post meant committing to a belief in France's capacity to fight, if necessary; any other stance would draw an accusation of defeatism or incompetence. As Narbonne himself admitted in his speech of acceptance, "to refuse the Ministry of War in the circumstances in which we find ourselves may be seen as a lack of trust in France's forces."[46] On the other hand, as the war appeared every day more likely, it was difficult to ignore the danger of a defeat, and its potentially dramatic consequences:

On what course of events are we embarking ourselves? Paris desires that, at whatever cost, the refusal by the Elector of Mayence to disperse the émigrés be answered by a declaration of war. It will be necessary in the end to give in to this national aspiration, on pain of being shamefully forced to do so. Will the Austrians and Prussians sustain the German princes? One trembles at the precipice into which we are throwing ourselves. We begin a war without money and without officers. And yet this is inevitable, as this long uncertainty about lives and properties is impossible for a nation to sustain. It is the greatest combination of evils one can possibly imagine.[47]

In the same letter, commenting on the speeches the new minister of war had made at the assembly on 7 and 10 December (to which she had seemingly contributed),[48] she observed: "The début of M. de Narbonne has been brilliant, but what of the future? I trust the courage, the talents of M. de Narbonne. If he saves this country, however, it will be a miracle, not a work of genius."[49]

The only residual hope left to the government was that the conflict might be circumscribed, if not avoided, by active diplomatic interventions. Thus, in parallel to the secret negotiations conducted by the court with the émigrés and with the emperor, in January 1792 the new minister of foreign affairs de Lessart sent, as unofficial envoys, Talleyrand to London and Ségur to Berlin, with the task of negotiating the neutrality of, respectively, England and Prussia.[50] As a close friend of Talleyrand, Staël must have been aware of—if not directly party to—these diplomatic missions, which in the end proved ineffective. She was certainly involved in the mission entrusted to the young general Adam Philippe de Custine, who was sent to the duke of Brunswick with the request—which he declined—that he take up command of the French army against the European powers; though Louis XVI was persuaded to sign the letter, this was very much Narbonne's and Staël's initiative.[51]

For three months Narbonne battled on in order to achieve his miracle, inspecting fortifications and troops and reorganizing recruitment. His commitment to ensure that France was ready to fight led him inevitably to a political rapprochement with the Fayettistes and the Girondins—the two groups on the left of the Legislative Assembly who advocated military intervention (unlike the Jacobins, who at this stage were against it). At the same time, his policy of integration of the regiments of volunteers into the regular army led to an open conflict with the minister of the navy, the die-hard royalist Bertrand de Molleville. Following an escalation of disagreements and disputes, the king asked for Narbonne's resignation on 3 March. After leaving his post, he tried for the last time to justify before the assembly his position in relation to the war: "No one wants the war, I believe, on the ground of futile provocations, or from the desire to cause troubles that might be entertained by the enemies of the constitution; but no one wants peace at the cost of liberty, preparing it by spreading the belief that France is unable to sustain a war. I hate the ferocious design that leads some people to wish for war, if this can be avoided. I despise the compromise of weakness, which states that war is impossible."[52] However reasonable, this balancing act had obviously proved unsatisfactory to all parties; it certainly fell short of the "miracle" Staël had evoked.[53]

The resignation of Narbonne and, shortly thereafter, the replacement of the Feuillant cabinet by a Girondin one marked the end of Staël's hopes that the moderates might regain some control over the political situation through the action of the executive. At the end of April, shortly after the declaration of war, accusations against the former minister of war and his mistress, originally voiced by the royalist journal *Correspondence politique*, were set forth at a meeting of the Jacobins' club: Narbonne and Staël, together with some deputies of the Gironde, had been attempting to overturn the monarchy and to create a protectorate, with Narbonne as protector, in view of establishing the republic.

This is how the *Bulletin de minuit* reported the discussion of 25 April:

> MM. Robespierre, Chabot, Collot d'Herbois have denounced, during the last meeting, MM. Brissot, Condorcet, Fauchet, Guadet, Vergniaud, Narbonne, and Mme de Staël as having the design to create a protectorate in France with a republic. M. de Narbonne would become the protector; the king would be placed in a very bad position. M. Robespierre had offered to produce the proofs in his possession, and gave his head as a guarantee of the truth of what he denounced . . . M. Robespierre has then professed his loyalty to the constitution: as the constitution wants a king, such is his own wish.[54]

Quite apart from the fanciful character of the alleged plot (a short while earlier it had been suggested that the same group of conspirators were trying to place the duke of Brunswick on the throne), there is no reliable evidence of any direct contact between Staël and the deputies of the Gironde who were associated with her in the accusation. Unsurprisingly Robespierre, who claimed to possess evidence of the plot, never actually produced it. In spite of the absence of evidence, it is plausible that some sort of rapprochement with the Girondins, in order to secure a wider support for the minister, might have occurred at the time. But if so, this did not imply any significant shift as to how Staël saw the prospect of a war, even less a premature conversion to republicanism on her part.

The most important effect that the Narbonne episode apparently had on her political position was to increase her skepticism about the power of political institutions. Executive power under the new constitutional monarchy had proved as incapable of providing guidance and leadership as the parliamentary factions had been at the time of the Constituent Assembly. In particular it was unable to keep the country out of a disastrous war. To some extent this failure could be ascribed to a poor constitutional design, which obstructed the proper functioning of the executive and limited its powers. But this was only part of the explanation: Staël knew only too well that the confidence people placed in any government was not just the product of constitutional mechanisms. Indeed, since the beginning of the Revolution political institutions, good or bad, had been systematically undermined and wrecked by the relentless pressure of public opinion, which swept everything in its path. As she had confided to Gouvernet only a few months before, "I wonder whether opinion does in fact displace powers, whether the decrees it will pronounce are going to be the only effective means to govern or to disorganize the kingdom."[55]

In the circumstances, it is perhaps understandable that Staël should look for a shortcut, an instant substitute for the long process otherwise necessary to stabilize the new institutions of representative government: a popular, energetic personality in the executive might just succeed in rallying a dangerously volatile public opinion. She was very perceptive in her intuition that the French were not likely to recover entirely from the loss of a powerful monarchical image—that they would remain susceptible to the attractions of a charismatic presence at the head of the state. But the exercise was a risky one. Obviously the patriotic citizen-minister she had in mind would respect the limits of the constitution, not use his popularity to overturn it. Necker had never planned to topple the monarchy (though he was often accused of having done just that); and possibly Narbonne had no intention of doing so either, assuming he were given the opportunity to become France's Oliver Cromwell. Yet the temptation of a pursuit of popular consensus at the expense of constitutional forms, in order to avoid the evils of anarchy and popular uprising, was not likely to go away; it would continue to haunt the political choices of the moderates until the collapse of the Directory.

CHAPTER 3

Politics as Propaganda

DEFENDING THE QUEEN (1793)

THE PAMPHLET *Réflexions sur le procès de la Reine, par une femme* (Reflections on the trial of the queen, by a woman)[1] is the only known work Staël published during the period of revolutionary terror. At the beginning of her exile, at the end of September 1792, she had begun drafting a treatise on happiness and the influence of the passions, but this ambitious philosophical work, still incomplete, was not published until 1796. Another text that she planned to write in collaboration with Narbonne, an account of the conduct of the constitutional monarchists during the Revolution designed to explain and justify their position to European observers, was soon abandoned.[2]

The year that had elapsed since her flight from Paris during the massacres of September 1792 had been an especially difficult one in Staël's life, and not just because of the troubled historical circumstances. In the space of a few months the position of Narbonne had changed from prominent minister to wanted suspect threatened with imprisonment and execution. Hidden for a while inside the Swedish embassy, he had finally managed to leave the country at the end of August, thanks to forged documents the ambassadress had obtained for him. She had stayed behind, counting on the protection offered by her diplomatic status, but had been forced to leave for Coppet at the beginning of

September, when the violence in the streets of Paris had spiraled out of control.[3] In Switzerland she had given birth to a second son by Narbonne (Albert) and soon after had joined her lover for a few months, from January to May 1793, at the English residence she had secured for him and other émigré friends, Juniper Hall in Surrey.[4] But in spite of this short reunion, she was gradually forced to recognize his indifference and obvious desire to end their liaison—a discovery to which she reacted with characteristic storms of frustration and misery, carried across the Channel by a constant stream of frenzied letters.

Her relations with her parents had also become very strained. While her father was mainly concerned with keeping her away from the dangers of Paris, her mother disapproved very strongly of her too-public affair with Narbonne, showing herself—her daughter observed bitterly—more tyrannical than the Jacobins.[5] Both, for different reasons, wished to see her reconciled with her husband, who had joined them in Switzerland at Necker's invitation. Because he appeared to be too favorable to the Revolution, Erik-Magnus had been suspended from his function in January 1792 and recalled to Sweden; the assassination of Gustav III in March added to the uncertainty of his prospects.[6] Clearly the loss of his position as ambassador would have unpleasant consequences for his wife in terms of both status and income.

There were also growing concerns about the Necker family's financial circumstances: in May 1793 the Convention had placed the former minister on the list of those denounced as émigrés (though Necker was in fact a Swiss citizen who had been officially authorized to return to his country); this meant the confiscation of all his revenues and properties in France, and the seizure of the two-million-franc loan he had made, during his ministry, to the French crown. Besides being kept away from Paris, Staël saw her circle of friends and acquaintances dispersed and scattered across Europe, some of them in hiding or in prison, if not already dead. She spent a considerable amount of time trying to maintain contacts, assisting friends in difficulty, petitioning on their behalf all manner of authorities, monitoring the map of Europe to find the safest routes for traveling and the quickest way to send money and letters. *Reflections on the Trial* was written in this climate of insecurity and restlessness, marked by the uncertain news of the war, and by the daily horrific reports of arrests and executions.

Presented as an appeal to the Jacobin government and the French public to spare the life of Marie-Antoinette, the pamphlet was published in Switzerland and England (the French edition was seized and destroyed) a few weeks before the trial and execution of the queen on 16 October 1793. Although it carried no signature, the identity of the author was generally known, a fact that probably contributed to ensuring a cold reception from various political quarters. Staël learned from her friends that the French authorities were "furious" with her for publishing it, and decided to postpone for a while her ever-cherished project of returning to Paris.[7] Royalists, on the other hand, were far from satisfied with a defense of the queen that—in Axel von Fersen's words—betrayed the author's "constitutional" opinions and presented Marie-Antoinette herself as a sympathizer of the Revolution, indeed as a *Jacobine*.[8]

Writing to the novelist Isabelle de Charrière in Neuchâtel, a week after the queen's death, Staël herself admitted that the pamphlet had proved "a pointless effort."[9] It is indeed unclear what political purpose she thought it might serve, as she could not seriously have expected that it would make any difference to Marie-Antoinette's fate. No doubt she felt a moral obligation to speak out against what she regarded as a senseless—as well as heinous—crime. Her correspondence suggests that her compassion for the plight of Marie-Antoinette—an old political enemy she had no personal reasons to like—was sincere and deeply felt. (Before the captivity of the royal family at the Temple, she had repeatedly offered to organize their flight from France, using a method of escape she had successfully tested on other occasions, but her offers had been coldly declined.) Curiously her sympathy for the queen carried some elements of self-identification: like her, Marie-Antoinette had been the constant victim of vicious attacks in the press, and especially of sexual insults, ecumenically produced by all political sides. As she had confessed to Nils von Rosenstein two years before, in less troubled circumstances, "The license of the press is one of the most horrible disadvantages of this new regime, and it is to be said that aristocrats use it at least as much as the democrats, and what is astonishing, in a party that calls itself the party of chivalry, are their attacks against and their persistent hostility to women."[10]

Her misery at Narbonne's desertion and her recurrent suicidal fantasies (for months she carried around with her a lethal dose of opium) made her especially sensitive to the experience of suffering and death. The pamphlet had, however, broader political implications than an immediate appeal for mercy. By writing it, the author wished to make clear to the European public that professing constitutional opinions—that is to say, opposing aristocratic privilege and royal absolutism—did not mean condoning in any way the politics of terror and the crimes that were committed by the revolutionary regime. This clarification seemed necessary, as during her exile in Switzerland and England the ambassadress had been confronted with the bitter hostility that her own "democratic reputation"[11] provoked in émigré circles, and with the prejudices and suspicions of foreign observers. But the text also carried a warning to the Jacobins, threatening them with the consequences of their actions, for which they must sooner or later be accountable, both at home and in the wider international arena.

On the whole the text suffered from the imperfect combination of two different approaches, resulting in a few discontinuities in the argument, and in some unevenness of style. The defense of Marie-Antoinette was deliberately formulated in nonpartisan terms, calling on "republicans, constitutionalists, and aristocrats" alike to unite in support of the queen. Marie-Antoinette herself was presented as a victim, a woman, and a mother suffering a terrible fate, rather than as a political personality. At the same time *Reflections on the Trial* addressed the factors that had led to the politics of terror, and the possible consequences for France of pursuing the practice of proscriptions and persecution.[12]

With these objectives in mind, Staël adopted a different argumentative strategy from the one employed by Necker in his pamphlet of 1792, *Réflexions présentées à la Nation française sur le procès intenté à Louis XVI* (Reflections presented to the French nation on the trial of Louis XVI).[13] While Necker discussed the constitutional implications of the king's trial, questioning its legitimacy, Staël chose to set all constitutional and legal arguments aside. As she explained in the pamphlet's opening paragraphs, legal forms were only conventions on which the people and its rulers agreed at a particular point in time: since the queen's trial was essentially political, the task of the writer was not that of raising legal or constitutional objections, but of interpreting and discussing its political meaning—in her own words, "addressing opinion, analyzing politics."[14] To that end, it was necessary to understand the nature of the popular passions that had led to the queen's imprisonment, and the implications that the trial might have for the future prospects of the revolutionary government.

AN INTERESTING VICTIM

Staël introduced the discussion of the conduct and possible responsibilities of Marie-Antoinette by asking why popular sentiments toward the queen had changed so radically within a few years, from initial enthusiasm to violent hostility. As Edmund Burke had done before her in his *Reflections on the Revolution in France* (1790)[15] she played on the contrast between the enthusiastic reception accorded to the dauphine at the time of her marriage, in 1770, and the fury of the mob of which she had become the target some twenty years later. She stressed how this change in popular attitudes had occurred in a relatively short space of time, if just before the Revolution the queen was still the object of acclamations by the crowds during her rare public appearances in Paris. Such a sudden reversal of fortunes could hardly be the result of any radical transformation of the personality and conduct of Marie-Antoinette, but must necessarily have other causes. In her meteoric trajectory from cherished princess to imprisoned and hated monarch, the queen was the victim of external forces upon which her real conduct had very little impact.

To justify this view, the writer presented Marie-Antoinette as a blameless and politically noninfluential personality: a mother devoted to her children, a woman whose main public role consisted in charitable activities; a pretty woman, a little too frivolous in her youth, and possibly too generous toward undeserving courtiers, but innocent of any vice or malice; a meek sovereign, who had never caused any of her subjects to be imprisoned, punished, or killed; a dutiful wife, loyal to her husband, who had played a very subordinate role in public affairs, and who had in fact proved generally sympathetic to "patriot ministers" such as Turgot and Necker. This representation of the queen's position was at best a compound of half-truths: though never an intimate of Marie-Antoinette, Staël had been in contact with her on various occasions, and had personally experienced her haughty and uneasy patronage; she had also witnessed at close range the misguided political pressures the queen exerted on Louis XVI, and the tenacious hostility she had shown to Necker and to the cause of constitutional reform. All of this the writer deliberately omitted from her account. On the other hand, she was sincere when she claimed that Marie-Antoinette could hardly be held responsible for the bankruptcy of French public finances, and when she affirmed that the queen's influence upon Franco-Austrian relations was very marginal. As to the wild accusations of debauchery and sexual misconduct, Staël knew enough about life at the court (and had herself sufficiently suffered from similar calumnies) to reject them as complete fabrications.

There were obvious strategic reasons for minimizing, in the pamphlet, the responsibilities of Marie-Antoinette; but for Staël the main point was that, whatever her original faults, the queen had redeemed herself by the fortitude and piety she had shown in facing terrible ordeals, such as the execution of her husband, the gruesome death of some of her closest friends, and, worst of all, the separation from her son. Like Burke's pamphlet, Staël's *Reflections on the Trial* set forth an idealized image of Marie-Antoinette; but while Burke's queen inhabited a medieval fantasy of royal heritage and chivalry, Staël chose to turn her into the timeless symbol of vulnerable womanhood, ennobled by her grief. In the text she illustrated Marie-Antoinette's sacrifice with an array of heterogeneous literary references: some passages describing the queen's imprisonment (the tower, the secret prison, the severed head of the princess of Lamballe appearing at the window) evoked the dark atmosphere of the gothic novel, a literary genre that was finding new inspiration in the experience of revolutionary terror.[16] Some fragments of dialogue inserted in the narrative recalled the historical dramas Staël had always loved, in particular her own tragedy of 1787, *Jane Grey*, which recalled the fate of another unfortunate princess, also the innocent victim of overwhelming historical events.[17]

On the whole, however, the dominant inspiration for the pamphlet's style was unquestionably the sentimental novel.[18] The descriptions of Marie-Antoinette on her knees, clasping the children to her breast, weeping floods of tears, falling into fainting fits, experiencing "unspeakable torments of the soul"—all this cast her vividly as a character out of Rousseau, a Julie who had imprudently strayed across the border from the peaceful Swiss countryside into besieged royal palaces. It also made her into a forerunner of the heroines of Staël's own fiction, Delphine and Corinne. Unfortunately, the finishing touch—the undying devotion of the queen's lover—had to be omitted, for obvious reasons, from the narrative, but it featured prominently in the writer's own correspondence. There Narbonne's cruel inconstancy was unfavorably compared to Fersen's exemplary loyalty to his mistress. Should Narbonne refuse to see her again, she wrote on one occasion, "such a decision would be even more atrocious than the fate of that woman [Marie-Antoinette] renowned for her misfortunes. Her executioners have exhausted all manner of torments, but M. de Fersen was not among them. She has been able to call his name without horror, and died assured of his regrets."[19]

While the depiction of Louis XVI as a Christian martyr became a commonplace in émigré literature, Staël preferred for Marie-Antoinette the improbable role of republican heroine. Burke had been the first to introduce a "Roman" theme in his narrative, suggesting, with surprising nonchalance, the possibility of the queen's suicide, claiming that "with the dignity of a Roman matron" she would never fall by "ignoble hands."[20] Staël instead placed great emphasis on the "republican" dimension of the queen's character, offering her courage in the face of adversity as an example of Roman fortitude: "Instead of hating her, look at her example. If you are republicans, respect those virtues that you should imitate: this soul, which will not bend, is the kind of soul that would have loved Roman liberty."[21]

This dramatization of the queen's character in the fashionable languages of sentimentality and ancient virtue was essentially a rhetorical device designed to capture the sympathy of the readers. It was also, however, a means of shifting the argument away from the particular question of Marie-Antoinette's personal responsibility to the general one of the consequences of terror and the human costs of the Revolution. The queen's life, Staël argued, was by no means more valuable than the many other lives that were destroyed every day by the terrorists. Yet her spectacular downfall from a condition of privilege and happiness, the amplitude of her losses, gave to her suffering a particular poignancy, turning her into an especially "interesting" victim, worthy to become the symbol of all victims. Here the reference to Rousseau was crucial, because Staël believed that his awareness of human suffering was the dominant trait in the philosopher's sensibility, indeed the cornerstone of his moral doctrine.[22] Compassion was, she argued, the most basic of virtues, the foundation of human sociability, since a community in which people were unable to feel pity was no longer truly human. "If you win, if you manage to push the enemy back a second time from your territory, you might think you have triumphed; and yet at this very moment, if you persist in your cruelty, if you sacrifice the queen, your victories will have come to nothing."[23] Thus Marie-Antoinette stood before her judges as the ultimate test of their residual capacity to step back from the precipice of barbarism, restoring France to the proper condition of civilized society.

A PASSIONATE PEOPLE

If the queen's conduct was not the origin of the change of attitude on the part of the people, who or what was responsible for it? What could make popular sentiments turn so suddenly from admiration and enthusiasm to hatred? "Only five years ago— and by then all her political life, anything that could deserve love or hatred, had already occurred—five years ago I saw the whole of Paris crowd eagerly to witness her passage. This enthusiasm, the memory of which must make her plight more bitter, this enthusiasm, the memory of which must also trouble the French, and make them doubt their new judgments, is rejected today as a mistake."[24] The question of what caused popular beliefs and expectations to change and fluctuate was central to Staël's understanding of the revolutionary phenomenon. In the article "From What Signs" she had described how French public opinion retreated, from its initial wholehearted support of the reform movement, to a state of fear and uncertainty, thus favoring the growth of extreme political forces. Here she attempted to explain the dramatic swing from the traditional popular attachment to royal persons and the symbols of monarchy to the new ugly mood of disaffection, suspicion, and open hostility. Indeed, between 1789 and 1793 the very nature of opinion seemed to have changed, and what had originally manifested itself as an enlightened force, the voice of common reason, had rapidly turned into the irrational expression of brutal emotions and violent ideologies.

In 1791 Staël had argued that, in order to understand the dynamics of popular passions, one had to separate what happened in normal circumstances from what occurred in the exceptional context of a revolution. At the best of times the exercise of governance had to contend with the unstable balance of private interests and popular emotions: but, in ordinary circumstances, well-established regimes and institutions managed, to some extent, to control and canalize these unsettling forces. A revolutionary situation was one in which this unstable equilibrium of emotional states was severely disrupted, leading to anarchy and violent confrontations. It remained to be seen to what extent the disruption was caused by a failure in governance, by the impact of spontaneous and irresistible forces, or by the deliberate action of some political groups.

The book on passions that Staël had begun writing in September 1792 was an attempt to systematize this complex matter, considering first the influence that passions had upon the happiness of individuals, then the nature of collective passions, and the way in which these shaped the political life of nations. There is evidence that in the early months of 1793, the writer was already working on this project and reading passages of her new work to those friends who shared her English exile at Juniper Hall.[25] Although the version she published in 1796 in Lausanne, under the title *De l'Influence des passions sur le bonheur des individus et des nations*, was organized as a broad philosophical discussion, the original core of the work was based upon her direct observations of the French revolutionary experience.[26]

Thus the text of *Reflections on the Trial* stood in close proximity to the elaboration of the treatise: though it was not designed to present any systematic conclusions, it anticipated a number of insights about the emotional dynamics of the revolutionary process. Staël retained in her analysis the notion—originally set forth by the tradition of sentimental moral philosophy—of the presence in human emotions of alternating phases of excitement and tranquillity. Like individual passions, collective popular moods also had a tendency to follow patterns of movement and rest, agitation and peace: the writer employed the terms "enthusiasm" and "exhilaration" to describe the pleasurable excitement that crowds experienced at moments of collective mobilization. This emotion was not especially discriminating in its objects: in France, before and even at the beginning of the Revolution, it had manifested itself in the joyful acclamations of the royal family on the occasion of their public appearances, while later on it would produce violent antiroyalist and antiaristocratic protests and riots. In September 1791, commenting on the new "patriotic" attitude displayed by the king and queen, Staël had described to Nils von Rosenstein the general enthusiasm manifested by the Parisian crowds for the celebrations of the new constitution:

> From morning to night there is endless dancing, illuminations, and feasts. In short, they believe themselves happy, and vanity makes them wish to parade their happiness in front of their enemies. Actually, there is nothing very satisfactory in lacking money or work, but this new regime amuses them. All these military uniforms, maneuvers, and endless events take them away from the monotony of their lives, and sometimes I think that they are attached to the new order because it takes them away from the boredom of their usual occupations.[27]

The desire to escape from the experience of *l'ennui* (boredom), that major theme in Old Regime libertine literature, was clearly not confined to the aristocratic sensibility: it turned out that the poor were getting bored too, though for somewhat different reasons; but unfortunately in their case the search for diversions was rapidly getting out of hand.[28] Staël thought that the French, being by nature a "passionate people," were especially prone to being easily excited. In normal times these states of excitement were not likely to last for long: once whatever had occasioned them was over, people generally returned to their usual occupations, and to a state of tranquillity. However, the Revolution had changed all this: by encouraging the expression of emotions, by liberating public speech, by allowing every possible license to the press, and by multiplying opportunities for popular gatherings and mobilizations, it had turned these occasional moments of enthusiasm into a permanent condition of delirious exaltation.

CRIMINAL STRATEGIES

Initially Staël had followed Montesquieu in associating the emotional need for "movement" with the aspiration to liberty: in this respect it was probably to be expected that a process of political change should lead to a degree of unrest in the population. But in *Reflections on the Trial* she clearly attributed responsibility for keeping the people in a permanent state of agitation to a deliberate political design. The popular fury that had engulfed Marie-Antoinette, together with the other symbols of the Old Regime, was by no means a spontaneous popular response. It was the product of a series of relentless campaigns directed at spreading calumnies, lies, threats, and false accusations against anyone who was perceived as a political enemy. Aggressive propaganda and intimidation—rather than the ordinary practice of political confrontation—were the means by which, in this new context, political objectives were promoted, and parliamentary battles won. Two years earlier, Staël had described to Gouvernet the daily pressures exerted by the Jacobins to discredit the new constitution of 1791: "They have in their clubs three thousand spectators, and by shouting from morning to night, with an appearance of reason, that the court is in bad faith, they make the party of the republic grow in Paris."[29] Once the Jacobins had come to power, this practice of bombarding the public with relentless propaganda had been transformed, by the terrorist government, into a powerful machinery of surveillance, intimidation, and denunciation. "All human passions have been set free in order to direct them against the former power, against those objects the people remembered to have envied, and that they now had no longer reason to fear . . . What fury, what insults, what cunning, what means, alien from the truth, and yet more influential than the truth upon a passionate people."[30]

In the *Spirit of the Laws* Montesquieu explained how in a free country—England—the members of the legislative excited the people against the executive, whenever it suited them to put pressure on the government, spreading alarming allegations and agitating imaginary threats. Then, having obtained the desired result, they exercised their influence to placate the people and restore civil peace.[31] Montesquieu warned his readers that such manipulative tactics on the part of the legislative were viable only within a stable constitutional framework, where the representatives of the people acted as a buffer between popular fear and fury, on the one hand, and the government on the other. If, however, "the terrors [excited by the legislative] should emerge on the occasion of the overturning of fundamental laws, they would prove insidious, lethal, atrocious, and may lead to catastrophes." Now, what the Jacobins accomplished in the revolutionary process went clearly beyond this calculated exploitation of popular emotions on the part of enlightened politicians, who acted within a moderate regime. What the French revolutionary leaders had done instead was to excite large masses of people (who were not in a position to judge and to reason for themselves), directing and empowering them to act on the ground of imaginary threats and false beliefs:

That class of society that has no time to oppose analysis to assertion, examination to emotion, will govern as it is led, unless, in attributing to such a class great power, it is also estab-

lished as a firm rule that falsity is a national crime. Verisimili-
tude is nothing to the man who has not taken time to reflect;
on the contrary, the more he is surprised, the more he will like
to believe.[32]

Initially the unleashing of popular passions had served to promote and sustain the cause of radical political change; but as the
Jacobin regime progressed on the path of subversion, persecution, and crime, the involvement of large crowds in their actions
came also to be a defensive strategy on the part of the revolutionary leaders. The latter knew only too well that, in the case of
defeat, they would be held personally responsible for all that had
occurred, and they wished to implicate as many people as possible in their actions so as to be able, on the day of reckoning, to
share and to spread the blame. The Convention had adopted this
strategy at the time of the trial of Louis XVI by encouraging and
promoting antiroyalist petitions from the departments, and by
seeking the complicity of the army. The same attitude was now
being adopted to implicate the mass of the people in the condemnation of Marie-Antoinette:

> The leaders of a popular party try by all means to bind the
> people to their cause; they know that in all revolutions glory
> and defeat belong to the leaders; and, afraid that the people
> might rest upon this certainty, they wish to identify with it in
> all possible ways; they try to persuade it that it is the real au-
> thor of those acts, from which there is no hope of return.[33]

Staël stressed that those guilty of such dangerous, and even
criminal, implication of the masses in the initiatives of the terrorist government acted not as the legitimate representatives of the
people but as chiefs of factions, exercising an arbitrary power.
While Louis XVI had been judged by the Legislative Assembly,
Marie-Antoinette was summoned to appear, like any ordinary
suspect, before the revolutionary tribunal. Thus, in addressing
the queen's future judges, the writer made a point of reminding

them that they were not "the representatives of the nation," nor were they invested with any mandate on behalf of the people. Consequently they were at liberty either to obey their own conscience or to be dictated to by the "cries of the assemblies of Paris." The power built upon the "dark fury" of popular passions was no longer recognizable as anything but mob rule and arbitrary domination.

NATURAL AND ARTIFICIAL PASSIONS

The exploitation of popular emotions by unscrupulous political leaders did not necessarily mean that the manipulators were acting in a controlled, rational manner. No doubt considerations of interest, as well as political calculation, explained to some extent the risky tactics of popular mobilization employed by the Jacobins, as it was the most effective means they had found to secure power. But at the heart of their strategy there was also an irrational element, which manifested itself in the self-destructive course upon which the terrorist government had now embarked. Staël described this irrational element as "the fanaticism of political opinions," a lethal disposition that undermined the residual instincts for self-preservation of the revolutionary political class.

Later on, in the treatise on passions, the writer developed a detailed account of the passion she called "spirit of party," in terms that recalled David Hume's discussion of the subject in the *Essays*, but with the added flesh and blood of recent French events. The spirit of party was the irrational dimension of party allegiance, one that depended not on considerations of affinity or interest, but simply on the fanatical attachment to certain beliefs. While in normal circumstances this disposition might have no serious consequences, certain "exceptional events" might stimulate it, turning it into a force far more deadly than any of the other passions that were generally disguised behind it—such as pride, vengeance, or fear.[34]

In *Reflections on the Trial* Staël did not provide an extensive analysis of partisanship but clearly identified fanaticism, the irrational attachment to a cause, as the most irresistible and destructive component in the emotional storm raised by the Revolution. She also saw it as the prime mover in a process of distortion and corruption of public morality. The reversal of popular attitudes toward the monarchy, and toward Marie-Antoinette in particular, was not in fact the only consequence of the manipulations undertaken by the revolutionary leadership. Their actions also had another, more fundamental effect, namely, the perversion of the "natural" emotions of the people and their replacement by "artificial" ones. The strength of the early ideals of the Revolution had been that they promised a return to the principles of nature. Instead the "terrible influence of fictive passions" led to the paralysis or distortion of natural responses, so that in the end the entire community lost "all sense of humanity."[35] "What more terrible reversal of the innate sentiments of the human heart than the ostentation of cruelty, than the kind of eloquence that is sustained by threats, than those solemn oaths that promise only death?"[36]

The paradox of the French experience was that a revolution originally inspired by the desire to uphold natural values and natural sentiments had ended in the corruption or suppression of these. Compassion had been replaced by cruelty, humanity by hatred, courage by the wish for death, liberty by enslavement. The excess of excitement created by the Jacobin propaganda, the constant artificial stimulation, in the people, of violent instincts, had resulted in a state of emotional fatigue and, finally, in a condition of apathy that engulfed leaders and ordinary people alike. Like the excess of pleasure, the excess of violence and cruelty generated a sort of emotional indifference. This process of desensitization of the public had gone so far that the possible execution of Marie-Antoinette would no longer provide a rallying point, or a source of encouragement, for the revolutionaries: it would simply be yet another pointless crime.

While the trial and death of the king had generated profound emotion—and presumably satisfied the desire for vengeance of those who condemned him—no such response could be expected any longer. The country, exposed to so many tragic events, had sunk into a state of indifference so profound that it would hardly pay any attention to an additional victim. Indeed, if the Jacobins expected from the condemnation of Marie-Antoinette some propaganda triumph, a new wave of enthusiasm for their cause, they were deceiving themselves: "Do they imagine they could double the courage of the people by intoxicating it with the blood of a new victim? But such a terrible resource is now exhausted: everyone is so accustomed to the idea of death, oppressors and oppressed alike have become so familiar with it, that to give it would no longer provoke any kind of emotion."[37] The Revolution was associated with a condition of emotional disorder, and this disorder led, inevitably, to a confusion in moral judgment, to a perversion of the collective sense of right and wrong. Staël stressed this point a few months after the execution of Marie-Antoinette in a letter addressed to the Swiss theologian Jean-Gaspard Lavater (the theorist of physiognomy), who had requested a copy of her pamphlet:

> Here is the defense of the queen you have asked for. At present I can no longer look at it: the kind of hope it inspired in me at the time makes my regrets even more bitter. The death of a king, who was also the most honest of men, has produced in Europe a more vivid sensation. However, I do not believe that any other act combines so many elements of barbarism than the long torments of that unhappy victim. Ah, what horrors committed in the name of the holiest of ideas, liberty, and how can we have a clear notion of justice and injustice when they have been so artfully confused?[38]

The Jacobins' reckless attempt to rule on the strength of undisciplined passions had granted them unexpected political influence, but at the cost of undermining their original project of a society built around the recognition and assertion of natural laws and natural principles.

MASTERING FRANCE'S FUTURE

In evoking the character and the sufferings of Marie-Antoinette, Staël had appealed to the heart of her readers, engaging their emotions with a series of touching, tearful tableaux. Feeling sympathy and compassion for a woman who was no longer a monarch, but simply a defenseless widow subjected, with her children, to the cruelest persecutions, meant restoring natural sentiments to their rightful place in a civilized community. In the concluding pages of the pamphlet, however, the writer adopted a different tone, addressing the French government and its supporters with the voice of reason, urging them to consider, through the queen's fate, the future prospects of their regime and of their country. As the argument shifts, one can almost hear the cogs and wheels in the practical politician's mind as they start clicking and turning again, moving toward the next goal.

One of the side effects of the state of emotional excitement generated by the Revolution was that those who experienced it rapidly lost touch with external reality. They became so absorbed by their own domestic drama that they believed that the entire world must share their exaltation. This, however, was not the case, as elsewhere in the world people continued to lead normal lives, and to conform to ordinary standards of behavior and morality. Wrapped up in their collective dream (or nightmare), the French were unaware of the degree of indignation and horror provoked by their actions among other nations. And yet sooner or later they must face this dismal reality:

> In the sort of intoxication that a revolution creates, one believes that the rest of the world has also changed; but what will be his fate when he wakes up and realizes that he has become an object of hatred for his fellow men![39]

Unlike some of the friends who shared her exile, Staël was always rather skeptical about the possibility that the Revolution might be terminated by foreign military intervention. Her skepticism probably betrayed an element of wishful thinking on her part, as she could not bear the thought of France being occupied by foreign troops and given over to counterrevolution—a sentiment she was to express very vividly twenty years later on the occasion of Napoleon's defeat. But apart from her obvious distaste for this prospect, and although the news of the war remained confused and uncertain, she thought it would be unrealistic to expect an armed solution to the French political crisis. In the pamphlet she acknowledged the recent French military "triumphs," urging her compatriots not to dishonor their well-deserved glory by murdering the queen.

She argued that even a victorious France must sooner or later come to terms with the other European powers, and that an act of mercy toward the surviving members of the royal family could make the nation's bargaining position much stronger. She also suggested that Marie-Antoinette might prove a valuable hostage in dealings with the Austrians, while her death would enrage them and make them far less well disposed in the event of a negotiation. The suggestion that the queen be used as a hostage has been dismissed as far-fetched by some commentators on Staël's pamphlet.[40] And yet there is some evidence that the possibility of a deal involving the person of Marie-Antoinette was seriously discussed by the Committee of Public Safety before they decided to put the queen on trial.

At a meeting of the committee held on the night of 2 September 1793—reported to Lord Grenville's office in London by a clerk who was a British agent—Pierre Joseph Cambon argued against initiating the trial, proposing that Marie-Antoinette might prove useful in an effort to negotiate some form of amnesty in the case of a military defeat.[41] He failed to convince the committee, in particular Jacques René Hébert, who dismissed the suggestion on the ground that no one, of all those present at the meeting, was likely to survive the Revolution, let alone find himself in a position to make terms with the enemy.[42] This reaction—if the report is accurate—would confirm Staël's feeling that the queen's execution was an indication that the revolutionary government was irredeemably pursuing a self-destructive course.

Against this kind of collective death wish, the writer argued that it was still possible to reverse the trend of terrorist policy and draw back, before the final fall into the abyss. No doubt the European monarchs had felt somewhat threatened by France's rejection of aristocracy and royalty; but these political choices alone would not have provoked a military reaction on their part. What the other European nations reacted against was the barbarism of the terrorist regime, and the atrocities it had perpetrated:

> Do not deceive yourselves: the destruction of royalty and of the privileged orders has perhaps irritated, and turned against you, the majority of European governments; but what makes the nations rise up against you is the barbarism of your proscriptions. You govern by death; the strength that your government, by its very nature, lacks, you find in terror, and where a throne used to stand, you have erected a scaffold![43]

If this state of affairs continued, and if the terrorists were to add to the list of the crimes already perpetrated the death of the queen, then those foreign powers, Austria in particular, would not rest, and France could never feel secure. Only by resisting "the passions of the moment," by an act of mercy that marked at the same time a return to rationality, could the French hope to become masters of their own future.

DEMOCRACY AND LIBERTY

Staël's double appeal to mercy and reason was bound to remain unheard. In Paris, not only was her pamphlet destroyed, but the Swedish embassy was raided and searched, papers belonging to the absent ambassador and his wife were seized, and two employees were temporarily arrested. As Sweden was not at war with France, the reaction of the two sections of the Paris Commune responsible for the raid was clearly disproportionate, a sign that the ambassadress's provocation had hit its target, though possibly not in the way she had wished. If she was profoundly distressed by the news of Marie-Antoinette's execution, Staël began to feel that the end of the terrorist regime was only a matter of time, and that the position of the Jacobin leadership was becoming increasingly vulnerable. On 13 April 1794, a week after the execution of Danton and his group, she wrote to her husband:

> You see that Danton and others have been decapitated. Robespierre is marching toward dictatorship. All that is left in France is the power of the nine members of the Committee of Public Safety, who are entirely led by one man. Does Signeul [M.de Staël's secretary and a Jacobin sympathizer] continue to call this democracy and liberty? This does not change in any way the question of the external war, which seems increasingly decided in favor of the French: but if the government takes the form of a *dictatoriat*, it seems to me it will be easier to change it.[44]

The real question, at this stage, was not whether the rule of Robespierre, or of some other leader, would come to an end, but what, if anything, could be salvaged from it, what future was left in France for "democracy and liberty." The defense of Marie-Antoinette set forth in *Reflections on the Trial* was at the same time a recognition of the fact that, in a few years, the experience of Jacobinism had profoundly altered any previous understanding of the impact of popular emotions and beliefs upon the authority of constitutional government. The role played by unruly popular passions in creating anarchy and promoting tyranny was of course a familiar phenomenon in the Western political tradition, as was the practice of manipulation exercised by demagogues and faction leaders upon popular opinion. But recent French events had given to the conjunction of these well-known factors an entirely new dimension.

The scale of what the Jacobins had achieved was very impressive: starting from a minority position, and from a limited geographical area (the city of Paris), they had come to dominate public opinion in a large modern country of over twenty million people, establishing their influence through a vast network of political associations, meetings, journals, and other publications. They had also succeeded in overturning secular loyalties—such as the traditional allegiance to the crown—and in maintaining popular support on their side in the face of overwhelming odds, like the threats of famine and war. As a result, the first French example of modern constitutional government had been defeated and destroyed on the very ground on which it believed itself to be strongest, that of intellectual and moral leadership and popular consensus.[45]

Staël's analysis of the Jacobins' performance raises the question of the role she attributed, in the revolutionary process, to what she referred to as "the people" or "the nation." On her account, if the mass of the people harbored the needs, fears, and expectations that agitated French society, these shapeless emotions and aspirations acquired political significance only though the initiative of some active minority groups. The Revolution itself appeared to be the work of rival elites who pursued different political designs, each of them claiming to act according to the wishes, and in the interest, of the whole nation. Because in France the masses were largely unprepared for any active political role—owing to a lack of tradition, habit, and education—even if they were nominally invested with the power to govern themselves, they would still rule "as they were led," following the slogans and directives of some influential minority.

For Staël this interaction between the French people and its ruling elites was at best problematic. Because the country lacked a tradition of free government, in France the normal relations between a free nation and its elected representatives had not yet taken shape. The shaky reputation that the Constituent Assembly had enjoyed in the eyes of the same "nation" by which in theory its members had been elected was an indication of this bond's fragility. When in power, the moderates had proved unable to win the trust of the mass of the people and to interpret their expectations. For their part, in attaining popular support by means of manipulation and deception, the Jacobins had made the prospect of a free government even more remote: they had empowered the masses but had not enabled them to choose for themselves.

While Staël believed that the people were not able to decide for themselves, this did not mean that the popular role in the Revolution was just a passive one—that the nation was destined to be either patronized by enlightened rulers or led astray by agitators and demagogues, as was assumed by conservative critics such as Burke. The basic aspirations that the French people embodied at a particular point in its history represented the ultimate limit to the action of any political class, and to the ambitions of any leadership. No real popular sovereignty and no freedom would ever be possible unless this limit was taken into account. Later on Staël would place the "quietly murmuring" majority, desirous of peace, order, and prosperity, at the center of her vision of representative government. Here the sense of limit took the form of the fracture described in the pamphlet between the vocal minority of the Jacobins—with their shouting gatherings and resounding speeches—and the irresponsive mass of ordinary citizens, sunk into mute stupor. The ominous silence of the nation in the face of Marie-Antoinette's death stood as the barrier against which the tide of revolutionary passions was doomed to break.

CHAPTER 4

Addressing William Pitt (1794)

IN LATER years Staël was to describe the fifteen months or so that elapsed between the fall of Maximilien Robespierre on 27 July 1794 (9 Thermidor) and the establishment of the Directory in October 1795 as "an epoch of true anarchy" for France.[1] But in the immediate aftermath of the anti-Jacobin coup, as, from her Swiss exile, she tried to make sense of the confusing information that filtered out of France, her judgment was far from clear-cut. No one at the time was able to predict the consequences of the arrest and execution of Robespierre and of his close entourage; indeed, it was several months before observers convinced themselves that the terrorist regime had actually come to an end with the elimination of the Jacobin leader.

For Staël the anticipation of a new state of affairs in Paris—whatever this might be—was not just a matter of general interest but carried immediate consequences for her own future plans and prospects. During her exile she had occasionally imagined herself beginning a new life elsewhere: in England with Narbonne, in Germany or Denmark with her new lover, Adolphe Ribbing (a Swedish nobleman who had been exiled after taking part in the assassination of Gustav III),[2] or even in America, where Necker had acquired some landed property.[3] However, her real ambitions remained firmly focused upon the chances of returning to Paris and to the heart of French politics. Characteristically, while it was far from clear if, when, and on what terms this return might be possible, she anticipated events, making a symbolic comeback with the timely publication of a provocative work.

Composed toward the end of 1794, and published at the beginning of 1795 in Switzerland, England, and France, the pamphlet *Réflexions sur la paix, addressées à M. Pitt et aux Français* (Reflections on peace, addressed to Mr. Pitt and to the French)[4] was a strikingly bold and confident piece of writing. Although (with one exception) all editions were unsigned, well-informed readers could be in no doubt as to the author's identity. Far from showing the strain of two years of exile, relative isolation, and existential anxieties (the disintegration of her relationship with Narbonne, the death of her mother after a long illness, the threats to her father's fortune), the writer spoke with the voice of one who meant to make an impact upon the European debate. To complete the effect, she selected as her main interlocutor, somewhat surprisingly, the head of the English government, William Pitt, identifying him as at the arbiter of France's and Europe's future.

The central question addressed in the pamphlet was that of the consequences of the war between France and the European coalition from a variety of perspectives: the internal situation of the French republic, the demands of the émigrés, the interests of Continental powers, and the domestic, as well as international, position of England. By illustrating these different viewpoints, the writer meant to show that reaching some peace settlement as soon as possible was the most desirable solution for all concerned, indeed the only means of restoring order and stability in Europe. But if the restoration of European order was the ostensive object of *Reflections on Peace*, the pamphlet presented in addition some significant insights on the nature of representative government in France and England. For the first time the writer confronted the new French republic not as a temporary aberration but as a serious political object, one that might outlive the terrorist regime. She also looked at Pitt's wartime government in critical terms, trying to distance herself from the unconditional admiration of English institutions she had always felt until then.

MISSING ROBESPIERRE

While modern historiography has conventionally adopted the coup of Thermidor as marking the end of the French Revolution, for most contemporaries the possible consequences of the event were far from clear. If in Paris the execution of Robespierre was the occasion for celebrations in the prisons and in the streets—as well as the start of a long trail of vengeance against the former terrorists—observers abroad reacted to it with more alarm than relief. It was generally feared that the elimination of the Jacobin leader—like the execution of Georges Danton a few months before—might be just another episode of partisan infighting, leading not to the end of terror, but to the dictatorship of a new faction and to further violence.[5] Diplomats and ministers, in Austria, Prussia, and England, however hostile to the fallen Jacobin leader, had regarded Robespierre as the true master of France, somewhat overestimating his personal power and his control over the Convention and the Parisian mobs. Because of his initial opposition to the war, they also expected him to be open to the prospect of peace negotiations.

In Switzerland in particular—as Staël explained in a letter to her husband at the beginning of August—Robespierre's disappearance caused great anxiety, as he was generally seen as a friend and "protector" of the Confederation.[6] In November 1793 he had in fact presented to the Convention, for the Committee of Public Safety, a report on foreign policy that confirmed France's intention to respect neutral countries.[7] It was now feared that the new leadership might adopt a more aggressive attitude and eventually invade Swiss territory. For Staël personally the situation in Switzerland was already sufficiently uncomfortable without the added complication of a French occupation.

A few weeks before Robespierre's fall, a popular insurrection in Geneva had established a revolutionary regime, and the new government had condemned Necker to a year's imprisonment and a suspension for three years of his citizenship.[8] This sentence, though representing no immediate threat to the person of Necker—who had prudently removed himself from the town, anticipating the new leadership's hostility—had potentially serious financial consequences for the family. The French government had already seized all their properties and revenues in France, treating the former minister as an "émigré" despite the fact that he had never been a French citizen: in the circumstances Necker's status as citizen of Geneva was an essential condition for contesting the confiscation. There were other problems: the government of the Republic of Berne, anxious to avoid any occasion of conflict with France, was expelling from its territory (which included the Pays de Vaud, where Staël was living at the time) all the émigrés under the age of forty: an initiative that could deprive her of the company of her closest friends, including Ribbing himself. Moreover, given the unstable political situation in Sweden after the king's assassination, Staël's husband had been suspended from his post of ambassador and recalled to Stockholm; thus the writer's own privileged status as the wife of a foreign diplomat was now also in question.

In her correspondence, during the summer and fall of 1794, Staël wavered in her assessment of the French situation between caution and optimism. In Paris the gradual release of prisoners, the trials against the most exposed of former terrorists, and the newfound freedom of the press were all reassuring signs, showing "the strength of public opinion." However, in other parts of France, circumstances were still quite confused, and a general uncertainty remained as to the nature of the new regime. "If I dared," she wrote to Ribbing in October, "I would tell you the news from France is perfectly good, but I am afraid to bring bad luck . . . In Paris the freedom to write and speak is complete.

People are released and acquitted . . . Yet without a government we shall see variations in the public spirit, but no real security."[9] Two months later, however, she had overcome her doubts and confided to the same correspondent (who was now contemplating settling in Denmark) how much the idea of returning to Paris still attracted her: a "perfect freedom of the press," she claimed, was now reigning in France, making the capital "an ideal place in which to live."[10]

Another major unknown at the end of 1794 concerned the pursuit of the war. Robespierre's regime had been overturned just when the revolutionary army, after some initial reverses, was on a winning streak, enabling France to occupy Belgium and the left bank of the Rhine, threatening Germany and Holland. The question now was whether the Convention, under its new leadership, would choose to pursue the war, extending French territory to and beyond its supposed "natural frontiers," or whether it would prefer to come to terms with the European powers.

Staël's initial opposition to the war in 1792 had been chiefly motivated by the belief that France was unprepared to fight and was doomed to suffer a defeat: a defeat, moreover, that would mean the return of the Bourbons and a counterrevolution, mercilessly enforced by foreign armies.[11] She had not been entirely unsympathetic to the patriotic sentiments that were driving public opinion toward a military intervention, especially in view of the provocations of the émigrés; but she still thought that in the circumstances indulging them was demagogic and irresponsible. Two years later, the danger that France might be crushed by counterrevolutionary forces had been forestalled, albeit at the cost of terrible sacrifices. But the same patriotic élan and shared national sentiment that enabled the republic to resist against her enemies had now become the main obstacle to the end of the Revolution and to a return to normality. The war had turned into the real engine of the Revolution, the crucial factor that still kept the nation united in support of the existing government. It was for this reason that all European powers—especially England, identified by Staël as the *dominus* of the coalition—should try by all means to secure peace.[12]

While she had selected as her privileged interlocutors William Pitt and the French people, Staël could not resist the temptation to remind the coalition forces of their grave strategic errors: the credit they accorded to the vain and unreasonable pretensions of the émigrés,[13] their belief that the revolutionary leadership could be simply bribed or intimidated, and especially their failure to support "the party opposed to the republic," that is to say, the constitutional monarchists, who alone, inside France, might have stopped the Jacobins. The "enemies of France"—she argued—must finally understand the true nature of their real adversary: revolutionary ideology. The "chimerical system of equality" that inspired the Jacobins was a kind of "political religion"; like all religious doctrines, it was bound to be reinforced, rather than destroyed, by persecution and martyrdom. Only the passing of time and a condition of "rest"—a state of security and stability—might hope to calm its enthusiasm and eventually weaken it. Peace was the necessary precondition for this process, because the end of the war would finally deprive the revolutionary government of the nation's patriotic support. It was essential that this commitment to peace combine with a willingness to "follow the times," accepting the fact that France had moved on from the Old Regime, rather than engaging in a "backward struggle" to restore the past.[14]

RULED BY IDEAS

Though commentators have generally failed to remark on it, the single most striking feature of *Reflections on Peace* was the juxtaposition set forth in the text of the French nation, on the one hand, and the English minister on the other: "Mr. Pitt and France, a man and a nation, it is them we need to persuade."[15] This rhetorical appeal created from the start an interesting contrast, as it placed on the same level a particular individual and a whole population. Throughout the pamphlet England was represented by one man, an elected ruler, who embodied the will and interests of his country. On the French side, on the other hand, the government of the Convention and the mass of the people behind it were blended and conflated into a single collective entity. These radically different political subjects—the all-powerful minister, on the one hand, and the anonymous mass of the French nation on the other—provided the focus for Staël's arguments.

To begin with, she observed that Robespierre's disappearance made it especially difficult for the enemies of France to decide their strategy and to undertake any kind of negotiation. The void at the top of the French state was not in fact a passing phase, associated with the transition from one leader to another. The truth was that the French no longer obeyed anyone's personal authority and followed only a set of abstract ideals: "If any man had influence upon the French, a knowledge of his character, the study of his ambitions, could easily provide the means of dealing with him; but in France it is ideas that rule rather than individuals."[16] For a time, she argued, Robespierre had created the impression of a powerful personal leadership; his elimination by the Convention proved that this image of strength was deceptive: the French, having rejected the traditional, and therefore unassailable, authority of the king were as yet unprepared to accept a substitute ruler, whose power must necessarily come from talent or reputation:

> The French have too much vanity to succumb to a chief; the king was confused with royalty: it was his rank, not his talents, that placed him above all others; but a man chosen, deliberately followed and trusted, would be acknowledged as superior to others for his talent, and this kind of recognition is not French.[17]

Here the writer returned to one of her favorite themes, the inability of the Revolution to produce any true leaders, in spite of the presence on the political scene of men who were far from mediocre or inept. One after the other Necker, Mirabeau, and Generals La Fayette and Dumouriez had briefly enjoyed the favor of public opinion, only to be set aside and forgotten a few months later. For a while Robespierre had seemed the exception. Staël had actually met the lawyer from Arras when he was a low-profile deputy of the Third Estate; unfortunately, she described him only much later, in the *Considerations*, where she projected onto his person her passionate condemnation of his politics, transforming him into a greenish, ranting monster:

> I once conversed with him at my father's house, in 1789, when he was known merely as an advocate of the province of Artois who carried to extremes his democratic principles. His features were mean, his complexion pale, his veins of a greenish hue; he maintained the most absurd propositions with a coolness which had the air of conviction; and I could easily believe that, at the beginning of the Revolution, he had adopted sincerely certain ideas, upon the equality of fortunes as well as of ranks, which he caught in the course of his reading, and with which his envious and mischievous character was delighted to arm itself.[18]

It is quite likely that her first impression of him had been less sinister, though obviously she had not found him very interesting or charming. In any case she argued that if the people had rejected him, it was not because of his faults or his crimes, but simply because at some point he had tried to oppose the Convention, separating his own personal judgment from the collective one: "The people, disoriented, has taken sides with the Convention against Robespierre, simply because it always prefers an assembly to a man."[19]

This preference of the French for impersonal, collective authority had a direct impact upon the prospects of the conflict. The powers at war with France might be inclined to believe that, after Robespierre's disappearance, the revolutionary government would be weaker, and the country ready to succumb, if only her enemies pressed their advantage. This expectation was, however, dangerously misleading: the strength of the revolutionary government did not depend on a particular leader; it did not reside in a few politicians or generals, but in public consensus. The creation of a militant opinion, fanatically committed to a given set of political objectives, was at the heart of the revolutionary experience: "All the power of the Revolution in France consists in the art of impressing a fanatical impulse to opinion (*fanatiser l'opinion*) into the service of some political interests."[20] This fanatical impulse did not necessarily represent the views of the majority of the people, and large segments of the French population were rather in favor of a return to peace and order. Had France not been involved in a conflict with the rest of Europe, these two camps—the fanatical revolutionaries and the moderate lovers of order—might have confronted one another in a civil war. But while the country was at war and under the threat of a foreign invasion, popular opinion remained united in support of the Convention: "There is in France the potential for a civil war as a reaction to Terror, but while France is threatened by foreigners, people will fight to defend it."[21]

The motives behind this unity were varied: the former terrorists were bound by their complicity in the crimes of the Revolution; many blameless people were simply afraid of a foreign invasion and intimidated by the threats of the émigrés. There was a widespread sense of loyalty across the country toward relatives, neighbors, and friends serving in the army; many citizens harbored sincere feelings of patriotism and national pride, and none of them, whatever their attitude toward the Revolution, wished to see France defeated or humiliated. Indeed, hatred of the prospect of a foreign invasion was the only idea that kept together a nation otherwise "ready to dissolve." As a result of these shared sentiments of national solidarity, the Convention—regardless of what party or leaders dominated it—could count on all the country's energy and resources: "[France's] treasures are the fortunes of all private citizens; its soldiers, all the Frenchmen able to fight; its resources, the production of the French soil."[22]

One obvious question emerged from this analysis of the collapse of personal authority in France, so obvious that the writer could not help asking it herself: what was wrong with preferring collective institutions to personal power? If the experience of being "ruled by ideas" was associated with a fanatical attachment to abstract principles, the preference for an elected legislative assembly over individual leadership could hardly be rejected in the same way. How could one fail to approve the democratic identification between the people and the body of its representatives, especially considering that it conferred such strength on the revolutionary regime? After all, by siding with the Convention against Robespierre, "the people intended to be and believed they were fighting for themselves; what they defended in the Convention was the union of their representatives, while there is nothing democratic about the power of a single individual, whoever he might be."[23] While she recognized the merits of this identification between people and assembly, Staël argued against the "anonymous" rule of the legislative: her reason was that such collective exercise of power, however effective it might have been during the Revolution, was not compatible in the long run with stable government, at least not in the circumstances of France. It was natural to imagine that the "invincible opposition" to the authority of a single man would be conducive to freedom, but unfortunately it was not so; on the contrary, the rejection of personal authority proved "incompatible with the stability of the social state, and destructive of the same freedom of which it was believed to be the basis."[24] After this categorical statement, Staël did not develop any further the question of the instability of collective institutions in France; the main reason for her elusiveness was probably her desire to remain as vague as possible on the kind of regime France might adopt in the aftermath of Thermidor, while things were still unclear. What she did present instead was the counterexample offered by the position and prerogatives of the English government's head.

THE SOLITUDE OF THE ENGLISH MINISTER

> It is Mr. Pitt who must be called to account for the destiny of Europe.[25]

From the first line of the pamphlet Staël identified William Pitt as the most important actor on the European stage. This leading position derived, in her view, from two factors: the first was the influence England was reasonably expected to exercise upon a military coalition heavily dependent on English money; the second was the considerable power attached to Pitt's ministerial office. Thus the minister was portrayed as a lonely figure at the helm of the state; a leader invested with a responsibility that placed him above all personal and partisan interests; a man who, confronted with the dramatic alternative between peace and war, must find a solution "in solitude," by listening to the voice of his own conscience:

> It is necessary, in order to judge this great cause, to detach oneself from one's position as a man of ambition, a minister, and even an Englishman . . . at times when the spirit of party dominates, to see and to follow the truth requires an effort of reason that is almost never possible for a nation—given all the passions that agitate it—or for a man exposed by his position to the clash of individual interests.[26]

While the image of England as the banker of the anti-French coalition was common enough among foreign observers, the same was not true of the association of the English minister with the exercise of strong personal power. As a rule, admirers of the English constitution were likely to stress features such as the separation of powers and the defense of civil liberties. Its detractors, on the other hand, would emphasize the "undemocratic" nature of the English representative system, pointing at the undue influence of the crown, the power of the aristocracy, and the corruption of parliamentary institutions; the position of ministers as such did not attract any special attention.

Staël ranked unquestionably among the admirers of the English political system: a visit to the House of Commons during a journey to London with her parents in 1776 had consecrated, for the ten-year-old Germaine, a cult of English institutions that would last all her life. Like her father, she was very knowledgeable about English history and the country's constitutional tradition, and she was more than familiar, practically since her childhood, with the major sources on the subject. As a confirmed Anglophile, she was generally inclined to see every aspect of English politics in the most flattering light, and ready to minimize or justify any drawbacks. At the same time Staël knew more about the current situation of English politics than most Continental writers, though she had had little opportunity for any direct observation: as an adult she had been in the country only once, in the early months of 1793, in the company of Narbonne, who had fled to England after his short-lived ministerial experience.

Most of the information she had about the situation in England during the war came from her contacts with the political group she felt ideologically closest to, those Whigs who remained loyal to Charles Fox. One of the consequences of the French Revolution had been to divide and wreck the traditional network of Whig affinities, pushing Lord Portland's faction into a coalition with Pitt. During her visit to England in 1793, because she was living with a man who was not her husband, Staël had behaved with (for her) great discretion, restricting public contacts and keeping an unusually low profile. She had, however, allowed herself a private meeting with her political hero, Fox, spending three hours with him, as she revealed in a letter to the famous historian (and family friend) Edward Gibbon, without disclosing the content of their conversation.[27] She naturally identified with the minority of the Whig Party who had supported the French Revolution and opposed the war, remaining faithful to their original positions. Just like the model of the English constitution, the idealized image of a moderate but uncompromising force of opposition—the Foxite Whigs—played a major role in shaping her political imagination.[28] As a result of this particular bias, the position she adopted in the pamphlet was somewhat contradictory: on the one hand, she defended Pitt's right to exercise the considerable powers attached to his position as acting head of the executive, as she saw this as yet another instance of the superiority of the English constitutional system over the French one. At the same time she sided with her Whig friends in denouncing Pitt himself as a self-serving party leader, driven by objectionable factional interests.

With her contacts mainly confined to some Whig grandees, Staël had met William Pitt only once, in Fontainebleau, in 1785. The occasion of their meeting was of the most improbable kind: at the time the second son of Lord Chatham—already embarked on a promising political career—had been briefly considered by her parents as a possible candidate for her hand. In the absence of more specific evidence it seems likely that the project was nothing more than a suggestion, set forth by common acquaintances in view of improving the young man's financial prospects. But the Neckers at least did take the possibility very seriously: when Necker was dismissed by the king in 1789, both he and his daughter came up separately in their correspondence with the remark that Louis XVI would not dare to treat the father-in-law of the English minister that way.[29]

In any case the episode created no lasting connection, and Staël's view of Pitt the politician, far from being in any way sentimental, was generally inspired by the opinions of his political enemies. To begin with, she saw him primarily as an ambitious party leader, who exploited the war to promote the interests of his own political side. This notion was certainly very distant from the image Pitt had of himself: he famously claimed to be "an independent Whig" rather than a Tory (he had begun his parliamentary career on the side of the Whig opposition), and never showed much interest in partisan issues or ideological causes. His position of power derived far more from a network of personal contacts and loyalties than from any party structure or allegiance.[30]

On the other hand, Staël was right in thinking that the war had contributed to strengthening and extending the already-considerable powers attached to Pitt's office. It has been suggested that, whatever the historical precedents for this role, the younger Pitt was the first English politician to exercise in practice the full powers of a modern prime minister. A variety of factors contributed to this state of affairs: from King George III's protracted illness and his inclination to favor Pitt to Pitt's own determination to exclude from the cabinet anyone who failed to support his policies, imposing on his government what was at the time an unusual discipline and unity. But it was above all the impact of French events that allowed the minister to extend to a considerable degree his support and influence, both within the Commons and among the public. A growing fear of domestic radicalism, combined with the prospect of the war, led a substantial part of the Whig opposition to join Pitt's majority, giving him unprecedented control over Parliament; at the same time the war naturally enhanced the patriotic sentiments of the nation, creating wide popular support for the government in place.[31]

Interestingly, Staël's hostility toward Pitt, just like her admiration for Fox, was built upon a somewhat idealized vision of the English party system. At a time when parties in England were no more than unstable alliances of aristocratic affinities, she imagined them as they were to become, to some extent, only a few decades later, more stable organizations mobilized around shared principles and objectives. Somehow she needed to convince herself that her preferred vision of political conflict—the open and peaceful competition of two opposed parliamentary parties—though unthinkable in France, must be a reality at least on the other side of the Channel. In *Reflections on Peace* she duly rehearsed current Whig arguments when she questioned Pitt's motives for leading England into the war. His aim—she argued—was not to defend liberty in Europe, but to promote the interests of his own party. Now that France had ceased to represent a threat to the rest of the Continent, his only reason for continuing the war was simply to remain in office and to keep out the opposition: "War keeps Mr. Pitt in his position as minister; peace would recall to it Mr. Fox: here is the real alternative of which the English must be made aware; there is no other threat to fear, but this is what Mr. Pitt is afraid of; should his nation think like him?"[32]

It is unsurprising, given the content of her arguments, that Fox should refer appreciatively to Staël's pamphlet in one of his speeches against the war at the House of Commons. In reality both Pitt and his minister of public affairs—his cousin Lord Grenville—had struggled to preserve England's neutrality until the pressure from their Continental allies, the deterioration of diplomatic relations with France, and the impact of the execution of Louis XVI left them no choice but to join the coalition. Indeed, Grenville's correspondence for 1792 (including his exchanges with Pitt) suggests that his assessment of the possible consequences of the war was not very different from Staël's: like her, he believed that the impact upon France's domestic politics would be disastrous, and that it would only contribute to radicalizing the Revolution.[33] Now, however, two years later, a different pragmatic consideration—the threat that France had come to represent for English interests in the Low Countries—made Pitt's government reluctant to engage in peace negotiations.

Because she disapproved of Pitt's policies, Staël had been especially dismayed by the way in which the circumstances of the war had steadily increased his parliamentary majority, eroding the influence of the opposition and granting him an almost-uncontested control over Parliament. In the spring of 1793, in the same letter where she revealed her meeting with Fox, she described to Gibbon how dull London seemed in the absence of any real political debate, now that the war had forced Whigs and Tories into a patriotic entente:

> Imagine that London has become the most boring city in the universe, since there is only one political party left, the Ministerial one! God knows if I find happy for England this union of minds that, without altering the constitution, confers on the government that temporary dictatorship of which all governments are in need at such times. But the charm of society is destroyed by this despotism and this uniformity of opinions.[34]

As the war went on, she anxiously watched the dwindling numbers of the opposition, clearly feeling that more than just the charm of London society was now at stake. In December 1793, as the French recaptured Toulon, which had been for four months under the control of the English fleet, she wrote hopefully to her husband: "This taking of Toulon might overturn Pitt, and I would like England far better after that."[35]

But in February of the following year, she lamented to the same correspondent: "You see that England is in the same situation as last year: the opposition left with forty votes and the majority of the nation in favor of the war."[36] Dismayed as she was by the Whig opposition's loss of influence, Staël did not share the view, frequently expressed by Fox, that the threat of the French Revolution was just an excuse to draw public attention away from the real danger, represented by Pitt's attempt to vest "all power in the hands of the crown"—in other words, by the dominance of the executive and the consequent undermining of English liberties.[37] Although she regarded the exceptional imbalance between government and opposition as a regrettable state of affairs, and hoped it would soon end, she did not feel that the fundamental principles of the constitution were put at risk. As revealed by the letter to Gibbon cited above, she saw—somewhat inconsistently—in equally benign terms the sentiments of national solidarity, which led factions to rally around the crown, and the loyalty to their principles that kept the Foxites in opposition. Because all of this occurred "without altering the constitution," both reactions appeared to her as the signs of an essentially balanced and solid political system.

The assessment of Pitt's political performance presented by Staël in the *Considerations*, written about ten years after Pitt's death in 1806, shows that her attitude toward the English statesman had somewhat mellowed through time. She still judged him too fond of power, too inclined to Machiavellian calculations, and on the whole a far less engaging personality than Fox; but in the light of Napoleon's final defeat, he had become the symbol of British resistance against despotism, and she was prepared to acknowledge the great services he had rendered to his country and to Europe. But even in the more polemical vein that characterized *Reflections on Peace*, she never accused him of corruption or abuse.[38]

In the immediate aftermath of Thermidor, Pitt simply represented a direction in international politics that Staël was set to oppose; emphasizing his great personal influence was another way of stressing the immense responsibility he carried, and the fact that he had the power, if he wanted, to alter the course of events. What did not change for Staël was the positive appraisal of the power of the office of the "English minister": an elected, and yet strong personal authority, tempered and kept in check by public opinion. The experience of Napoleon's regime could only confirm this judgment: for all his personal influence and his commitment to the war, the English minister had kept his role of civil authority, with no military ambitions and no desire to subvert existing institutions. It was France, not England, that had generated the new Oliver Cromwell.

THE CONTAGION OF FRENCH PRINCIPLES

Setting aside the specific instrumental reason she attributed to Pitt for continuing the war—his desire to stay in power—in the winter of 1794 Staël saw only one fundamental motive that justified the pursuit of the conflict on the part of European powers. This motive was to prevent the "contagion" of French principles among their own populations, confusing the legitimate aspiration of the French to constitutional government with the Jacobin policies of insurrection and terrorism.[39] It was only the fear that their countries might be tempted to follow France on the path of revolution that had reconciled European rulers to the sacrifices required by the war effort, and to the increasingly heavy price of economic loss, destruction, and death. As England was now virtually alone in sustaining the cost of the war, it was in the name of this menace that Pitt was still able to retain the support of the ruling classes, whose agricultural, commercial, and financial interests were severely disrupted and threatened by the conflict.

The belief that, by pursuing military operations, the European monarchies could hope to eradicate from their subjects' minds the attraction of the French revolutionary example—this was simply a fallacy. On the contrary, the movements of troops and population associated with the war, as well as the suffering it inflicted on the common people, created the ideal ground for the spreading of anarchy and rebellion across Europe. The only way open to European rulers to fight the influence of French principles was to offer alternative examples of good government, demonstrating to their peoples that their lives were more secure and prosperous under the existing institutions than those of the French. Thus *Reflections on Peace* expressed for the first time a view that became central to Staël's assessment of the unification of Europe under French rule: the importation of political institutions from abroad could be successfully vetoed or promoted only by the spontaneous choice of the people themselves; they alone could decide what to imitate or to reject. Any attempt to employ force or deceit in these matters, however effective it might seem in the short run, was doomed to fail. In the specific instance, prolonging the war would not discourage the potential imitators of the Revolution and could only stimulate the patriotic resistance of the French.

But how was France likely to respond to peace negotiations? Could the new French government be trusted to respect any peace agreement they might subscribe to? This was the crucial question for the forces of the coalition, given that the character and intentions of the new rulers were largely unknown. Staël's answer to this was that the issue of the war and the uncertainty about the new government's intentions were inextricably connected. Unless the war stopped, those moderates in the assembly who had supplanted Robespierre would be unable to impose a stable rule. By creating a situation of permanent emergency, the war in fact authorized all manner of derogation from the law, perpetuating the state of unrest and disorder:

> The continuation of the war serves the project of anarchists; impetuous motions, atrocious councils, violent measures, anything that disorganizes the state, is confused by the people with the military spirit; all that is dangerous and unexpected in the vicissitudes of the war seems to offer freedom from the disciplined burden of the laws.[40]

France and Europe had a symmetrical interest in reestablishing peace; on the one hand, the European powers could not expect to eliminate the French problem unless they allowed France to achieve a stable, moderate regime; on the other hand, France could not hope to sustain her war effort indefinitely against the rest of Europe: quite apart from the consequences for the nation's domestic stability and economic resources, the success of the French army depended on a large popular mobilization, an advantage that would disappear in the near future, as the other European countries would be forced to adopt a similar degree of

militarization. France's extensive social and economic engagement in the war effort was actually one of the main practical
obstacles to peace: this is why Staël stressed that the gradual de-
mobilization of the French army, rather than its sudden disband-
ing, was essential to ensure a return to peace and normality,
while avoiding the risks of social unrest.

While exhorting French public opinion to peace, Staël was
very guarded in addressing the question of what exactly was
going on within the French government; understandably at this
stage she was unwilling to risk any bold anticipations. She described the men who had brought about Robespierre's downfall
as "the leaders of the moderate party,"[41] deliberately ignoring the
fact that many of them were former terrorists, now scrambling to
escape from the consequences of their past actions. Posterity—
she argued—would find it difficult to imagine what it was like to
have an entire nation threatened with the scaffold: in such circumstances those moderate deputies who had terminated terror
must be regarded by all as their liberators. Under this moderate
leadership France was expected, in due course, to give itself a
"just, free, and durable" new constitution.

By now Staël had become reconciled to the idea that this new
constitution was likely to be a republican one; the real question
was that of what type of republic might prevail. A republican
government might last only if it reflected "the real social basis"
of the country—that is, if all dangerous democratic utopias were
rejected. Any attempt to return to the more radical ideals of Jacobinism was bound to end in a civil war and probably, after much
unrest, in the return of the monarchy. What the "real social basis"
of France dictated was a republic modeled on the American one,
that is to say, a moderate representative government, free of feudal legacies and articulated in a federal structure:

> If . . . the party of moderates triumphs, it is possible to find in
> the American constitution a form of republic truly applicable;
> the principles of universal justice and the austere virtues of a

republic will be established in France; governments will be at peace next to a neighbor who will no longer have royalty or feudalism, but will be free of that anarchy which alone is fatal to the tranquillity of Europe.[42]

Thus Staël echoed the Neckerian creed: a large state could become a republic only by adopting a federal form. At this stage, however, all constitutional subtleties seemed to her rather out of place. The only thing that was required of the new government was the basic achievement of any government: "the safety of property and persons"; or, as she put it more vividly, "protecting men from the ax of assassins."

CHATHAM'S GHOST

A great admirer of English drama, Staël could not resist introducing into her text a little Shakespearian touch: in the concluding paragraph of the section dedicated to Pitt, she called on the ghost of the Earl of Chatham (who had died in 1778) to intervene on behalf of peace, persuading his misguided son to change his mind:

> Ghost of Lord Chatham, show yourself to your son, enlighten him with your genius or, from your grave, ask him to renounce your name.[43]

One can see that, as a politician, the elder Pitt embodied Staël's ideals far better than did his son: he had been a Whig and a brilliant parliamentary speaker; like his son, he had held the government during a long war against France (the Seven Years' War), without ever exposing himself to accusations of corruption or of authoritarian ambitions.[44] Unfortunately, the ghost of the late statesman was unable or unwilling to oblige, and the younger Pitt, far from experiencing Hamlet-like doubts, remained firmly committed to the war, even when other European powers were ready to sign peace agreements with France. In England the dividing line between government and opposition hardened into an ideological barrier that would last for decades, outliving both William Pitt's and Charles Fox's leadership. In July 1794 an article in the *Morning Chronicle* observed, "Mr Pitt has completely triumphed in breaking to pieces that great body to whom the people looked up with confidence as to men who would never sacrifice their love of the Constitution to the views of the Court."[45] A month later, in a letter addressed to his nephew Henry Lord Holland, Fox complained bitterly of the failure of his party to manage the situation as well as of the disloyalty of his political friends.[46]

It is of course impossible to tell in retrospect whether the expectation of a durable peace with France at the turn of 1794–95 was at all realistic; certainly Staël was not alone in thinking, at the time, that the moment of exhaustion and disorientation caused by Robespierre's disappearance would make the Thermidorian government especially receptive to peace proposals. Realistic or not, the view that pursuing the war was "mad" did not prevail, and, as the new directorial regime took shape and consolidated, the opportunity to take advantage of France's confusion by imposing peace was lost. If her *Reflections on Peace* failed to persuade Pitt and European opinion that an armistice with France was both desirable and possible, the work did at least fulfill Staël's aspiration to attract significant attention, at least from the English side. She was especially proud of the fact that, addressing Parliament on 25 March 1795, Fox cited her pamphlet, describing the anonymous author as an "excellent man," and skillfully weaving some of her arguments into his own speech. In particular he borrowed her argument about the narrow-minded attitude of the coalition, who had failed to take advantage of General Dumouriez's defection; he also adopted one of her favorite religious metaphors, claiming that the émigrés were so bigoted as to reject even those who had "converted" to their cause.[47]

Staël's work also elicited some reaction from Pitt's camp, in the form of a reply, *Reflections on the War. In Response to the Reflections on Peace addressed to Mr Pitt and the French Nation*, written by the Genevan expatriate Francis d'Ivernois.[48] In exile in England, following the same revolution in Geneva that had led to Necker's condemnation, d'Ivernois had become a prolific author of pamphlets in support of the English government: in his work he questioned Staël's assumptions about France's reliability in any future peace agreement, demanding that the French surrender all the occupied territories before any negotiation might be considered. Obviously well aware of the identity of the author of *Reflections on Peace*, he adopted toward her a mildly patronizing tone, citing back to her the authorities of Necker and Delolme (an attitude of superiority hardly justified by his own groveling praise of Pitt):

> Some men of state . . . thought that in order to save their people from this contagion, it was best to arm them, were it only to divert their attention, and to give them the time to sober up; may be such men of state, having had the courage and the spirit to lead their compatriots towards an ordinary and reparable evil, in order to protect them from the extraordinary and irreparable evil of a revolution, have acquired a more durable entitlement to the gratitude of future generations, raising themselves above the passing cries of the present ones.[49]

While working on *Reflections on Peace*, Staël had indulged in one of her favorite exercises in political daydreaming: "My father [she wrote to Ribbing] sends me a gazette with a proposal from the Elector of Mayence, who requests the mediation of Sweden and Denmark to negotiate peace. Right now I am making up a fantastic plot: Monsieur de Staël is nominated for the congress, the congress takes place in Basel, and I pacify Europe."[50] France, Prussia, and Spain—though not England—were indeed going to sign peace agreements in Basel in April 1795 (Staël's fantasies were seldom very distant from reality), but without the assistance of the Swedish ambassador and his wife. However, just at the time when the treaties were signed, Erik-Magnus was finally able to return to the Swedish embassy in Paris, after being reconfirmed in his diplomatic post by the duc de Sudermanie (Gustav III's brother, now regent on behalf of the minor Gustav IV). On 23 April he presented his credentials to the French government: the ceremony, and his speech on the occasion, were widely reported in the press.[51] Though not impressed by her husband's fulsome praise of French achievements, Staël managed to be reasonably polite, congratulating him on his speech: "Your speech was not one I would have made, but perhaps all the better for it; and it was with great emotion that I read of the great and sincere applause with which it was rewarded."[52] The motive for her graciousness toward him was only too transparent: now that their position was secure, she wished to return as soon as possible to France at his side; the ambassador's feeble attempts to keep her away were doomed to fail in the face of her determination to resume her place at the center of the Parisian stage. Elsewhere, however, she expressed a different reaction to her husband's performance. Writing to Ribbing, she eagerly disclaimed any responsibility for the speech, and explained:

> I am less patriotic and especially less ordinary (*commune*); but how could you believe that I am not interested in the success of the republic? First of all I never failed to adopt the opinion [of the object of my preference] . . . M. de Staël, if I remain with him, is entirely dependent on the success of the republic. The constitution [of 1793, my note] is impossible; and if royalty were to return, it would arrive with such a strong impulse that it would certainly not stop at what we would call the right point. I desire the republic as the only government that would suit you while not dishonoring France.

After reproaching her correspondent for some hints, in one of his letters, about her proximity to monarchical positions, warning him that such allusions, put in writing, might be dangerous, she concluded dramatically:

> I am under the wheels of the carriage you drive, and that leads straight to the republic.[53]

Setting aside her emphatic claim to be "driven" by the "carriage" of Ribbing's republican faith (probably a half-truth: she would soon attribute a similar influence to her new "discovery," the Swiss aspiring writer Benjamin Constant), we find in this letter a clear expression of the constraints weighing on her choices. Her only chance of returning to public life—the continuation of her husband's diplomatic career in France—was dependent on the preservation of the republic: she was under no illusion as to the consequences of a return of the Bourbons upon her and her husband's joint prospects, as their conduct had been perceived by the court since the beginning as dangerously compromised by their involvement in the Revolution. The republic was the only path that remained open to the establishment of a stable, moderate regime, given that constitutional monarchy was no longer a viable option. But in order to succeed, the republic needed two things: peace and the guarantee that the Revolution was indeed over.

CHAPTER 5

The Advent of Modern Liberty (1795)

IT IS only at the end of May 1795, almost a year after the fall of Robespierre, that Staël could finally realize her long-cherished ambition to return to Paris. She knew only too well that the political circumstances were still unsettled, and her own position vis-à-vis the revolutionary government far from secure; but while she had persistent doubts about the wisdom of her decision, the attraction of Parisian society and politics proved irresistible. "Here I am, my dear friend"—she wrote on 23 May from Nogent sur Seine to her husband, who had desperately tried to keep her in Switzerland—"in spite of you, in spite of events, in spite of my own self."[1]

Her arrival coincided with the failure of the insurrection of *prairial* (20 May), the second attempt that spring, after the similar uprising of *germinal* (1 April), to reestablish the power of the Parisian Commune and of the people of the *faubourgs* over the Convention that had toppled Robespierre. While the outcome was a reassuring proof that the strength of revolutionary Jacobinism was spent, Staël had underestimated the degree of attention that her presence in the capital would soon attract. From Paris she wrote to Adolphe Ribbing in Switzerland: "I arrived . . . in the middle of the famous *journées* at the beginning of *prairial*. To begin with, I was rather frightened, but the triumph of the Convention reassured me . . . This time the Jacobins are, I hope, destroyed, and the tranquillity of Paris rests upon strict and severe measures." Then she added: "Here I am, ridiculously suspected of opinions I do not share; they are all afraid of me."[2]

Her hope in returning to Paris had been that her status as the wife of the Swedish ambassador (Sweden having maintained friendly relations with France throughout the revolutionary period) might be sufficient to legitimate her position. In addition she had come prepared to offer her full support to the Thermidorian government, and to endorse the new republican constitution that must soon be created to replace the radical constitution of 1793 (Year I). Her political views were shared by her new friend, the talented, if still unknown, Swiss writer Benjamin Constant, who had accompanied her in her journey to Paris. Writing to his aunt, Mme de Nassau, Constant gave the following account of the insurrection's aftermath: "The triumph of the Convention has been as complete as their courage has been sublime. The assassins (*hommes de sang*) are crushed, the *faubourgs* in revolt are disarmed, anyone guilty is imprisoned and judged . . . We hate the Jacobins, we laugh at and despise the royalists, we want order, peace, and the republic, and we shall have them."[3] While the evidence on Staël's political contacts during these months is patchy, it seems clear that at this stage she was siding with the supporters of the Thermidorian regime, rather than attempting to play a role in opposition. Predictably, she gathered around her the surviving constitutional monarchists and canvassed to obtain the pardon of those of her friends who were still exiled as émigrés. However, she also opened her salon to individuals of other political orientations, including former Girondins and Montagnards (who represented the left wing of the former assembly) in the attempt to promote a broader consensus across the old dividing lines between factions.[4]

Yet this prudent strategy did not prove a sufficient protection. As soon as she crossed the border, Staël became the object of suspicions from all political parties, and the target of fanciful allegations of conspiracy that reverberated from Switzerland to Paris and back, reaching as far as Stockholm. In due course she was publicly accused, in the press and at the Convention, of associating with various prominent émigrés in view of preparing a coup d'état against the republic. Following the repression of the royalist insurrection of *vendémiaire* (5 October)—an insurrection she regarded as suicidal, and in which she had no part—she was once again threatened with a sentence of exile. Confronted with her protests and the ambassador's, in order to avoid a diplomatic incident with Sweden, the government accepted instead her voluntary retirement to the spa town of Forges-les-Eaux. But it was only a short reprieve: in December the ambassadress gave in to the pressures and finally resigned herself to following Constant back to Switzerland, where she remained, living between Coppet and Lausanne, for the whole of 1796.

The main casualty in this episode of collective political paranoia (one of many that marked her life) was the essay Staël had written during the few months she managed to spend in Paris, sometime between June and September 1795: *Réflexions sur la paix intérieure* (Reflections on domestic peace).[5] As this was due to appear in print just at the time of the *vendémiaire* unrest, the author prudently decided to withdraw it from publication. Contrary to what is generally assumed, *Reflections on Domestic Peace* was not a work dictated merely by the immediate political circumstances of the time, endorsing the author's official "conversion" from constitutional monarchy to republicanism. The form of the constitution that the Thermidorian government must adopt, in order to put an end to the revolutionary regime, was naturally a matter of interest for Staël, as her correspondence during the summer of 1795 indicates. However, her pamphlet focused less on the design of the future constitution of 1795 (Year III) than on the substantial values that must sustain it in order to make it politically viable. Once again Staël claimed that, in order to unify the nation under a republican government, it was necessary to identify the durable interests and aspirations of the majority of the French people. Now, however, the question of what the majority wanted was defined with greater clarity than in the past. The unity of the nation under the republic must be founded upon the general demand for liberty: not, however, the patriotic, participative liberty, inspired by the model of ancient republics, that had been revived by the Jacobins with such destructive consequences, but a new kind of liberty, based on the modern needs for security, prosperity, and peace.

THE FORCE OF CIRCUMSTANCES

In *Reflections on Domestic Peace* Staël returned to a favorite theme she had already addressed, in very different circumstances, in 1791: the question of the partisan divisions present within the nation, and of the possible reconciliation of rival parties. In the opening paragraphs she recognized that all appeals to unity, after years of ferocious factional struggle, must sound like hollow rhetorical phrases; and yet the only hope of survival for the new government was the creation of a broader social and political consensus. But unity of what forces, and to what political purpose? Staël made it clear that two groups were bound to be excluded from any project of reconciliation: the first group consisted of those royalists who worked for the restoration of absolute monarchy; the second included those republicans who advocated the "demagogic tyranny" of the mob. With these factions, moved by fanatical, uncompromising beliefs, any understanding was impossible. Both were "strangers" to the nation: the ultraroyalists because, by choosing to emigrate, and by fighting alongside foreign armies, they had literally placed themselves outside the frontiers of the French nation.[6] As to the radical republicans and former terrorists, they were simply criminals, and as such they were the natural enemies of any social order.

Setting aside these "extreme" factions, the two major forces that could, on the other hand, form a viable political alliance were described as the royalist "friends of liberty"—in other words the partisans of constitutional monarchy—and the republican "friends of order": those who advocated a moderate regime committed to social stability and the defense of property. These two parties obviously differed in their original allegiance to, respectively, the monarchical and republican ideals; and yet their objective interests and basic aspirations were very similar: resorting to one of her favorite metaphors, the writer explained that they both recognized "the same cult in different rites."[7]

Staël's peroration was primarily addressed to the first of these two parties: her own political group, the constitutional monarchists. Here, finally, was her opportunity to vindicate their conduct during the earlier stages of the Revolution—something she had been longing to do since 1792. But now the retrospective justification of their choices—so harshly judged from both left and right—went together with the bold proposition of a new political line. In order to preserve the substance of their original project for a free and stable government, the Constitutionnels must renounce their original attachment to the monarchy and endorse the existing republican regime. In 1789 the establishment of constitutional monarchy in France had seemed the obvious answer to the nation's demand for liberty. This choice was supported by the authority of many enlightened theorists: "a crowd of political writers," from Montesquieu to Mirabeau, had argued that France must follow England's example, progressing from absolute to limited royalty. Even those writers who were ideally in favor of republicanism were convinced at the time that the nation was totally unprepared for the drastic change from monarchy to republic. Indeed, when this change actually occurred in 1792, it was made possible only by the use of coercion and violence. While one might deplore this outcome, now that the republic had been forced upon the nation at such high cost of disruption and death, switching back to royalty would prove at least as difficult and would no doubt once again require the employment of violent means.

Besides, who could be cast now in the role of constitutional monarch? The legitimate successors of Louis XVI, his brothers, were fiercely committed to the uncompromising restoration of

the past, and to the return of absolute monarchy: clearly no opening toward a moderate regime could be hoped from them. As to
the possibility of establishing a new dynastic line, what was
probably still possible in 1791 could no longer be envisaged now:
a new king called to rule in the place of the legitimate heir Louis
XVIII would be unable to command the loyalty of the partisans
of the old dynasty and could hardly expect the support of republicans. Another major difficulty was that one could not restore
royalty in France without reestablishing "the institutions of nobility" naturally attached to the crown; but the restoration of
aristocratic distinctions and privileges was incompatible with
the newly established principles of equality and would excite the
resistance of a large part of public opinion.

In light of these considerations the Constitutionnels must resign themselves to the idea that at present a monarchical regime
was no longer possible in France, at least not without a second
revolution, which was bound to prove more destructive than the
first. Should constitutional monarchists be regarded as opportunists and traitors if they decided to support the republic?
Staël's answer was that, in this instance, endorsing the inevitable
meant simply accepting the principle that the French people
were free to choose: if the nation did not wish to be ruled by a
king any longer, all good citizens must respect its will. However,
the most forceful part of Staël's argument was a point of method.
In the domain of political science—as Montesquieu had extensively shown—there were no mathematical theorems or universal rules. The viability of all systems of government was largely
dependent on the specific circumstances of a country at a particular time. Now, if this was true, the Revolution must necessarily be taken into account as an event that had created a totally
new context:

> What circumstance is more influential than a revolution?
> What character of population, what extension of territory,
> what diversity of climate can make states more different from

one another than these stormy times, in which all passions are agitated?[8]

The Revolution had simply changed everything, radically altering all those conditions that made a particular regime possible at a given time. It had also provoked an unprecedented acceleration both of the process of historical change, and of the evolution of public opinion, "concentrating in a day the experience of centuries." Those political actors who thought they could stand still, clinging to their old convictions in the raging storm, could hardly hope to succeed in reaching their goals.[9]

A CONSTANT IDEA AMID THE STORMS

"Forgive me if I remind you [so Staël addressed the Constitutionnels] that without you the Revolution would never have existed."[10] This was a responsibility (and indeed a merit) that constitutional monarchists could not deny: they had created the circumstances that made the Revolution possible, and had initiated it. But why had they done it, to what purpose? The aim they had pursued in 1789 was not the establishment of a particular regime as such, though they had expected the advent of constitutional monarchy; it was the conquest of greater freedom for the whole nation. The institutions of monarchical and republican government were only means to an end, and it was the end that really mattered. The end was liberty: liberty was the true object of the Revolution, an object that could not now be abandoned: "If we wish to find some grandeur amid the troubles that lacerate France, if we want to find a constant idea amid the storms, discover through the blood and the ruins an object that elevates us and continues to emerge through the centuries, it is this will to be free, a will no doubt shamefully disfigured, but upon which even the most ferocious tyranny must rest."[11] It is true that the motives behind the French nation's aspiration to liberty were not the same for all; indeed, people were moved by a variety of emotions and expectations, according to their experience, their beliefs, and their position in society. Nonetheless the ideal of freedom represented a common ground:

> Different sentiments lead, for different reasons, to the general desire of establishing freedom in France: hatred of despotism, enthusiasm for the republic, fear of revenge, ambition for the talented, all these impulses make people wish for the same thing. It is therefore in the name of this liberty that it is possible to unite the largest number of French citizens.[12]

While the aspiration to freedom was widely shared, there was a great deal of confusion as to the kind of liberty that was most desirable. In particular, what many failed to recognize was the crucial difference between civil and political liberty. Civil liberty—Staël argued—was the true object of most people's aspirations, the source of security and substantial benefits for all; all the advantages citizens could reasonably expect from the government derived from it: "No taxes that are not proportional. No arrest or judgment except within legal and universal forms. No privilege of any kind." In the relation between civil and political liberty, it was the former that served people's interests, while the latter was merely its instrument:

> Political liberty has the same relation to civil liberty as the guarantee to the object it protects; it is the means, not the end. What has contributed to make the French Revolution so chaotic is the confusion of ideas on this subject. Political liberty has been pursued at the expense of civil liberty: as a result there has been an appearance of liberty only for the governed, and a hope of safety only for those in power, while what should happen is just the reverse.[13]

The writer stressed that the enjoyment of civil liberty did not necessarily include access for all citizens to political rights—the right to elect and to be elected. This exclusion of political rights from the attributes of civil liberty did not imply the reintroduction of privilege, as it was quite possible to overcome it by the acquisition of property: "Political rights do not represent a form of privilege, given that they can be obtained by acquiring a small but independent property. Whatever is a source of competition and not an obstacle to personal merit; whatever is a target, and not an exclusion, cannot be considered a privilege."[14] Rather than being a privilege, political rights represented an obligation, a form of public service; exercising them was a duty, such as the duty of keeping watch in the face of some impending threat. Thus only those ambitious men who aspired to power wanted political rights for their own sake. Civil liberty, on the other hand, mattered to all quiet, peaceful men who did not want to be dominated and enslaved. Staël illustrated further the distinction between political and civil liberty by referring to the experience of ancient republics. Political liberty was associated with the spirit of patriotic virtue and sacrifice typical of the ancient city-states. Modern societies had totally different needs: the main concern of modern citizens was protecting what they had and securing their own private advantages.

> Ancient republics were founded upon virtue and maintained by sacrifices; citizens were united by their common devotion to their motherland. But with our customs, with our century, it is necessary to reform men and society by the fear of losing what they have; one must talk of rest, safety, property to those men whom a revolutionary power may crush, but without whom no constitution can be established.[15]

While Staël's assertion of the superiority of civil over political liberty echoed the traditional antirepublican themes originally set forth by Hobbes and Montesquieu, the experience of the terrorist regime gave a new significance to the association of political liberty with ancient republicanism. Thus the writer was ready to acknowledge the sacrifice of those true republicans who, during the Revolution, had given their lives in emulation of the patriotic virtue of the ancients. But on the whole the imitation of antiquity during the Revolution had served to justify new forms of despotism and servitude: "Since power has begun to call itself 'liberty,' a crowd of people think of themselves as Romans just because they flatter it."[16] Anticipated by Emmanuel Sieyès before the Revolution to justify the preference for representative, rather than participative, democracy, the distinction between civil and political liberty had acquired, through the experience of the Terror, a far more immediate and compelling urgency.[17] The phrase "liberty of the moderns" does not actually appear in *Reflections on Domestic Peace*; yet all the components of this notion, which Constant subsequently reformulated in his works, were already clearly expressed in Staël's analysis: the view that for modern citizens political participation represented a burden, rather than a desirable opportunity; the stigmatization of Jacobinism as anachronistic and dangerous in its pursuit of ancient republican values; the insistence on independence and the enjoyment of wealth as central to the experience of modern citizenship.[18]

DEMOCRACY OR THE REPUBLIC?

The impossibility of bringing back the monarchy, and the identification of civil liberty as the durable achievement of the Revolution, were the premises upon which the new government must be founded. Circumstances made the preservation of the republican form inevitable; but what kind of republic should be envisaged in order to achieve a stable rule? Having made her choice in favor of the republic, Staël was naturally forced to set aside her preferred model of limited government, the one offered by the English monarchy. The alternative example of representative government to which France must now turn was the American one: what the country needed was a republic "modified on the principles of the American government." By referring to the American model, the writer did not imply that France should turn into a federation, as she believed this might be desirable in principle but impossible in practice, for all manner of historical reasons. What she meant was that the republican constitution should respect two basic conditions: the separation of powers and the restriction of active political rights to property owners.

But first it was necessary to clear the ground of all misunderstandings by refuting the belief that the existing republican constitution was responsible for the years of violence and instability France had experienced. Recent events—Staël argued—had created great confusion in the minds of observers, who often mistook the effects of the revolutionary regime for those of its republican institutions. It was now necessary to separate, once and for all, "what belongs to democracy, and what belongs to the republic; what derives from the revolutionary government, and what might be feared from a republican constitution."[19] Whatever its excesses, the revolutionary regime had enjoyed all along a certain degree of legitimacy. The proof was that the legal activity of government had been carried on without major disruptions throughout the Revolution, while the army had continued to take its orders from the National Assembly. There had been conspiracies within the government itself, but not against it. On the whole the country had never found itself in a condition of total anarchy; on the contrary, "commandment and obedience existed, social order could be maintained."

What had caused the derailment of the revolutionary government were not its republican institutions, whatever their defects, but the actions of a particular political group that Staël described as "the democratic sect." The fatal error of this faction had been "to reject the conditions of property" as the basis for the exercise of political rights. Had they not made this choice, or had they been less prominent within the government, the "political machine" might have continued to work. In other words, the downfall of the Jacobin regime had been caused by the democratic turn that its leaders had imposed on the republic by seeking the support and encouraging the aspirations of the propertyless. Even now the men of Thermidor were inclined to repeat this error, anxious as they were to preserve the republic from the threats of the royalists:

> As nonproprietors seem right now fiercely opposed to royalty, republicans are strongly tempted to rely on them; however, they fail to realize that nonproprietors do not agitate against this or that form of government, but against any order that protects property . . .
>
> How can you place within the constitution men who are only looking for prey? Men whose interests can be served, by those who represent them, only by the concession of the first of all benefits, the property they lack?[20]

Here Staël expressed without any mitigations a set of assumptions that durably shaped her understanding of political stability: the identification of property as the true basis of social order; the danger represented by the predatory tendencies of the mass of the people; the folly of entrusting power and authority to those who would naturally use them to despoil proprietors, wrecking the peace and prosperity of the nation. "The equality of political rights seems far more dangerous than the state of nature: in such a bizarre society, property would be tolerated only to excite hatred against it; proprietors would survive only to play the role of potential victims; legislation would serve to organize persecution."[21]

There was, however, a major difficulty associated with the project of establishing a republic of proprietors in France: while in America the large majority of the people were property-owners (at least this was what European observers believed), in France it was the propertyless who formed the largest social group. But if property was so unequally distributed, what was the legitimacy of a model of representative government resting upon proprietors alone? How could such a regime claim to defend the interests of the mass of the people, when its institutions represented only those of a minority? Staël's answer was that one must distinguish between the interests of the "majority of the moment" and those of the "durable majority." In the short term, it was clearly in the interests of the poor to get hold of a share of property at the expense of the rich. But in the long run a policy of spoliation—regardless of whether it was effected by violence or by law—would threaten everyone, generating insecurity and discontent among all classes, and undermining social peace. Particular individuals or groups might get richer or poorer without serious consequences for public order, but society as a whole could be maintained only if the security of existing property arrangements was ensured.

There are some obvious analogies between Staël's views on property and those expressed in his writings by Jacques Necker.[22] But here she went beyond the simple echoing of inherited prejudices about the advantages of aristocratic liberty and the merits of wealthy notables as a ruling class. In her analysis she placed the issue of economic inequality firmly at the heart of the process of the Revolution's radicalization, attributing to it greater importance in the downfall of the Jacobin regime than to other factors such as, for example, the unchecked hegemony of the legislative, the suspension of civil liberties, or the enforcement of emergency rule during the war. Obviously the poorer people who had taken part in the revolutionary movement had not necessarily done so in the hope of economic gain; no doubt, their motives for revolting against the monarchy were both more diverse and less coherent.[23] Yet in the end it was against this particular obstacle that the revolutionary process had finally crashed: democracy was simply not possible in a large state characterized by a very unequal distribution of wealth. Thus, just as constitutional monarchists had to resign themselves to the loss of hereditary royalty as the price to pay to restore social peace, moderate republicans must renounce the temptation of democracy in order to preserve the republic. The security of property was the common ground for the foundation of a consensual and durable political regime: "To end a revolution one must find a center of balance and a common bond. The balance is property, the bond, personal interest."[24]

If in advocating a republic of proprietors Staël adopted a conservative reading of representative government, *Reflections on Domestic Peace* shows that she did not envisage a static system ruled by a closed elite. While the present need for tranquillity was a natural consequence of years of unrest, one of the main advantages of republican government was, on the contrary, that it allowed social mobility and rewarded individual capacity and merit: "What government is more favorable to the promotion of talent than a republic?"[25] Monarchies—she argued—had no use whatever for merit, while the republic "needed men distinguished for their talents and their virtues." Here Staël returned to one of her favorite themes, the absence of prominent personalities and the systematic undermining of individual reputations that had characterized the revolutionary period. One of the priorities of the new republic must be to recruit capable, dedicated men, regardless of their past history and of the party to which they originally belonged. Thus in Staël's mind the stabilization of postrevolutionary French society's economic interests was paired with the reconstruction of its ruling class: a reconstruction in which ability, dedication, and personal qualities must prevail over class distinctions and partisan prejudices.

BETWEEN CONSTITUTIONS

Staël's insistence on the necessity of uniting the nation around a set of common interests suggests that she was more preoccupied with the preservation and stability of the republican government than with the particular shape of its institutions. In describing to Ribbing the heated debate raised by the proposal (finally adopted) confirming that members of the Convention were to constitute no less than two-thirds of the new Legislative Assembly, she observed: "This country is agitated by the reelection or nonreelection of two-thirds of the Convention. There is against the reelection the moral character of the deputies; in its favor the great interest in the preservation of the republic."[26] It was above all the need to preserve the republic that led her to accept the measure in spite of its obvious drawbacks, in particular the re-confirmation of the mandate of many former terrorists. Her correspondence shows that she closely followed the making of the constitution of 1795, occasionally expressing views on particular issues—but always with a certain pragmatic detachment as to the specific solutions that were being discussed. In *Reflections on Domestic Peace* she confined herself to indicating some general principles that the new constitution should satisfy: a legislative divided into two branches, the independence of the executive, and the establishment of property restrictions for the suffrage.

In his illuminating study on the constitution of 1795, Michel Troper argues persuasively that the leaders of Thermidor were not at first convinced that the republic needed a new constitution.[27] To begin with, they considered the possibility of reviving the constitution of 1793: approved by a popular referendum (though one that attracted relatively few voters: under two million, with over four million abstentions), this constitution had been suspended by the Convention on account of the war before it could be implemented. One of the main requests of the insurgents of *germinal* and *prairial* was precisely that it should finally be enforced.

Before the riots the Thermidorian government, in the absence of a shared political line on the subject, had been playing for time. Thus the Commission of the Eleven (Commission des onze) was created at the end of April 1795 with the official mission of preparing the laws that were required for the application of the "suspended" constitution. Significantly Sieyès, in his capacity as France's most prestigious constitutionalist, had declined the opportunity to sit on the Commission of the Eleven, choosing instead to remain on the Committee of Public Safety (Comité de salut publique), the two posts being incompatible: an indication that he did not expect the Commission of the Eleven to do any serious new constitutional work. It was the fear of a return of Jacobinism generated by the insurrections that tipped the balance in favor of the introduction of a new text. In the circumstances the constitution of 1795 was mostly the work of the moderates Pierre Daunou and François-Antoine de Boissy d'Anglas (who was also designated as *rapporteur*, on behalf of the Commission of the Eleven, to the Convention).[28]

Troper's reconstruction of the sequence of events undermines the traditional view of a political class determined from the outset to end the Revolution by burying the "democratic" constitution of 1793 and replacing it with a resolutely "antidemocratic" one. In the light of the hesitations and ambiguities of the Thermidorian leaders, it is indeed easier to recognize the elements of continuity between the two constitutions: the preservation of the republic, the endorsement of the declaration of rights (though in a somewhat modified version), the choice of a collegial executive, and a degree of separation of powers. While the hypothesis of an uncertain—and to some extent circumstantial—transition from the 1793 to the 1795 constitution is quite convincing, the fluctuations of the Thermidorian government did not reflect Staël's own position, since she was from the start in favor of a resolute break from the past. Writing to Ribbing before her arrival in Paris, she had described the old constitution as "impossible."[29] It is easy to identify the elements that led her to this negative judgment. In addition to the excessive opening to popular participation, the constitution of 1793 suffered in her eyes from the weaknesses that had led to the implosion of the constitution of 1791: an unchecked legislative power exercised by a single chamber and an executive without real prerogatives and heavily dependent on the legislative. Moreover, the fact that the constitution of 1793 had been introduced in a revolutionary situation meant that the legitimacy it derived by the popular vote (a strong argument in favor of its preservation) should be regarded as dubious.[30]

Staël's objections to the 1793 constitution are illustrated by a draft found in the Coppet archives (and only recently published) entitled *Idées pour une déclaration des droits* (Ideas for a declaration of rights).[31] Consisting of a set of fragmentary annotations, it was probably written in parallel with the debate on the revision of the Declaration of Rights that accompanied the making of the 1795 constitution. One annotation stated that political rights do not form part of the citizen's basic entitlements: "the making of laws is not a natural right." Another passage indicated that the authority of the general will is, in any case, limited, since it cannot by definition oppose itself to the "very aims of the association" (such as, presumably, the protection of life and property). The implication of this was that the rejection of the constitution of 1793 was fully justified, in spite of its endorsement by a referendum: "What right did we have to change the constitution we had? Because it was contrary to natural rights, and because we had not agreed to it."[32] In the same text she rejected the idea of the right of resistance—which had been introduced by the constitution of 1793 but removed from the 1795 one—using the current argument that "a constitution cannot inscribe the means of its own destruction." Staël's decisive position in favor of a new constitution's adoption coincided with the awareness of the enterprise's difficulty. Was it really possible to produce a moderate constitution, based upon the limitation of powers, in what was still a revolutionary context?

> How can one enforce the separation of powers? How is it possible to write a chapter of Montesquieu on the banners of rebellion?[33]

On the whole the new constitution was far from perfect; it was, however, as she wrote to Ribbing "quite tolerable" and could "improve with time."[34] One of the areas of improvement was the question of bicameralism. The two new legislative councils, the Five Hundred (Cinq-cents) and the Elders (Anciens), were not exactly two separate chambers—more like the two subsections of a single one, as their modes of election and their competences were very similar (the only difference being that the Five Hundred had the initiative to introduce new legislation, which was then submitted to the approval of the Elders). Staël's hope was that the Elders might be consolidated into a body whose members would have lifetime tenure, a "conservative power" (*pouvoir conservateur*):[35] a transformation that did not occur at this stage. The collective executive—the Directory—did have reinforced powers when compared to the executive council of the constitution of 1793, since it could issue decrees (*arrêts*), but it had no right of veto and was still subject to the legislative.

Some of the difficulties connected with the new constitution's design were essentially technical and concerned the instruments that should be used in order to achieve the desired result. Such was, for example, the intricate and difficult question of the separation of powers: Staël was strongly in favor of the principle but struggled to identify the right institutional structure to achieve it. This is apparent in the (often-cited) letter on the subject that she addressed to Pierre-Louis Roederer.[36] The letter was sent in response to some remarks on the executive Directory that Roederer was to publish a month later in the *Journal de Paris*. As an expert on constitutional matters, Roederer had been advising the Committee of the Eleven without being a member:

> Thinking about your difficulties, so well presented, about executive power, I had a thought I wish to submit to you. There is much talk of the division of powers while the most difficult problem is possibly their union. An executive power that has nothing to do with the making of laws is the natural enemy of those who impose upon it decrees contrary to its views and means of execution. This is why the royal veto seemed necessary. It is impossible to confer such great influence on a republican executive. Should not ministers then be chosen among the representatives of the chamber and senate?[37]

Another puzzling technical issue concerned the best means to achieve a restriction of the electorate. In a letter to Alexandre de Lameth, Staël candidly admitted that a "disguised" form of restriction might be preferable to an openly stated one, provided the latter ensured the right result:

> I am ready to agree with you on the great principle of property; but I do not know whether the two degrees of election give the same result as the conditions of property. It is a question to be examined: if it was true that a system of election that did not treat proprietors as a separate class would nevertheless get them always elected, would it not be more adroit to organize things in such a way that they did get elected without having to claim in advance that they alone would be chosen? It is a political problem that needs analyzing, but the aim is unquestionable. Government must proceed by the aristocracy of the best, but what attaches me to the present constitution is the repugnance I feel for the reestablishment of heredity in any form.[38]

In the *Considerations* Staël described the constitution of 1795 as "more reasonable and better arranged" than the constitution of 1791, but she pointed at the weakness of its executive, the Directory, as being at the origin of its failure: "This executive power did not have the necessary authority to maintain order; it lacked several indispensable prerogatives, the absence of which led . . . to destructive convulsions." And she concluded: "There was some grandeur in the attempt of establishing a republic . . . but the attempt failed essentially because of the kind of men who occupied exclusively those positions [of directors]; the party to which they had belonged made them odious to the nation."[39] This, however, was a judgment expressed with the benefit of hindsight. In 1795 the writer believed that the new constitution was as good as could be expected in the circumstances; indeed, the fact that the Committee of the Eleven, the expression of a political class that was still "naturally revolutionary," could produce something like it seemed to her "little short of a miracle."[40]

THE GUNS OF PUBLIC OPINION

"I approve, as far as it is possible, the suspension of my work."[41] Thus, on 7 October 1795, two days after the failed insurrection of *vendémiaire*, Staël signified to her friend François de Pange, who was in charge of the edition of *Reflections on Domestic Peace*, her decision to withdraw her work from publication. As the phrase suggests, she was obviously unhappy with having to sacrifice her text, but she was also very anxious about the possible impact its appearance might have upon her position. Three days later, she urged her husband to make sure that a set of copies—for some reason still in circulation—had been safely locked up.[42]

Her decision to remain silent was a last attempt to persuade the government that her presence in Paris was not, and had never been, instrumental to any conspiracy against the republic. She had already spent the previous months refuting over and over again the same accusations, and providing the same justifications for her conduct. As soon as she had arrived in Paris at the end of May, she had thought it expedient to publish—in a sympathetic journal, *Les nouvelles politiques*—a declaration in defense of her own intentions toward the republican regime.

> The strange celebrity some insist on forcing upon me, the childish fear of a twenty-six-year-old woman who comes to join her husband, compel me to express my political opinions. I declare I do not share the prejudice that leads to supporting a certain form of constitution from considerations other than the happiness and will of the nation that adopts it; that I sincerely wish for the establishment of the French republic on the sacred foundations of justice and humanity, since it is clear to me that in the present circumstances only a republican government can secure peace and freedom to France.[43]

In the same statement she admitted keeping in touch with friends "persecuted by Robespierre," that is to say, émigrés. She was in fact canvassing to reverse the decision whereby Necker was

treated as an émigré, to ensure the return of exiles such as Talleyrand and Narbonne, and to secure the release of General La Fayette, held in captivity by the Austrians since 1792. But she firmly
refuted allegations that she had organized any "political confer-
ences" or that she had been at all involved in "public affairs"
during her Swiss exile. Her declarations failed to obtain the desired effect, and she continued to be accused in the press and
even at the assembly of acting as an agent of unspecified royalist
activities, including the gathering of troops at the Swiss border.
Suspicions about her conduct were shared by the French and
Swedish authorities alike and were fed by whatever foreign contacts she kept and by any social gatherings that took place at the
Swedish embassy. Predictably the *vendémiaire* coup gave apparent substance to what had been until then vague and unsubstantiated allegations.

The insurrection—quite disorganized and lacking a clear
plan—was mainly the effort of young constitutional monarchists
and of a crowd of Parisian bourgeois alarmed by the readmission
of former terrorists into the sections of the Commune. (More experienced, hard-line royalists kept prudently out of it.) It was
easily dispersed by the troops of the Convention and not too
vigorously repressed (by Bonaparte's famous "whiff of grape-
shot"), so that most of those involved could escape. Staël had
never thought for a moment that the revolt of a random collection of moderate citizens could hope to succeed against a government of seasoned revolutionaries. All it would do was to trigger
a new wave of repression, favoring the return of the Terror or
opening the path to counterrevolution. At the end of September
1795, she wrote to her husband: "I am very worried, my dear
friend, about all this movement in Paris, and never has the *res
publica* appeared to me to be in such great danger."[44] When she
realized that some concerted action was taking shape, she tried
very hard to convince its supporters in her own entourage
(mostly younger men who had not lived through the earlier
phases of the Revolution) that their initiative was extraordinarily

ill timed—the constitution had just been ratified—as well as doomed to fail. Indeed, its most likely effect would be a revival of Jacobinism, a dangerous force of whose terrible power they were simply unaware.

One of the young men in question, the royalist journalist Charles de Lacretelle has left a very vivid record of the "speech" the ambassadress allegedly addressed to the aspiring plotters, as their intentions were discussed at a dinner party at her house. Lacretelle's account is probably somewhat fictionalized (it is difficult to imagine Staël addressing her dinner guests as if she were addressing an assembly, but then perhaps she did . . .). Yet the substance of the argument is close enough to the opinions she manifested elsewhere to be worth citing:

> You speak, gentlemen, of ending the Revolution, and yet you are taking the best route to restarting it. Are you dealing with men ready to surrender their place to you? Are perhaps those disciples of Danton, those *old cordeliers*, unable to see that for them it is a matter of life or death? They will fight you with the absolute power they still hold, and with weapons you do not know, those of the Revolution. You are very naive when you talk of *sovereignty of the people*: you are stammering in a language they master far better than you do, a language they fabricated for their own use.

According to this account, she was particularly scornful of the view that the support moderates enjoyed in the forum of public opinion could be of any help if they decided to jeopardize that support by resorting to the use of force:

> Just now Monsieur de la Harpe had no doubts about your victory, since public opinion is on your side; but be wary of compromising it with acts of violence; the Parisian sections, after 4 *prairial*, have given back their guns to the national Convention, as they mistrusted, with good reason, their gunners; these guns are now going to be turned against you: I ask M. de la Harpe, what is the caliber of the guns of public opinion?[45]

Yet, for all of Staël's hostility to the projected coup, it is easy to see how she was compromised by it: after all, some of the agitators were close friends of hers (Benjamin Constant and François de Pange, though not implicated, were briefly arrested);[46] there had been very public gatherings at her house attended by some of the suspects; the relentless campaign of allegations and rumors against her had finally found some substance. Moreover, the insurrection offered the opportunity to the more radical members of the Thermidorian government to raise suspicions about the loyalty of their moderate colleagues. Thus men like Boissy d'Anglas and Jean Denis Lanjuinais, who were on friendly terms with Staël, were politically weakened, as they themselves became the target of accusations of complicity with the insurgents.

Her diplomatic status allowed the ambassadress a short reprieve, in the form of a voluntary retreat from Paris to the spa town of Forges-les-Eaux in Normandy (though her husband's interventions in her defense had been so lukewarm as to shock Boissy d'Anglas, who had been in charge of the negotiations). On her return to Paris, after some weeks spent under police surveillance, Staël finally resigned herself to return to Switzerland in the company of Constant. As she confided bitterly to her friend Mme de Hénin: "Ah, how that 15 *vendémiaire* damaged us, and the fury and stupidity of that impotent struggle against an authority confident of triumphing! Well, we must bear it, but we have lost much ground on the front of reconciliation and peace."[47] The rapid evolution of political events meant that *Reflections on Domestic Peace*, with its prefigurations of the notion of liberty of the moderns, was put aside for good, to see the light only after the author's death.

CHAPTER 6

Condemned to Celebrity

THE INFLUENCE OF PASSIONS (1796)

THE YEAR 1796—the year of Staël's thirtieth birthday—was once again a time of acute existential dissatisfaction. When she had been forced to leave France for Switzerland, following the events of *vendémiaire*, she had hoped to placate the government's hostility by a short strategic absence. Instead she was stranded there for the whole year, staying with her widowed father at Coppet, or living with Benjamin Constant at various residences around Lausanne. While the members of the newly appointed Directory varied in their individual attitudes toward her, ranging from Lazare Carnot's open enmity to Paul Barras's friendship, they remained collectively opposed to her presence in Paris. Indeed, in May 1796 she learned that her name appeared on a list of suspects who were to be arrested on entering France. Though the French government later claimed that it was just a matter of mistaken identity, the implicit threat was obvious enough, and the ambassadress's movements and contacts continued to be closely monitored by the authorities on both sides of the border. The fact that her husband's diplomatic post in Paris was once again in jeopardy created a further obstacle to her return to the capital. In order to improve her relations with the Directory, Staël encouraged Constant to publish his first political essay, *De la force du gouvernement actuel de la France et de la nécessité de s'y rallier* (Of the force of the present government of France, and of the necessity of rallying to it),[1] a pamphlet in support of the Thermidorian regime that echoed some of the themes she had set forth in her unpublished *Reflections on Domestic Peace*. Though Constant's work was quite well received in Paris, helping to establish his reputation, it did little to change Staël's position with the French government.

Prevented from returning to the French political scene, Staël decided to use the time of her exile to complete the book she had begun after her flight from Paris in September 1792, a study of the influence of passions on individual and collective happiness. Following what seems a recurrent pattern in her life, frustration over some immediate practical object led her to invest in some more durable intellectual project.[2] At the beginning of October 1796 the first of the two volumes she planned (the second was never written) was published in Lausanne under the title *De l'Influence des passions sur le bonheur des individus et des nations* (Of the influence of passions on the happiness of individuals and nations).[3] As she explained in the preface, since she was "condemned to celebrity" while nothing was really known about her, she must have the chance to be judged as an author, on the merit of her own writings.[4] Unlike the pamphlets she had published during the Revolution, *Of the Influence of Passions* was conceived as a philosophical work, rather than as an occasional intervention in the political debate—though in the end the content of the text was probably closer to contemporary political issues than the writer had originally intended. By the time the book appeared, her collaboration with Constant was producing another unplanned result: she was pregnant by him (her daughter Albertine was born in June of the following year), the pregnancy representing another potential obstacle to her return to Paris. Luckily her friends' relentless pressures on the Directory, combined with Barras's personal support, finally had some effect: by Christmas 1796 she was back, if not in Paris, at least in France, in Constant's country property at Hérivaux.

A FRIGHTENING MIXTURE

Staël's study of human passions, though frequently referred to by commentators, has received, on the whole, scant critical attention when compared to the rest of her oeuvre.[5] The book was not especially successful at the time of its publication, though the author's contacts secured some favorable reviews in the French and English press; it also failed to make a lasting impression upon posterity. The main reason for this lack of success was probably that, in spite of the volume's suggestive title, the nature of the project behind it was not very clear: in particular there was a discrepancy between the plan of the work outlined in the introduction and its actual content. Far more than Staël's later writings, *Of the Influence of Passions* was phrased in the language of eighteenth-century moral philosophy, suggesting a somewhat belated contribution to the Enlightenment tradition of the morality of sentiments.[6] However, this impression of a rather conventional, even derivative work is quite deceptive. The professed subject of the book was indeed a classic topic in moral philosophy: the obstacles that passions present to the achievement of human happiness, and the remedies that philosophy can offer against their disruptive influence. It is also true that Staël's approach to the issue acknowledged the central role of emotions and sentiments in shaping human morality, in line with the position of Jean-Jacques Rousseau and with the views of Adam Smith, whose fashionable *Theory of Moral Sentiments* she duly cited in her text.[7] But while the general approach in *Of the Influence of Passions* was quite conventional, the perspective from which the subject was addressed was that of the radically new context created by the French Revolution.

As the author explained, the aspiration to happiness as a natural entitlement for individuals and for nations was at the heart of the philosophical and political project of the Enlightenment; as such it had become the focus of a vast movement of renewal for mentalities and institutions alike. "In our age," she claimed, "the hope or need of happiness [has] raised the human race."[8] Yet the realities of the Revolution had brought these aspirations to a tragic end, through the advent of terrible evils: destruction, war, terror, and even crime, "a frightening mixture of all human atrocities." Thus the natural desire of all human beings to be happy had turned into the unbridled display of fear, hatred, and cruelty. Explaining the degeneration of this original claim to a better condition for individuals and society alike was the initial motivation of Staël's work. Her leading assumption was that the project of a happier—more free, just, and humane—society was still valid, and could be rescued from the negative experiences of the Revolution, combining "the execration of the past" with "the hope for the future." Analytically the task was a difficult one, since it involved identifying why the expectations of 1789 had failed to materialize, separating the accidental factors that may have contributed to it from any intrinsic flaws of the project itself.

In the opening paragraphs the writer professed her intention to approach the subject with detachment from the immediate context, relocating it instead in a broader historical and theoretical perspective. She admitted, however, that she was emotionally very deeply involved with the issue, since, like the other "partisans of republican liberty," she had suffered most from the betrayal of the ideals in which she had passionately believed:

> It seems to me that the true partisans of republican liberty are those who hate the most the faults that have been committed in its name. Their adversaries may no doubt experience a just horror of those crimes; but since the same crimes can serve as arguments to confirm their position, they do not suffer like the friends of liberty, for whom the pain is greater.[9]

While the political scope of Staël's enterprise was clear enough—a partial rehabilitation of the ideals of 1789—her book's design did not quite conform to the outline she announced in the introduction. Her plan, as she described it, was to address the impact of passions in two different dimensions, those of private morality and of political institutions: thus the first part of her work discussed the influence of passions upon individual happiness, while the second part was to have analyzed the difficulties that passions represented for the establishment of free and stable political regimes:

> Passions, that impulsive force that drives man independently of his will, here is the true obstacle to individual and political happiness. Without passions, governments would be a machine as easy to operate as a system of levers, whose strength is proportionate to the weights they must lift; while man's destiny would be a just balance between his desires and the possibility of satisfying them.[10]

The volume that appeared in 1796 was presented as the first part, namely, the discussion of individual happiness; the second part, the study of the happiness of nations, with its political and constitutional implications, was to have been published at a later date.[11] In spite of this announced division of the subject, the volume frequently abandoned the discussion of the individual experience of passions to stray into political considerations: this is apparent in the chapters on glory, ambition, vanity, partisanship, and crime, which together form the bulk of the work. Probably this uneven structure was the result of Staël's anxiety to complete a project on which she had already worked intermittently for several years. In her haste to publish she may have anticipated arguments that had originally been intended for the second volume. In the absence of specific information about the sequence in which the chapters were written, it is impossible to be more definite on this point.

GOVERNING PASSIONS

It would be misleading to infer, from the dominance of political themes in *Of the Influence of Passions*, that Staël was not interested in the philosophical issue of individual happiness. On the contrary, as she approached her thirtieth birthday (she had already begun taking a year or two off her age whenever she referred to it in writing), she experienced a state of profound misery and frustration, which she attributed to her own "very passionate" nature. Different factors contributed to what had apparently already become a state of permanent, if latent, depression: the death of her mother and her beloved father's decline, her strained relations with her husband, and the end of her long-term passionate liaison with Narbonne. Above all she suffered from her condition of forced inactivity, and from the deprivation of Parisian society: she even went so far as to attribute the failure of her most recent love affairs (with Adolphe Ribbing and later with François de Pange) simply to her own physical absence from Paris. Anxious to escape from a condition that she described vividly to a correspondent as "inactive pain," she was willing to explore the means of achieving a greater inner balance, and to become emotionally more independent.

The problem was that, as she explained in the book's opening pages, vulnerability to passions varied too much from one individual to another to be captured by general principles: people were just too different in their response to emotions for their behavior to be predicted with any degree of accuracy. Nonpassionate people were generally capable of being satisfied in any setting, while the happiness of very passionate characters—such as the author herself—"was entirely dependent on what went on inside them." There were of course partial remedies that moral philosophy might recommend to this unfortunate minority of "very passionate" people, to distract them from their obsessions: pursuing intellectual interests, studying, meditating, or engaging in charitable activities. But it was impossible to offer an effective cure for their afflictions.

The outlook was more promising if the issue was addressed from the perspective of society at large. While the passionate impulses of single individuals differed considerably from case to case (therefore proving difficult to classify), their distribution across the population must necessarily show certain statistical regularities. Staël cited as example the fact that the incidence of divorces in the canton of Berne, or that of murders in Italy, seemed to follow stable patterns. Thus in considering how popular passions could be governed by appropriate laws and institutions, one was on relatively solid ground, since it was possible to identify some direct correlations. Staël explained this point in terms that were strongly reminiscent of David Hume's essay "That Politics May Be Reduced to a Science":[12]

> This is what must lead us to think that political science could someday acquire a geometric self-evidence. Morality, every time it is applied to a particular man, can be wrong in its assumption about him; instead the organization of a constitution is always founded upon fixed data, as a large number of cases in all domains leads to results that are always similar and predictable.[13]

Because of these recurrent patterns in collective behavior, the use of constitutional instruments to curb the destructive effects of passions was a viable political project. Indeed, one could say that the government of passions represented one of the central objects of constitutional theory, and also one of its main challenges:

> Passions are the greatest difficulty for governments: this truth does not need to be developed; it is easy to see that the most despotic social arrangements would be equally acceptable to passive, inert men, happy to remain in the place allocated to them by fate, while the most abstract democratic theory could be implemented among wise men guided exclusively by their reason. The only problem of constitutions is therefore to know to what degree passions can be excited or compressed without compromising public happiness.[14]

The aspiration to a balance between the compression and the stimulation of passions—between rest and movement, tranquillity and excitement—had been a leading theme in eighteenth-century moral and political reflection. It was associated with the Renaissance ideal of "mediocrity," the identification of an intermediate emotional disposition, and of a middling social condition, as the most conducive to individual happiness.[15] It was also central to the doctrine of moderate government as theorized, most influentially, by Montesquieu.[16] Staël placed herself in direct continuity with this tradition when she defined happiness—for individuals as well as for nations—as the reconciliation of contrasting states:

> Happiness, such as we desire it, is the union of all opposites: for single individuals it is hope without fear, activity without anxiety, glory without calumny, love without inconstancy, the type of imagination that embellishes in our eyes what we have, and diminishes in our memory what we have lost . . . The happiness of nations should be to reconcile the freedom of republics and the tranquillity of monarchies, the emulation of talents and the silence of factions, the deployment of military spirit in foreign relations, with the respect of the laws at home.[17]

While she endorsed the traditional ideal of the balancing of opposites, Staël believed that the Revolution had provided new insights on the dynamics of private and public passions. The eruption of uncontrolled impulses and violent emotions the French people had experienced in recent years had left indelible traces upon the emotional makeup of survivors. Even if the present mood of French society favored the return to order and civil peace, the wounds left by the Revolution could not be simply set aside and forgotten. Understanding what had happened was an essential precondition not just for achieving immediate civil reconciliation, but also for the stability of any future regime.[18]

THE DEMOCRATIC YOKE

Staël followed Hume in assuming that, while human passions may be constant through time, their deployment in particular settings was bound to vary according to specific historical traditions and circumstances. In the case of France, the abrupt transition from a monarchical regime based on privilege to a democratic republic based upon the equality of rights had turned usually controlled or latent human impulses into dangerously disruptive forces. Among these potentially explosive impulses was the desire to rise and to occupy a prominent role in society. The writer identified three passions associated with it: love of glory, ambition, and vanity. Throughout the seventeenth and eighteenth centuries these notions had been at the center of a vast philosophical reflection: debates initially focused upon the moral value of individual qualities and efforts, but gradually extended to the implications of these individual achievements for society at large, questioning the true worth of fame and reputation. In the postrevolutionary context, as the very foundations of society had been shaken, and public values undermined, the same concepts appeared in a different light.[19]

Staël had originally addressed this issue in her unpublished essay of 1789 "Eloge de M. de Guibert" (Defense of Guibert).[20] Commenting on the unhappy career of the comte de Guibert, a military strategist and one of the great reformers of the French army under the monarchy, who had died in disgrace at the beginning of the Revolution—she had questioned the view that glory, be it military or civil, was a notion of the past. Guibert had been criticized for using the term "glory" too often in his speech on the occasion of his admission to the Académie française in 1786. But was his insistence on "this great idea, this worthy reward" really so outdated? Or was it the case that the pursuit of fame for its own sake was still a precious incentive for men of talent to serve their country?

In *Of the Influence of Passions* Staël called "love of glory" the disinterested aspiration to accomplish great deeds in the service of mankind, or at least of one's community (even more disinterested in the case of intellectual or artistic glory, as this generally came only after death); she called "ambition" the craving for power and what goes with it: social prestige, lucrative positions, wealth, and honors. While glory presupposed true genius and grandeur in those who achieved it, the rewards of ambition were readily accessible even to the most mediocre individuals. As the writer had already argued in *Reflections on Domestic Peace*, societies based upon rank and privilege—Old Regime monarchies and aristocratic republics—offered little scope to individual advancement. Men from the lower ranks could not rise without causing resentment in their social superiors and envy in their equals; the members of the privileged elite, on the other hand, could not elevate themselves above their peers without humiliating and offending them. On the whole military glory was the only form of distinction tolerated in the members of monarchical and aristocratic societies. In principle the abolition of aristocratic privileges in France in 1789 should have opened new prospects to the emergence of talent. However, another crucial limiting factor had come to replace the old barriers of hierarchy and rank: the new culture of equality did in fact resent and hinder any instance of individual success.

This new phenomenon, represented by a sort of legitimation of social envy, was enhanced by the considerable expansion of the free press. The constant scrutiny of the actions and character of any public personality exercised by journalists and pamphleteers had the effect of destroying the reputation of those who aspired to glory, criticizing their actions and magnifying their most insignificant faults:

When the freedom of the press, and even more the multiplicity of journals, makes public every day the opinions of yester-

day, in such a country what we call glory cannot exist . . .
There are in all characters defects that in the past were revealed only by the light of history . . . Today whoever wishes
to distinguish himself is at war with the self-esteem of all; at
each step he takes to elevate himself, he is threatened with
being pushed back, and the mass of enlightened men take a
sort of active pride in destroying individual success.[21]

In modern times, just as in the past, glory was subjected to the
"democratic yoke" that exposed it to the fluctuations of popular
favor: but modern, enlightened opinion proved more destructive
of individual reputations than the naive "judgment of the multitude" of less advanced societies. Only at the very end of the
chapter on glory did Staël admit that she had been thinking all
along of Jacques Necker: she had not forgotten how the minister's (in her eyes fully deserved) moment of glory in the summer
of 1789 had been poisoned by vicious attacks in the press and
followed by a rapid decline of public favor. The unfortunate experience of her father, she argued, illustrated the incapacity of
modern societies to express and encourage glory. It also helped
to explain a trait Staël had repeatedly stressed in her previous
writings, namely, the absence of truly influential and respected
personalities during the revolutionary period. Unfortunately,
where glory had become impossible and true greatness was not
recognized, there was ample scope for the negative counterpart
of the love of glory, ambition. Ambition did not depend in the
same way on popular approval: the ambitious man scorned criticism and was indifferent to any consideration other than the
acquisition of power; he had a self-centered personality and a
disposition that implied "a certain contempt for mankind."[22]
Needless to say, these negative characteristics were well suited
to the circumstances of a revolution:

At times of revolution, ambition alone can succeed. There are
still the means of acquiring power, but the kind of opinion
that can confer glory no longer exists; the people rules instead

of judging; by playing an active role in all events it takes sides for or against certain individuals. In the nation there are only enemies in arms; that impartial power that we call the public no longer shows itself. What is great and just in absolute terms is no longer recognized; everything is valued only in relation to the passions of the moment.[23]

The obsessive drive and lack of any moral concern that characterized the pursuit of ambition helped to explain why the chiefs of the Revolution were unable to perform the role of true leaders, inspiring and guiding the people. In order to keep their power they had to anticipate and follow the course of events, as any attempt to stop them, changing their direction, would result in their own destruction:

> In order to be ambitious in a revolution it is necessary to march always ahead of the impulse that has propelled events; it is a rapid descent in which it is impossible to stop; in vain one recognizes the abyss into which he is about to fall; whoever jumps off the carriage will be broken by the fall; to avoid peril is more dangerous than to confront it; one must lead on the path that drives to perdition, as any step backwards destroys the man who takes it without preventing events from taking their course.[24]

Thus rather than directing and leading the revolutionary process, the chiefs of the different factions had been ceaselessly seconding the expectations and moods of the crowds, becoming the passive followers of a process that escaped their control.

The third passion associated with the desire to attain recognition that became prominent during the Revolution was vanity. Staël admitted that vanity at first did not even look like a real passion, given that its object—to be admired—seemed too insubstantial to have a real impact. Indeed, it was difficult to believe that the same impulse that dictated the attitude of a frivolous woman in a ballroom could, in other settings, have serious political consequences. And yet the contribution of vanity to the progress of events in France—a country apparently more prone than most to this passion—had been decisive. Perhaps—Staël observed—it was excessive to claim that vanity alone led twenty-four million people to rebel against the privileges of two hundred thousand: there had been very good reasons of natural justice to justify such rebellion. Similarly, it would be going too far to attribute to vanity the resistance exerted by the aristocracy against the Revolution. And yet the vanity of political actors was one of the main impulses behind the sequence of events since 1789:

> It is in the inner march of the Revolution that one can observe the empire of vanity, from the desire of ephemeral applause to the need to impress, of that passion so typical of France, and of which foreigners by comparison have a very imperfect idea.[25]

Staël described in particular how the presence of a public audience at the debates in the assembly had all along conditioned the conduct of legislators. No doubt in the later stages of the Revolution, during the Terror, it was fear of the mob that drove deputies to endorse certain policies; but to begin with, it was just vanity, the desire to be at the center of attention. The wish to impress the audience led them first to make inflammatory speeches, then to vote radical and even criminal measures:

> A great number of opinions have been dictated by the wish to surpass the previous speaker and to be applauded after him; the admission of spectators in the hall where deliberations took place has been sufficient to change the direction of public affairs in France. At first certain phrases were sufficient to elicit applause; then, in order to gain it, it has become necessary to renounce principles, to propose decrees, even to approve crimes . . . It was not to satisfy sentiments of hatred and

fury that barbarous laws were voted, but to please the public in the galleries.[26]

At a different level, vanity, in the form of the ill-conceived desire to appear "original," had prevented French legislators from imitating the constitutional models of other nations, such as England and America. They had preferred to introduce improvised institutional arrangements of their own invention, rather than relying on safe and well-tested ones already in place elsewhere.

The combined forces of ambition and vanity had been a decisive factor in the radicalization of the revolutionary process. Anxious to gain popular favor, and jealous of one another's influence, political leaders had failed to resist the escalation toward growing insubordination and violence. But another important element that undermined the authority of revolutionary leaders comprised those very ideals they promoted in their eagerness to attain prominence, above all the exaltation of liberty and equality. Staël explained this point through a comparison with England: during the Great Rebellion Cromwell had been able to retain his power because the main impulse behind the English Revolution had been the demand for religious reform. Consequently his followers contested some forms of authority—such as absolute monarchy—but not authority as such, and were still disposed to submit to a chief. In the case of France, on the other hand, the very notion of a few men exercising power over the mass of the people went against the principles by which the Revolution was inspired:

> When the cause of a revolution is the exaltation of all the ideas of liberty, it is impossible for its first leaders to keep their power. They must excite the movement of which they will become the first victims; they must encourage the principles that will serve to judge them; finally, they can promote their opinion, but not their interests, as in a revolution fanaticism makes better sense than ambition.[27]

In other words, in France the guidance of men had been replaced very early on by that of ideas, and the authority of prominent individuals by that of partisan ideologies.

A PASSION WITHOUT COUNTERWEIGHT

From the analysis of the desire for self-advancement, Staël moved on to consider the passion that was more than any other at the heart of the revolutionary experience, namely, the spirit of party. Like vanity, party spirit was one of those passions that in many settings may remain dormant or manifest themselves in relatively harmless forms: Staël gave the example of certain obscure literary or artistic controversies, in which trifling rivalries or disagreements may elicit a disproportionate emotional response. One had to live in the age of some religious or political revolution to measure the truly frightening power of partisanship. The religious wars between Catholics and Huguenots in the sixteenth century were the only precedent in French history that seemed comparable in this respect to the revolutionary experience. One important characteristic of the spirit of party was that it could be found equally in mediocre individuals and in highly intelligent, enlightened ones. While it was not surprising that credulous, stupid men should rush to endorse extreme positions, it was more difficult to understand how clever ones might do so: indeed, partisanship apparently deprived even the best minds of all capacity to reason. Staël gave as an example of this disposition the philosopher Condorcet:

> A man celebrated for other reasons, Monsieur de Condorcet had precisely the character of the spirit of party. His friends claim that he would have attacked his own opinion, indeed that he would have disowned it and written against it, without confiding to anyone his secret efforts, had he believed that by this means the cause of that opinion might triumph.[28]

Two years after the philosopher's tragic death in captivity, Staël could still not bring herself to condone what she saw as his disastrous political choices.[29] As an aristocrat and a distinguished scientist committed to social progress, the marquis de Condorcet should have been a natural ally of moderate reformers. His young wife, Sophie de Grouchy, the translator of Adam Smith and Tom Paine, was a friend of Staël and, like her, hosted a literary salon. Condorcet's ideas on public instruction and political representation, such as he expressed them in his *Rapport sur l'Instruction publique* (Report on public instruction) of 1792, were not very distant from Staël's own.[30] However, with his election to the Legislative Assembly (of which he became chairman) in 1791, and to the Convention in 1792, the philosopher's attitudes revealed his radical republicanism. Close to the group of the Girondins, he shared their hostility to the monarchy, their support of the war, and their strong democratic aspirations. At the trial of Louis XVI, he did not vote for the king's death, as he was opposed on principle to the death penalty, but proposed that Louis should be sent instead to the galleys. After drafting for the Girondins the project for a democratic constitution (which was never applied), he succumbed with them to the persecution of their former allies, the Jacobins. Contemporary rumors of secret political meetings in the ambassadress's house between Condorcet and Narbonne, at the time of the latter's ministry, have never found confirmation in the existing evidence.[31] In Staël's eyes the marquis remained a dangerous political enemy, with the aggravating factor of his distinguished birth and intellectual talents. Although she was generally compassionate toward the victims of the Terror, she clearly thought, without quite saying so, that he had brought upon himself his own unhappy ending. Her severe judgment on Condorcet did not go unnoticed by the editors of the *Décade philosophique* (the journal representing the spiritual heritage of the philosopher), who, rather than publishing a proper review of *The Influence of Passions*, confined themselves to a short, frosty notice.[32] Naturally not all the excesses of civil wars and revolutions could be ascribed to the spirit of party, since in such circumstances loyalty to a cause served often as a pretext to disguise baser motives; yet no other passion that came into play could match it in intensity; it exercised a "sort of dictatorship" over people: "Pride, rivalry, vengeance, fear take the mask of the spirit of party; but such passion in itself is the most fierce: it becomes fanaticism and faith in regard to whatever object it is applied."[33]

Unlike other passions, the spirit of party was not open to compromise: an ambitious man might modify his conduct from considerations of prudence, or in exchange for some benefits; a fanatical one was unable to do that. Partisanship was essentially a "passion without any kind of counterweight." It was also a self-defeating disposition, since the unbending attitude of factions was often a major obstacle to the enactment of effective and useful political strategies. Staël cited the example of the ultraroyalists in the Constituent Assembly, who had stood by, allowing the Jacobins to seize power, rather than forming an alliance or even simply voting with the hated Constitutionnels. Whoever was moved by the spirit of party—she concluded—would prefer to fall, dragging down his enemies with him, rather than sharing any part of his triumph with them. In this reconstruction of the vicissitudes of the assembly, Staël clearly implied that such fanaticism was the property of "extreme" doctrines—such as belief in absolute monarchy or in democracy—rather than of any "intermediate" position.

Possibly the most frightening trait of partisanship was that, pushed by it, honest men could commit odious and even criminal actions while feeling at peace with their own conscience. In the *Essays* Hume had raised this point, arguing that loyalty to a faction may deprive men of all sense of morality and shame.[34] Staël now used the same argument to show how easy it was to justify atrocities and murders when they were committed in the name of a cause. Thus one common feature characterizing those responsible for the crimes of the Terror was the absence of any trace of remorse on their part. The few truly criminal personalities that had emerged during the Revolution could not regret their actions, because they were driven by an uncontrollable, frenzied impulse that grew with each crime. Such men were, however, a negligible minority. Their actions were seconded by a mass of honest, ordinary men, sincerely convinced of the legitimacy of their conduct. Neither the real criminals nor their followers experienced any regret or felt any compassion for the victims. And yet, Staël argued, it was during a revolution, with the breakdown of ordinary laws and legal constraints, that a sense of compassion for other people's sufferings would be most necessary to keep barbarism at bay:

> In a revolutionary crisis it is claimed over and over again that compassion is a childish sentiment, opposed to those actions that are necessary to the general interest, and that it must be set aside, with all effeminate emotions, unworthy of men or state or chiefs of parties; it is on the contrary during a revolution that pity must become a rule of conduct. Where justice is well established, one can do without mercy; but a revolution, whatever its aim, suspends social order, and it is then necessary to go back to the source of all laws, in a moment in which legal power means nothing.[35]

The leaders of parties believed they possessed supreme wisdom when they placed sectarian considerations above common humanity; but in fact they were preparing their own and the nation's destruction. In the concluding pages of her book, Staël placed compassion at the heart of human sociability. Such sentiment was "fertile of rich products for individuals and for nations. One must be persuaded that it is the only primitive idea attached to the nature of man, because it is the only one necessary to all virtues and all enjoyments."[36]

In a footnote, Staël criticized Smith for claiming that compassion was dependent on sympathy, that is to say, on the human capacity to participate in the feelings of others. On the contrary—she claimed—we must feel compassion even for those sufferings we fail to understand, or that we could never experience in the same way.[37] While this critique of Smith seems somewhat unjustified (the exercise of sympathy does not necessarily imply proximity to the experience of others, only the capacity to put ourselves in their place), Staël's insistence on pity for the sufferings of those with whom we cannot identify had direct political implications. The capacity to feel for others across ideological and social divisions was in fact essential to guarantee the rights of minorities, especially at times of civil disorder:

> Legislators often govern on the ground of too general ideas; the broad principle that the interest of the minority must always give way to that of the majority depends entirely on the kind of sacrifices that are imposed on the minority. If it is pushed to the extreme, one arrives at the system of Robespierre. It is not the number of individuals but the pain that must be calculated.[38]

THE GREAT NATION

There is a striking contrast between the picture of the new republic built upon a moderate constitution outlined in the introduction to *Of the Influence of Passions* and the one presented in the conclusion. The political model was the same, but while initially it was presented as the solution to a theoretical problem, indeed almost as a scientific finding, in the end it was shown to be the only path to safety out of a maze of difficult moral choices and emotional traumas. Staël had begun by arguing that while the moralist could not always hope to teach men how to be happy by mastering their emotions, the legislator must strive to approach as far as possible the model of a constitution that led to the balancing of passions. Unlike the discipline of individual temperaments (which was too dependent on particular factors), the stability of societies could count on the fact that large human groups were, on average, quite predictable in their emotional responses. Naturally, real political regimes could never quite match the ideal of a harmonious community, and yet such an ideal could be clearly defined through the appropriate reasoning, since "the greatest perfectibility of which [the human race] was capable was to acquire well-founded ideas on political science."[39] In the past people had believed that the best way of achieving a moderate constitution was to build it on the opposition of two main social forces, aristocracy and democracy.[40] This doctrine had been considered for centuries as the chef d'oeuvre of the science of government; and yet in practice it had caused the ruin of many regimes. The modern way of approaching the problem through the establishment of representative government was to abandon the idea of two opposed interests, and to imagine a society with a single combined interest, in which no category of citizens was separated from the rest by the privilege of birth:

> Is it not possible that mankind, witness and victim of this principle of hatred, of this kind of death that destroys so many states, should put an end to the struggle between aristocracy and democracy? Rather than insisting on creating an equilibrium that, because of its chief advantage—the place it accords to liberty—ends up by being overturned, should we perhaps consider instead whether the modern idea of representative government might establish a single interest, a single principle of life, rejecting whatever can lead to democracy?[41]

Staël made it clear that setting aside the traditional model of the mixed constitution did not mean rejecting the principle of the separation of powers within the constitution itself: on the contrary, the "division of powers" was presented as a valid alternative, which offered "all the advantages and none of the disadvantages" of the opposition of interests.[42] The main difficulty in this new conception of representative government was how to prevent a society in which there were no rigid class barriers from sliding toward a situation of dangerous equality, such as the one created by the Revolution. Staël's answer was the emergence of an "aristocracy of the best": a ruling class of superior men, to be picked out from "an immense nation" through a selective system of election that took into account their personal qualities, their economic standing, and their reputation in the community (acquired, for example, through some form of public service). In this way the new republic would be able to match the greatness of monarchies:

> These different reflections should lead to the main purpose of present debates, to the way of constituting a great nation in order and liberty and to combine the splendor of arts, sciences, and letters, so praised in monarchies, with the independence of republics. One should create a government that is open to the competition of genius, and yet able to contain factious passions; that might offer to a great man a scope worthy of him, while discouraging a usurper; a government that might illustrate, as I said, the only perfect idea of happiness, the union of all contrasts.[43]

Thus in the introduction the modern French republic was heralded as a novel political system able to accommodate private and public grandeur. It was presented as a solution dictated by the progress of the science of government and by reason: indeed, reasoning was identified by the author as the only means to persuade all former enemies to rally to it, since "only men who have been persuaded are truly defeated."[44] In contrast with her initial insistence on scientific evidence and reasoning, in the conclusion of the book Staël claimed that compassion for the people's past suffering was the only sentiment that could reunite the nation, ending the spiral of hatred and vengeance. The grandeur of the new republic, now triumphing over its foreign enemies, was to be measured by its capacity for generosity and clemency. Civil peace would come not from reasoning and persuasion alone, but from a single patriotic impulse embracing victors and vanquished alike: "A kind of impulse of the soul, made of enthusiasm and pity, can alone stop domestic infighting, and equally remind all parties, occupied at tearing one another apart, of the name of their motherland. Such an emotion can produce more in a day than all the political writings and strategies; man fights against his own nature when he gives to the mind alone the greatest influence upon his destiny."[45]

Seen from this perspective, the republic was described, in far more realistic terms, as an ultimate resort, a barrier against the evils that still threatened the nation: "What do we wish from the genius, the achievements, the freedom of republics? What is there to wish? A few less pains, a few more hopes."[46] Whether one considered it from a rational or from an emotional angle, the incarnation of representative government in a "Great Nation,"[47] a republican regime that retained some monarchical traits, was presented as an exclusively French phenomenon: a product of France's natural features (such as her large territory and numerous population) and of her history, past and present. Staël stressed that her defense of the new regime did not imply that she considered it as necessarily applicable to any other European country. This precision was introduced to reassure her monarchical readers that her conversion to republicanism came from pragmatic rather than from ideological reasons. It also showed how the study of passions, undertaken as a broad theoretical exercise, had led the writer to delve even more deeply into the specific historical circumstances of France, and to consider the chain of unpredictable events that had generated, with the Revolution, such unusual emotional developments.

THE TESTAMENT OF MY THOUGHT

In the introduction to *Of the Influence of Passions* Staël did not miss the opportunity to cite Constant's pamphlet *Of the Force of the Present Government* in highly praiseworthy terms:

Everything invites France to remain a republic; everything dictates that Europe should not follow her example: one of the most inspired works of our time, the one by Benjamin Constant, has addressed admirably the question of the present position of France. Two reasons of sentiment strike me above all: should we suffer a new revolution in order to overturn the one that has established the republic? And the courage of such great armies, the blood of so many heroes, have they been spent in the name of a chimera of which history shall remember only the crimes it has cost?[48]

The pamphlet, completed by Constant toward the end of March 1796, had been published in both Switzerland and France; the whole text or parts of it were also reprinted in the periodical press, in *Le Moniteur* and *La Sentinelle*.[49] In mid-April Constant traveled to Paris to promote his tract, as well as to apply for French citizenship in his capacity as descendant of a family of persecuted French Huguenots.[50] His work received some favorable notices but also generated the usual speculations about imaginary royalist conspiracies in which the Swiss author might be involved. (Offensive insinuations in the *Courier républicain* about the nature of his relations with Staël led him to fight a duel with its editor, Louis-François Bertin.)[51]

As the passage cited above suggests, the main argument outlined in *Of the Force of the Present Government* was indeed very close to that previously developed by Staël in *Reflections on Domestic Peace*, though Constant addressed the issue in his own distinctively terse and incisive style: both authors defended the view that France's republican government must be sustained in order to avoid the evils of a counterrevolution. Constant's pamphlet also echoed some themes that were prominent in *Of the Influence of Passions*: the author referred, for example, to the influence of vanity on the attitude of the French political class; he evoked the greater scope given to ambition in republican (as opposed to monarchical) regimes; he also offered a series of considerations on the role of factions and the spirit of party, a subject that was not prominent in his later works. The question of the textual similarities between Constant's and Staël's writings in this initial phase of their intellectual cooperation has been analyzed in great detail by the editor of Staël's correspondence, Béatrice Jasinski.[52] One can only agree with her conclusion that, beyond the obvious similarity in the two authors' political views, it is impossible to measure the precise degree of their influence on one another. In a letter to Roederer—who had reviewed, somewhat critically, *Of the Force of the Present Government* in the *Journal de Paris*—Staël gave her own version of her and Constant's respective positions: "I answer for what I write; but Benjamin's work is not my own. I am, it is true, very enthusiastic about his talent and I must confess I have felt some irritation at the way you talk about it." After a series of admiring comments about Constant's literary talents, she admitted she did not endorse the directness and sarcastic tone of some of his expressions. This reaction on her part concealed to some extent a difference in political sensibility: she found Constant too flippant and even brutal in his dismissal of the defeated monarchists. She also found him too lenient with the Directory when he condoned the promotion of some former Jacobins to important posts in the new government. She then concluded: "([Constant's] book and myself are two separate things. My life belongs to my friends, not my opinion, and I shall never deviate from the line that you yourself [Roederer] seem to follow more rigorously than anybody else."[53]

Setting aside the intractable question of the relations between the two authors, *Of the Influence of Passions* marked a new departure in Staël's work. Until then she had addressed current political issues in occasional articles and pamphlets. She had adopted the style of peroration to persuade, justify, and denounce, just as she might have addressed an assembly had she been given the opportunity to do so. Such pamphlets were designed as militant interventions in specific debates, and the author was quite prepared to abandon them if their publication seemed ill timed or politically counterproductive. Although *Of the Influence of Passions* was constructed as a set of separate essays, each discussing a particular human emotion, the author's intention was to produce a more structured, comprehensive work. As soon as the book was in print, at the beginning of October, she sent a copy to Roederer, presenting it in the following terms: "You shall see in the book I am sending you what I think about moral ideas; and in the second part that I announce, I will try to develop what I think about political institutions. It is the testament of my thought. I shall try to finish it before I turn thirty, to die at that age, famous and regretted."[54]

In spite of its somewhat ironical formulation, the letter suggests that Staël did really mean to produce a substantial theoretical contribution, one capable of making a lasting impression upon the public. The way in which she presented her book suggests that, initially at least, she pursued the ideal of a broad systematic discourse inspired by Montesquieu's *Spirit of the Laws*, a work that should combine a set of general concepts and principles with a variety of historical illustrations. It was a preference that she shared with Constant, who during his life invested considerable energy in planning ambitious (and generally unfinished) large-scale treatises. *Of the Influence of Passions* showed the limitations of such a model. In a short essay published in 1795, *Essai sur les fictions* (Essay on fictions),[55] the writer had already suggested that the best way of addressing individual emotions was through literary creation, since this approach made it possible to preserve at the same time their unique character and their universal exemplary significance:

> My position would seem absurd if I were to say that I pay no attention to history, to which I prefer fiction, as if invention did not come from experience, as if the subtle nuances that emerge in certain novels did not derive from the philosophical principles, from the main ideas offered by the great picture of public events. However, such morality can exist only en

masse; it is by the repetition of a certain number of cases that history offers the same results; it is not to individuals, but to peoples, that its lessons are always applicable.[56]

But how could such lessons of history be expressed? What emerged from the book on passions was that, in the study of collective movements, history did not serve merely to provide occasional illustrations of general principles but supplied the basic structure of any political doctrine. Examples of "philosophical history" were not lacking in eighteenth-century literature. But with the Revolution history had completely submerged all philosophical categories in the irresistible flood of events. The powerful narrative of the Revolution had become the foundation of any new approach to political thinking.

CHAPTER 7

The Republic in Theory and Practice (1797–99)

WRITING FROM Coppet to Pierre-Louis Roederer in the fall of 1796, Staël described her personal position in the following terms: "You must know that I would prefer to appear in front of the revolutionary tribunal, with equal chances to die or to escape, rather than never returning to France; that I suffer so much, in a thousand different ways, from this exile, and that I would risk anything to get out of it."[1] During the three years or so that elapsed between the date of this letter and the coup that brought General Bonaparte to power in November 1799, Staël managed to spend a total of no more than six months in Paris. Whenever her presence in the capital appeared too intrusive, or evoked comments in the press, whenever the precarious stability of the directorial government was threatened by a new royalist or Jacobin conspiracy, she was forced at best to retire to some country residence (Necker's recovered estate at Saint Ouen, or Constant's country house at Hérivaux), at worst to return to Switzerland. Sometime in the fall of 1799, just before she once again risked leaving Coppet for Paris, she wrote to her friend Mme Pastoret:

> Why do you say that you would feel more affection for me if my life were less agitated and brilliant? In what way is it agitated, apart from a few calumnies? And what is so brilliant

about it? I spend two-thirds of it in a solitary château . . . There was a time in my life when I was much engaged in some services; but for three years now what have I done other than defend myself when I am attacked, while living alone two-thirds of the time? If this can be described as an "agitated and brilliant" life, there is only the grave to hope for that might seem sufficiently quiet for me as a place of rest.[2]

Paradoxically Staël's presence on the Parisian political scene was never so prominent, never so remarked on or gossiped about by the public and the press, as during this period in which she felt so bitterly excluded and marginalized. Indeed, what we know about her activities at this time comes mainly from other people's testimony and records. Staël's own surviving correspondence deals almost exclusively with practical and personal matters: crucial among these were her successful efforts to recover Necker's properties in France, which had been confiscated by the revolutionary government.[3] She was also engaged, less successfully, in the attempt to secure French citizenship for Constant (so that he might be able to stand for office) and for herself. Although she was born in France—therefore entitled to French citizenship by the jus soli—in marrying a Swedish subject she had acquired her husband's nationality, a circumstance that allowed the authorities to treat her as a foreigner, causing her immense frustration, as well as making her more vulnerable to police measures.[4]

There are indications that Staël took active part in the establishment—in June 1797—of the Cercle Constitutionnel, a political club created to strengthen the position of moderate republicans, in which Constant was to play an important role;[5] yet much of the evidence about the political contacts that she supposedly developed around the club is hearsay, and is patchy or unreliable. A month later, in July 1797, she was apparently instrumental in the appointment of Talleyrand—back from his American exile—to the post of minister of foreign affairs: however, the narrative provided by the former member of the Directory Barras in his *Memoirs*, with a description of Staël making hysterical scenes in his house to secure from the government the nomination of her friend, is clearly a malicious invention.[6] Most of the time we see her through the filter of other people's inaccurate recollections and fanciful allegations, all born within a political climate of growing insecurity, suspicion, and conspiracy. More importantly, although it was during this period (probably between May and October 1798) that Staël wrote her most substantial contribution to political and constitutional theory—the text entitled *Des circonstances actuelles qui peuvent terminer la révolution et des principes qui doivent fonder la république en France* (Of present circumstances that can end the Revolution, and of the principles that must found the republic in France)[7]—her correspondence offers no insight on the making of this work. It also fails to shed any light on why precisely she decided to put the draft aside, unpublished, a full year before the experiment of the directorial republic reached its conclusion with the advent of the Consulate.

Like the other essays produced by Staël since 1791, *Of Present Circumstances* combined a series of observations on the immediate situation of France with more theoretical considerations, in this case a reformulation of the theory of representative government. This tendency to combine a theoretical perspective with pressing practical considerations is typical of Staël's writings about politics: it is precisely the fluctuation between these two registers that gives her prose its distinctively breathless, uneven pace, alternating passages of terse analysis with urgent perorations, often sacrificing the linearity of the argument to rhetorical effects. In this text, however, the relation between theoretical and practical considerations was not just a feature of the writer's style, the product of her reluctance to choose between two different ways of approaching the same subject: here the relation between theory and practice became the central focus of the work. For Staël the most difficult problem created by the Revolution—a problem that the French political class had been thus far unable to solve—was how to bridge the gap between a set of abstract notions and their application, between the demand for individual rights and popular sovereignty, and the means by which this demand might be converted into viable political institutions. In particular the distinction between ancient and modern republicanism, outlined in the text, reflected the distance between a set of inherited philosophical beliefs and contemporary realities.

A QUESTION OF METHOD

The starting point of Staël's reflection in *Of Present Circumstances* was one of method: she began by claiming that she could not recognize herself in any of the works produced recently on the subject of the French Revolution, even when these had some obvious moral or intellectual merits:

> Among so many works about politics, I have not yet found a single one that corresponds to my own approach. I have seen writings against the principles of the French Revolution, obviously inspired by the purest morality. I have seen violent philippics against the crimes of the French Revolution . . . I have seen writings that, while presenting what looked like a true and brilliant political theory, kept silent about everything that was done in the name of that same theory . . . None of these works express what I regard as the best opinions and sentiments.[8]

She then went on to explain that her disagreement was connected with one specific difficulty: it was wrong in her view to approve of any political doctrine that failed to offer clear guidance for action: "I believe it is not acceptable to praise a theory without formulating an opinion on the means of its application."[9] Further on in the text she explained at greater length how she saw the relation between general principles and action in politics:

In my view the man of genius in politics is someone who can
trace the path from the most basic principles to their physical
application; the dreamer conceives a system and fails to ver-
ify it by any material proof; the practical man observes facts
without connecting them to their cause . . . Theory without
experience is only a phrase; experience without theory is just
prejudice.[10]

Unsurprisingly the authorities Staël cited as examples of a sound
approach to the understanding of complex political issues were
Newton and Montesquieu: Newton as the founder of the experimental method in natural sciences, a method that could be extended to the study of human behavior in society; Montesquieu
for his ability to identify general laws and continuities in the confused sequence of "accidental combinations" that formed human
history, in such a way as to become "a historian of hazard."

Whatever the inadequacies of contemporary writers when
compared to these past masters, their failure was not just the
result of their own limitations; it was also the product of the
unique character of the object they were trying to grasp, namely,
the Revolution itself. The French Revolution, Staël argued, was
different from any other modern revolutionary experience because of the indeterminate, abstract nature of its object. Other
nations—America, Switzerland, Holland—had rebelled in order
to gain their independence from a colonial power or foreign rule;
in the case of England, the revolution had started as a domestic
confessional conflict, with essentially religious motivations—a
circumstance that had contributed to giving the rebellion a precise object and a specific focus.[11] In France, on the other hand, the
Revolution's main purpose had been to assert a set of abstract
principles; it was a movement promoted by writers and philosophers, and inspired by high sentiments such as the love of equality, the hatred of prejudice, and the belief in progress, rather than
by any specific political project.

The principle of the French Revolution is the progress of philosophy. Had Montesquieu lived in our times, he would perhaps have thought that philosophy was the principle of the French republic; no doubt virtue is also philosophy. But the principle of the republic is the war against all prejudices by the establishment of social institutions founded, as it were, on elements of positive calculation.[12]

Born of these moral and philosophical aspirations, the French republic was obviously committed to putting them into practice. However, the "elements of positive calculation," the exercise of translating principles into a new social order and new political institutions, had proved very hazardous, generating considerable confusion, abusive interpretations, and conflicts.

POLITICAL AND ECONOMIC EQUALITY

In Staël's view the main difficulties in the transition from the principles of the Revolution to their enactment in the new republican model came from the question of equality. The abolition of aristocratic privilege, and the establishment of the equality of all citizens, had been at the heart of the revolutionary project. The implications of the first part of the project—suppressing hereditary privileges—were clear enough: in practice it meant abolishing the legal and fiscal prerogatives of the nobility, and opening access to all public posts to the nonnobles. But what about those inequalities that were not inscribed in the legal status of a particular social group? Should they also become the object of a legislative and institutional intervention?

Predictably Staël stood in firm opposition to the view that equality meant the social and economic leveling of citizens, minimizing, if not abolishing altogether, all differences of wealth, social standing, or education. The interpretation of equality as the elimination of all social differences had been set forth by the

most radical currents within the Revolution, such as the Babeu-
vistes (the last surviving radical group led by Gracchus Babeuf),[13]
and by those conservative aristocrats who wished to discredit
the very idea of equality by pushing it to its extreme consequences. Staël thought, by contrast, that equality must be understood as *political* equality, that is to say, equality before the law; it
should not mean the suppression of social and economic distinctions, let alone the abolition of property or the redistribution of
wealth. No doubt, a well-organized society must be able to grant
all its citizens the means of their survival, and to assist those in
need. But the strategy of attacking property as such did not provide a solution to poverty, as the revolutionary experience had
shown; it only increased insecurity and generated further in-
justices. While aristocratic privilege created "artificial" inequalities, based upon heritage and status rather than upon personal
qualities, political equality allowed the emergence of "natural"
inequalities, those that derived from the superior merits and
abilities of certain individuals: "Political equality is simply the
reestablishment of natural inequality. All hereditary distinctions
create a fictitious inequality, which may correspond, but may
also be in contradiction, to natural inequality."[14] The combination of political equality and natural inequality was the precondition for the emergence of the most able and dedicated men.
Thus the new republic must provide a competitive setting, in
which rulers would be selected on the ground of their personal
intellectual and moral qualities:

> When you allow all men to compete for all positions, and you
> ensure the freedom of choice by means of good constitutional
> institutions, you will be certain that the most enlightened,
> honest, and respected individuals will be called by the people
> to govern . . . Thus it is not political equality we are fighting
> against when we celebrate the supremacy of virtue, of enlight-
> enment, of education, and even of property, qualities that by
> conferring on candidates a greater interest in the political as-

sociation, and more time to acquire instruction, make them worthy of the suffrage of their fellow citizens.[15]

Toward the end of 1793 the question of equality and its role in the Revolution had been the subject of an essay—*Réflexions philosophiques sur l'égalité* (Philosophical reflections on equality)[16]— that Jacques Necker added to a new edition of his work of 1792 *Du pouvoir exécutif dans les grands états* (Of executive power in large states).[17] In this text Necker returned to the questions of obedience and of the enforcement of the law that had been at the center of his book on executive power. The Revolution—he argued—had ended in chaos because the suppression of social hierarchies, combined with the mirage of equality, had undermined all respect for authority and destroyed public order. In a large, diversified society such as France, accustomed to high degrees of inequality, the order of ranks and the respect for honors and social distinctions were indispensable to preserve the legitimacy and stability of power. Instead the French revolutionaries had assumed that "the submission of a large population to the obligations imposed by a small number of men was a simple matter, a result that would automatically follow from the sanctions imposed on whoever violated public order."[18] Entranced by the wonderful phenomenon represented by the political and civil union of twenty-five million people, they had convinced themselves that "public order could be maintained in an immense country without those social differences that favor the sentiments of respect and obedience, without those distinctions that preserve authority from the familiarities that lower it."[19] Thus, according to Necker, the chimera of equality, preached to the uneducated populace and introduced without any precautions, could only generate frustration, insubordination, and confusion.

Staël's own analysis in *Of Present Circumstances* showed how far she had distanced herself from her father's views. Like him, she regarded the ideal of a truly egalitarian society as a dangerous utopia, a threat to individual liberty and to the security of property. Like him, she believed that political power was best placed in the hands of a prosperous, enlightened elite. However, she thought that the decline of hereditary privilege and the advent of civil equality were conquests from which there was no turning back; if in France they had been introduced too brutally and imprudently, they represented nevertheless the true founding principles of modern society.[20] While Necker's conception of rank was rather static—since he saw the preservation of social distinctions as a guarantee of stability—hers was essentially dynamic: the creation of an egalitarian society was indeed a dangerous illusion; but it was equally delusory to imagine that the social energies and ambitions liberated by the Revolution could be simply pushed back inside the old armor of hierarchy. On the contrary, the prospect of social advancement and the promotion of talents were the safety valves that could preserve postrevolutionary society from the process of rapid social implosion that had destroyed the Old Regime. Where Necker identified the ideal ruling class with a self-perpetuating elite of notables, Staël was closer to the modern notion of an expanding, upwardly mobile middle class.

FROM DEMOCRACY TO REPRESENTATIVE GOVERNMENT

Staël's dynamic notion of equality, understood as the equal opportunity for all to rise in society, had direct consequences for the way in which popular sovereignty must be understood and exercised. Political equality meant the right of every man who qualified for citizenship to contribute to the formation of the laws that governed him—that is to say, to take part, directly or indirectly, in legislative power. This participation could take two forms: the first one was pure democracy, a regime based on the "gathering of all citizens on the public square"; the alternative was representative government, a system that intervened whenever this practice of immediate participation was no longer possible. But what precisely was the relation between these two models?

The revolutionary experience offered conclusive proofs that the enforcement of social and economic equality was a costly and ultimately impossible objective, while the achievement of political equality represented a viable, realistic project. In the same way—Staël argued—it was now clear that the original principle of popular sovereignty could be realized, in practice, only by resorting not to democracy but to representative government. Pure democracy was, as it were, the theory, the abstract principle of popular sovereignty; representative government was the means of its application to real political systems in the modern world:

> There are many political reasons today that militate against those associations sufficiently small to permit pure democracy in the legislative. There are even reasons that, in the present state of Europe, discourage certain powers from adopting a federative system. In the necessity in which we find ourselves to contain the abuses of too numerous associations, there is no doubt that representative government is the only one that keeps intact the equality of political rights.[21]

In other words: in order to approach the results expected from the model of pure democracy, it was necessary to deviate from it in the forms of its application. The translation of the principle of sovereignty into representative institutions and practices implied certain necessary sacrifices, since the principle itself had to be modified and adjusted to specific circumstances. Representative government did not necessarily correspond to a single political model but was compatible with a variety of possible institutional arrangements. (In the case of France, for example, the constitution of 1795 satisfied the basic conditions of the model—absence of hereditary positions, popular election of the legislative, separation of powers—without being the most perfect, let alone the only possible, constitution for the republic.) Calibrating the sacrifice of the just portion of citizens' rights in order to ensure the efficacy of representative institutions was just like creating an appropriate system of taxation: one could not simply rely on some overall formula but must take into account, measure, and compare a variety of factors. But to what extent was it acceptable to limit the right of the citizens to participate in political decisions? How could one be sure that such a right would not be entirely emptied of its substance by the delegation of power to representatives? The solution for Staël consisted in adopting *interests*, rather than *persons*, as the real subject of representation:

> What principle can we find that may be the basis of these different adjustments, all dependent on localities and circumstances, and all made necessary by the very experience of the French Revolution and by the speculations of moralists? Here is what seems to me the essence of representative government: that it is the interests of the nation, not the individuals that form it, that are represented ... When you have admitted the principle of the representation of interests rather than of individuals, the modifications required by the different circumstances of localities, customs, and habit are all derived from the same causes and lead to the same result. The difference is only in the path taken: the starting as the final points are the same.[22]

This meant in the first instance that selecting representatives in the mirror image of the electors themselves was not a good idea, as in this way the interest of the nation as a whole would not be realized. Just as people entrusted their private affairs to individuals whose qualities they themselves did not possess (such as competence, experience, knowledge of a particular domain), the interests of the people should be committed to those most capable of interpreting and serving them:

> Everywhere the individual or individuals who cannot act by themselves try to transfer to someone else the motives and

means necessary to achieve their objective. Representation is nothing but the political application of the daily working of this personal interest. Representation is not the calculation of a reduction, so to speak, that gives the image of the people on a small scale; representation is the political combination that leads the nation to be governed by men chosen and organized in such a way that they carry the will and the interests of all.[23]

The delegation of private affairs to able procurators who possessed a specific competence (an image so often found later on in Benjamin Constant's writings) was not the only criterion for successful representation. Representatives must also have a vested interest in the enterprise: they could "carry the will and interests of all" provided these were very close, if not identical, to their own:

A representative government is one in which the nation is governed by accredited procurators (*procureurs fondés*) whose powers, number, and differences are combined in such a way that they have as their personal interest the general one. Just like able traders, [they] impose such restrictions on their shareholders, fix their numbers, give them a certain interest in the enterprise, a certain right to deliberate in proportion to their interest, so that they may be trusted to promote the cause of the association as a whole.[24]

In *Of Present Circumstances* the relation between democracy and representative government was placed in historical sequence. Representative government was the natural successor of democracy in the evolution of modern European political regimes, the only system that could offer to the large, populous societies of today the advantages of "grandeur": the enjoyment of a degree of wealth, military power, and artistic and intellectual excellence that small communities could not achieve. At the same time the fundamental principle of democracy (ensuring that citizens may be subject only to laws of their own making) was incorporated into the model of representative government, which became its practical support, its vehicle. As society progressed, the system could be gradually democratized (by extending the citizens' access to the suffrage), but always within the same "aristocratic" model. Thus the structure of the new republican constitution was not an optional alternative to a democratic one but the only way to ensure that the ideal of popular sovereignty might be realized in practice.

THE REMOTENESS OF REPRESENTATIVES

While representative government was better adjusted than democracy to the needs of modern society, there was at least one respect in which the new system was at a disadvantage when compared to the old, namely, its far more problematic relation to popular opinion. In ancient republics magistrates and citizens shared the restricted space of the city-state, in which they were in regular contact with one another as they took part together in assemblies, meetings, and public ceremonies. The moods and intentions of the people were thus immediately apparent to rulers; similarly, the small size of communities meant that the good or bad deeds of magistrates would soon be known to everyone. The establishment of modern representative government in large states interposed a far greater distance between the people and its rulers. The citizens were not necessarily informed about the actions of their representatives, while the representatives themselves often found it difficult to recognize and interpret popular sentiment. Freedom from public affairs, which was granted to the citizens of modern representative regimes precisely by this distance, must not be confused with democratic freedom:

> In order to benefit from the purest political liberty, you cannot have the association of thirty million people. Representative government provides in practice great freedom, because opinion presides over it, but there is no democracy in a country

governed by seven hundred and fifty deputies out of thirty million men.[25]

In modern nations public opinion—a different thing from the immediate presence of the citizens in the public square—emerged to occupy the space that separated the government from the people: opinion could no longer be "caught at the source"; citizens were made aware of magistrates' actions by the press, by other means of information, and by public debate; the will of the people, on the other hand, manifested itself intermittently on the occasion of elections. Staël observed that this state of affairs was to some extent advantageous for the citizens themselves, as it allowed them a welcome freedom from public responsibilities, together with the tranquillity and leisure necessary to pursue their own goals:

> It is a great good, I believe, for the majority of men, the possibility to exist independently of public affairs. This repose, unknown to the ancients, is the advantage of large human associations; it is an additional opportunity of happiness offered to the diversity of characters.[26]

However, there were also significant disadvantages associated with this separation between rulers and ruled, disadvantages that the Revolution had brought sharply into focus. In France public opinion, as the expression of popular expectations, had been the main force behind the revolutionary movement, generating a radical change both in institutions and in society at large. Indeed, opinion had *made* the Revolution—but the impulse that agitated and unsettled the country had gone too far. Initially led by enlightened philosophers, but then driven by partisan groups, fanatical demagogues, and unscrupulous pamphleteers, the expression of opinion had become an exercise in manipulation, increasingly distant from the real needs and aspirations of the people. In the end the reaction of the public had been one of fatigue: ordinary people had become unable to sustain the tension and agitation created by this relentless propaganda, and had finally withdrawn into an attitude of passive resistance. What the new republican government confronted now was a quiet but secretly disaffected and therefore potentially dangerous populace. The paradox was that, without public opinion, republican government could not exist: by its own nature, it had to be sustained and guarded by it.

At the heart of the difficulties confronted by the new republic was the issue of elections. Under representative government, elections were the natural means of expression of the will of the nation; and yet under the Directory elections had failed to perform this function. Briefly, the circumstances Staël was referring to were these: the constitution of 1795 had been accompanied by a decree that prolonged the mandate of two-thirds of the existing members of the Convention, restricting the choice of electors to the replacement of only one-third of the assembly ("decree of the two-thirds"). The reason behind this measure was the understandable desire, on the part of the survivors of Thermidor, to preserve the legislative from a sudden swing toward the Jacobin Left or the royalist Right. But the result had been a massive abstention of the electors from the referendum of approval of the constitution (about 80 percent) and an even greater abstention (about 95 percent) precisely from the vote on the decree itself; at the subsequent elections for the legislative in 1797 and 1798, participation had remained very low (around 25 percent); in 1797 the government had lost its majority in the assembly to the royalists, while in 1798 it had obtained only a narrow one against the Jacobins. On both occasion, the Directory had intervened to annul the elections in a large number of departments, and had proceeded to arrest or deport some representatives of the opposition on the accusation of conspiracy.[27]

A few years earlier, when the constitution of 1791 was approved, Staël had expressed the hope that the restriction of the electoral suffrage to the propertied classes might favor the emergence of a large moderate consensus.[28] In principle the constitution of 1795 was designed to produce (and indeed accentuate) the same effect. In practice, however, given the massive abstention at the elections, any corrective impact of this limitation of active citizenship was lost, and the will of the moderate majority failed once again to be expressed. By depriving the electors of a real opportunity to renew the assembly, the decree of the two-thirds alienated and discouraged them. As Staël was to observe in later years: "This decree produced a terrible effect upon opinion, and broke altogether the treaty silently signed between the Convention and honest people: the people were ready to forgive the *Conventionnels*, provided the latter gave up their power, but it was natural that they should wish instead to preserve it, if only as a safeguard."[29] On the whole the writer was not unsympathetic toward the motivations of the Directory: in her view it was understandable that they should try to protect themselves and the country from the effects of a radical change of legislative personnel, such as the disastrous one that had occurred on the occasion of the election of the Legislative Assembly in 1792. The problem was that the need for stability and the need to be legitimated by a free popular vote were not altogether compatible in these particular circumstances.

A similar difficulty in the relations between the system of representation and its legitimation by public opinion emerged when France invaded Switzerland in 1798.[30] Staël, who at the time was residing with her family at Coppet (a locality very close to the French border), was both alarmed and shocked by the Directory's initiative to occupy Swiss territory. As she wrote to her husband, Switzerland had been one of the very few allies of the French republic, and yet now the French "threaten to invade the country if we do not 'revolutionize' (*révolutionner*), with the result that people do try to 'revolutionize' in order to please them."[31] Staël was generally in favor of the constitutional design of the République helvétique, created by the French in the aftermath of the military occupation: all cantons were given equal status within a united representative republic (until then the Vaud—the region where Coppet was located—had been under the rule of the Republic of Bern), though she believed that something closer to the original federal autonomies should have been maintained. As she pointed out to the same correspondent:

> From Paris a constitution has arrived here for the whole Helvetic body, a single republic, one and indivisible, organized in twenty two-cantons, one of which is the Vaud. I myself find it very reasonable, and my view is that it should be adopted right away. But there are many prejudices here, and possibly it is not sufficiently close to a federal government. In the constitution that is presented to us it was indeed necessary to democratize the cantons, but to leave each of them free to regulate itself within its own limits.[32]

The République helvétique did not include Geneva: the city-republic was not at the time a canton but an independent territory and a French "protectorate"; with the occupation it was directly annexed to France, as part of the new department of Leman. The incorporation was decided by a special committee (Commission extraordinaire) on 19 March 1798, bypassing the existing legislative authority of the Conseil général, a procedure that seemed at best very questionable.[33] An additional problem was that the military occupation, by putting enormous strain on the resources of what were predominantly poor rural regions, destroyed in the eyes of the people any merits that the new, more democratic constitution might have possessed. As Staël argued quite fervently in a letter to Barras, the member of the Directory to whom she could speak more freely:

> What does the Directory want from us? Changes to the constitution of the Vaud? They are being made, they will be made; but the presence of the armed forces destroys all liberty in deliberations, and all tranquillity in people's mind. One cannot imagine the despair of the near totality of the inhabitants.[34]

In the same letter she cited the *Spirit of the Laws*, the assertion that Switzerland "paid to nature a higher price than all other peoples to their respective governments," stressing how difficult it was for most rural populations to secure the necessities of life in a mountainous country. She also expressed the belief that the Vaud would not oppose the French army's entry, but that some of the German cantons up in the mountains would attempt a resistance. Finally she recalled how even Robespierre had respected Swiss independence, while the Directory was apparently quite ready to violate it.[35]

THE USE OF POWER

The nature of the difficulties the Directory had to face was made clear by Staël in *Of Present Circumstances*, in a chapter entitled "The Use of Power." Once the new constitutional regime was secured and stabilized, republican institutions should be able to function without any interference. However, in this transitional phase everything depended on the actions of the executive:

> When in France a constitution is finally established, when it is felt that the Revolution is over, by the settling of all personal interests, the place of the government will be clearly delimited: the better the institutions, the less its action will be necessary. But at the moment in France everything depends on the government, order as well as freedom, victory as well as the administration, the triumph of the Revolution as much as its end. It is no doubt a great task, and the spirit of party, always unable to place itself at the center of ideas, is unable to conceive fully its difficulty.[36]

In other words, the executive was forced to intervene beyond its normal scope of influence, controlling elections and limiting the freedom of political opposition. Indeed, Staël went so far as to claim that the party in government—the republicans—must preserve their monopoly over the institutions:

A new system must now guide the governing party. It has been violent and disinterested, it must become ambitious and moderate; it must not, under any circumstances, give up its power, but rather rally gradually around itself a broader national consensus. I said: the governing party. I am not arguing that a specific group of individuals should, by illegal means, preserve their posts; what I am saying is that power must remain the prerogative of the republican party . . . It seems almost ridiculous to encourage a party not to deprive itself of power. Such recommendation is superfluous enough. But it is true that republicans, at least the democrats among them, have pushed their love of popular forms to the extent of jeopardizing the republic, and since now they wish to save it, they do so by creating shocks. The republican party . . . must make sure not to allow any other party within the state, defending the institutions by the action of those who founded them until they are able to return the favor.[37]

There was an obvious contradiction between the recognition of the need to preserve the continuity of republican hegemony and the criticism Staël expressed at the same time of the use of extraordinary laws against specific groups, who allegedly represented a threat to the republic, such as the émigrés and the refractory priests. In another section of the text, she wrote: "I desire . . . the establishment of the republic, but I see the guarantee in such and such civil and political institutions, not in revolutionary laws. I prefer to fortify the citadel rather than having its inhabitants killed in the breach. Revolutionary laws are simply a proof of impotence on the part of legislators."[38] Staël's opposition to the legislation still in force against those considered "émigrés" was dictated to some extent by personal motivations, since many of the people concerned were personal friends or former political allies (a point that the press hostile to her did not fail to point out). But what she actually objected to was the practice of extending the definition of "émigré" to many who (like herself) had left France not by free choice, or out of hostility toward the revolutionary government, but merely to save their lives. During the Terror many people were persecuted not because they were enemies of the republic, or had fought against it, but because (as in the case of priests) their social profile or political credentials were considered suspicious.

That the Directory should be forced to resort to exceptional measures in order to protect the republic from her opponents meant that the Revolution was not over, and that the government lacked the means of bringing it finally to an end. In particular the application of extraordinary legislation had one important consequence, that of placing civil government on the same level as a military one. There were, Staël argued, two means of promoting democratic principles, "reasoning" and "arms," opinion and force. If civil government was unable to sustain itself by opinion and had to resort to force, it would soon find itself in a position of inferiority as compared to the option of a military government. "In France it is necessary to confer grandeur on the government of the republic. The success of its armies has founded the glory of the nation and gained respect for its strength; but domestic institutions have not yet acquired dignity. The ancient consideration they enjoyed has been destroyed without being replaced."[39] Throughout the Revolution the army had proved far more successful than civil government: indeed, Staël thought it surprising that until then the military should prove so docile, submitting to a civil authority that was so unstable and discredited. Significantly it was by adopting the attitude of a civil magistrate that Bonaparte won the confidence of those politicians in the directorial government who conspired with him to bring about the Brumaire coup.

THE BRUMAIRE "REVOLUTION"

The analysis developed in *Of Present Circumstances* led the author into a sort of impasse as to the political prospects of the directorial republic. How could republican institutions be saved without violating the basic principles of a free constitution? Should one choose legality and the respect of rules at the risk of succumbing to the enemies of the republic? There seemed to be no good solution to this dilemma, and this may have contributed to Staël's decision to set her work aside. There is in fact no reliable evidence on why precisely she should have left unpublished the draft she had worked on for several months. The most obvious explanation is that, as with *Reflections on Domestic Peace*, she wished to keep a low profile after the accusations of conspiracy of which she had been the target in 1795 on the occasion of the attempted royalist insurrection of *vendémiaire*. But she might also have felt dissatisfied by the impossibility of proposing a clear and defensible line of conduct for the government without running into a maze of contradictions. At the time she was already engaged in composing the ambitious history of European cultural traditions that she was to publish two years later under the title *De la littérature considérée dans ses rapports avec les institutions sociales* (1800; I discuss this work in chapter 8);[40] she might have preferred to invest her energies in a project that seemed more durable and less dependent on the vagaries of political events.

The retrospective assessment of the experience of the Directory that Staël provided in later years was on the whole more sympathetic than one might expect. She argued that the regime suffered inevitably from some serious handicaps: its political personnel consisted of former members of the Convention, heavily compromised by the Revolution; there were among them no personalities of any great distinction; and finally the constitution adopted in 1795 was unsatisfactory in various ways. However, at least during the earlier period of their administration, the directors did manage to put an end to the financial crisis; they restored order within the country and enabled the army to win some significant victories abroad. In other words the failure of the republic was not the result of major errors on their part, or even of the bad design of the constitution, but simply the product of very unfavorable circumstances that did not permit the stabilization of the republican regime in its existing form.[41] In this respect Staël's judgment was very similar to the position prevailing today among historians on the subject.[42]

No doubt it was easier to formulate a balanced assessment in 1816, with the benefit of hindsight; but the fate of the abandoned *Of Present Circumstances* suggests that, by the end of 1798, a full year before the coup that brought Bonaparte to power, Staël considered the directorial republic a lost cause, and the advent of some kind of military rule a likely outcome.[43] Predictably her attitude toward what she interestingly described in the *Considerations* as "the revolution" of Brumaire was rather ambivalent, a combination of relief and resigned acceptance.

According to her own narrative of events, she found herself arriving back in Paris from Switzerland the very day (18 Brumaire, or 9 November 1799) that the legislative assemblies were meeting at Saint Cloud, the stage of Bonaparte's coup. As she was waiting for a change of horses before getting into town, she crossed path with Barras, whose political career had just been terminated, and who was traveling in the opposite direction, toward his country estate of Grosbois. She spent the rest of the day anxiously waiting for the news that "a friend" (Constant) was sending hour by hour on the progress of events.

> No doubt the majority of honest people, fearing the return of Jacobinism, wished for a victory of Bonaparte. My feelings, I must admit, were very ambivalent. Once a fight was engaged, a temporary victory of the Jacobins might lead to episodes of violence; and yet there was something painful in the idea of a victory of Bonaparte. I wept for the loss not of freedom itself, but of the hope of it.[44]

Two months earlier at the end of September, while still at Coppet, she had written to a bookseller in Lausanne, requesting "the collection of Machiavelli's works in Italian and the best available translation in French."[45] References to Machiavelli's work appear in her writings before then, but in such a way as to suggest that she might just have been quoting from other sources. Probably the desire to acquire a good edition just then is merely a coincidence, as is the fact that the letter with her order for the books has survived. Yet it is very tempting to imagine that she was preparing herself for the advent of the new prince.[46]

CHAPTER 8

Raising the Stakes

THE MEASURE OF AMBITION (1800)

IT HAS often been said that the year 1800 marked a turning point in Staël's life and work; yet the exact nature of this "turn" remains unspecified. The opening of the new century coincided for Staël with the appearance of her book *De la littérature considérée dans ses rapports avec les institutions sociales* (On Literature, considered in its relations to social institutions), after she had set aside unpublished the draft of *Of Present Circumstances*.[1] This new work marked a shift in the writer's perspective from political and constitutional theory to literature and the history of European philosophy and culture. The same year, following the coup of Brumaire, the Thermidorian republic was transformed into a Consulate, with General Bonaparte as first consul, initiating a series of events that eventually led Staël to a definitive exclusion from French politics and to a protracted exile.

Two closely interconnected issues seem central to the understanding of this new phase in Staël's life. The first is the nature of her attitude toward Bonaparte's power, an attitude that is bound up to some extent with the unfolding of her personal relations with the man himself, and with his immediate entourage. The second is the evolution of her intellectual preoccupations after the liquidation of the republican experiment, which had been until then the focus of her concerns. Naturally these two issues are intimately related: Staël's renewed interest in literature can be read as an escape from a political setting in which she no longer had a role to play, as an attempt to regain, in a wider arena, the influence she had lost in domestic French politics; it can also be seen as the natural development of her ongoing concern with the relations between political institutions and popular sentiments, between national governments and their cultural background.

The major difficulty in addressing these questions is that there is little direct evidence about how Staël felt at the time about current events, and about the priorities in her own work. What is left of her correspondence offers only a few patchy insights on the matter. Although she wrote extensively about Napoleon's appearance on the political stage, and about his subsequent career, she did so only several years later, in the declining phase of the empire and after its collapse. In retrospect her recollections and assessments were colored by the sense of failure of the imperial adventure, and by her personal experience of long years of bitter opposition. Inevitably she projected back into the uncertain, confused climate of 1800 her later, far more decisive and clear-cut judgments on Bonaparte's personality and political action; thus she was increasingly inclined to present herself as, from the outset, a critic and uncompromising opponent of the future emperor, while in fact she had assumed this role of dissident writer only reluctantly, and gradually, in the course of a few years.

If Staël's self-representation as heroic resister against Napoleon's tyranny was to some extent a simplification and an embellishment of reality, the "sour grapes" alternative set forth by some biographers seems even more misleading: the allegation being that Staël became an Bonaparte's enemy only after trying very hard, and failing, to gain his political and personal favor.[2] No doubt, like other moderate republicans in her entourage (Roederer, Pierre Daunou, Boulay de la Meurthe, Constant, Sieyès himself, to mention only some of them), she hoped initially that Bonaparte's personal influence might be contained within the limits of the new consular constitution, and like them she was soon to be disillusioned.

In this respect her position was not very different from that of the majority of the Thermidorian political class, who accepted the Consulate as a last, desperate stand against the impending threats of Jacobinism and counterrevolution.[3] The fact that the Directory had already resorted several times to extralegal measures—or, in other words, repeatedly violated the constitution (a fact that Bonaparte could throw in the face of the deputies at the most dramatic moment of his confrontation with them during the coup)[4]—made it easier even for moderates to accept yet another arbitrary change of regime, especially one that was effected without resort to violence. Like other intellectuals—for example, the group of philosophers and scientists known as the *idéologues*[5]—she was at first eager to offer guidance and inspiration to the new regime; like them, she was soon faced with the stark choice between docile collaboration with the consular, later imperial, power, on the one hand, and, on the other, marginalization or ostracism.[6]

All things considered, there is not much to be learned from the exercise of assessing once again the personal frictions between Staël and the first consul, or of measuring the purity of her anti-Bonapartist credentials. Setting aside the climate of fear and insecurity that led to the coup of Brumaire, there were important affinities between Staël's vision of republican government and the principles that founded the consular regime. The most important of these was the view that representative government stood in opposition to "pure" democracy: this meant that political equality and popular sovereignty were best achieved through limitation of democratic participation in government, so as to protect the institutions from the instability of popular consensus, and to preserve property from the assault of the poor. Other crucial common elements were the centrality of property as a basis for representation and the reinforcement of executive power against any attempted encroachment by the legislative. On all these points the ideology that guided the Consulate was not very different from the one that had inspired the Thermidorian republic.[7]

While the structure of the constitution of 1800 (Year VIII) may appear cumbersome and unnecessarily intricate when compared to that of 1795 (Year III), in principle there was no radical discontinuity in the spirit of the two charters.[8] Indeed, the chief author and sponsor of the new constitution, Sieyès, described it—in a set of annotations dictated to Daunou at the time of its drafting—as the full expression of the true principles of 1789, which the constitution of 1795 had only imperfectly embodied. At the time, the ill-judged (as he saw it) opposition to his proposals on the part of some of the other constituents had produced an unsatisfactory result that could now finally be set right.[9] As to the aims of this "improved" constitutional framework, they were the same as those that the Thermidorian republic had attempted, and failed, to attain: to restore order and stability, to guarantee the security of property, and to exploit France's military success to negotiate an advantageous peace with the European powers— or, in the words used by the first consul to proclaim the new regime, to end the Revolution, having finally secured the objectives that had originally motivated it.[10]

Another characteristic feature of the Consulate that tended toward Staël's desiderata was the novelty represented by the emergence of a strong personal leadership. In a famous passage of the *Considerations* she described how, on her return to Paris on the eve of the coup of Brumaire, she heard people everywhere repeating a single name—that of Bonaparte—whereas before they had referred only to impersonal entities such as the assembly, the people, or the Convention: after years of dominance by anonymous institutions, one individual now "monopolized fame for himself."[11] This observation is generally cited as the recognition on Staël's part of the beginning of tyranny in the form of personal rule, and she may indeed have meant it in this sense when she recorded it more than ten years after the fact. But in

1799 she had been far from regarding the emergence of personal leadership as an intrinsically bad thing.[12]

As we have seen, she had been deploring all along the absence of real political guidance during the Revolution, describing the men who ruled the Constituent Assembly and the Convention as the faceless, interchangeable mouthpieces of factions. Ideally she would have preferred a leader who (like her own father) had gained his reputation as a statesman, rather than as a military commander. However, while she was aware of the dangers that an excess of "military spirit" represented for free political institutions, she was also very sensitive to the crucial role that the army had played during the Revolution, to the remarkable success gained by the army in its later stages, and to their unquestionable loyalty to civil authority. As she had confessed poignantly to her friend Henri Meister in 1797, "without the armies there would be no hope left for the republic."

Thus in *Of Present Circumstances* she acknowledged the achievements of the French army, and almost marveled at their docile loyalty to a corrupt and unstable civil government. This appreciation on her part was well founded and is generally shared by later historians of the period. Even during the most difficult moments of the Revolution, the military had never shown any inclination to stage a putsch to replace civil authority; indeed, in 1792 and 1793 they had refused to follow, respectively, Generals La Fayette and Charles-François Dumouriez, when they had proposed marching on Paris at the head of their troops. While the military may have despised some of the civilian magistrates who ruled during the Revolution, they had always shown respect for the republican institutions they represented. As to 18 Brumaire, the initiative for and organization of the coup came from the political leadership of the Directory, while the military provided mere logistic support; and although the establishment of the Consulate and of the empire led to protracted wars, neither can be properly described as a military regime.[13]

At the time of the coup Sieyès (who had originally preferred another "sword" for the operation, that of General Barthélemy Joubert, who died fighting in Italy during the summer of 1799) famously described Bonaparte as "the most civilian of the generals."[14] Staël clearly agreed with this impression. In December 1800, a full year after the establishment of the Consulate, she wrote to Napoleon's brother Joseph, who had been away from Paris at the time of the royalist assassination attempt against the first consul known as *la machine infernale* (the infernal machine):

> All agree here on the fact that Bonaparte has never excited such a *popular* interest. He gave a very good reply to Kellermann, who was urging him to take a most military revenge:
> — . . . a general who is afraid is a coward; a magistrate who is afraid becomes a tyrant—.[15]

Even in later years Staël did not modify the view that Bonaparte, when entering politics, had carefully adopted the attitude of a civil magistrate, while the ineffective politicians around him displayed inappropriately bellicose postures. As she observed, "The warrior spoke as a magistrate, while the magistrates expressed themselves with military violence."[16] In any case the idea of the Consulate was precisely that Bonaparte would rule not alone but as part of a collegial executive of three people. In the aftermath of the coup, before the approval of the new constitution, he was seconded by two former directors, Sieyès and Roger-Ducos.[17] Of these Sieyès seemed to carry the greatest weight: he had considerable political experience, had recently won a significant victory (for the Left) at the elections of the spring of 1799, and was generally regarded at the time as powerful and influential. A few months earlier, commenting on Sieyès's nomination to the Directory, Staël had confided to a Swiss friend that Constant was very happy about it. His presence was in fact seen as a guarantee against a possible affirmation of the Jacobins in the councils, and as a prelude to peace negotiations with England.[18]

It was to Sieyès, rather than to Bonaparte, that Staël's friends (such as Constant) turned in the hope of securing some position in the new government. At a more personal level, Staël's relations with the members of the Directory—Barras excepted— were far from good; she was equally disliked by the Jacobins and the royalists in the councils, and had been pressured into a self-imposed exile by the suspicions raised against her by both parties. The prospect of a recentering of power around a new, moderate executive was not a priori bad news from her viewpoint. If Bonaparte did not seem to like her very much, and failed to admire her work, she was on friendly terms with various people in his entourage, including Napoleon's brothers Joseph and Lucien. Not being liked was not an especially new or intimidating experience for someone who had braved the enmity of the French royal court and of the Jacobins.

While there were promising elements in the new regime, the two years that elapsed between the coup and the eviction of Constant and other recalcitrant deputies from the Tribunat in January 1802 were more than sufficient to reveal its most unacceptable features. Paramount among them were the limitation of popular representation and the marginal role left to legislative power. Although the new constitution introduced universal male suffrage, electors could select candidates to public functions (such as local administrators or national representatives) only from preestablished, closed lists of *notabilité*. While on paper the two legislative assemblies—the Tribunat (Tribunate) and the Corps législatif (Legislative Body)—had, respectively, the prerogative of proposing and approving laws, in practice all the measures set forth by the executive were hurried along and applied before the legislative assemblies could even begin to examine them. The third assembly, the Sénat consérvateur (Conservative Senate), Sieyès's cherished invention, was not, as the name suggested, a legislative body but the prefiguration of a constitutional court.

The first consul made no mystery of the fact that he regarded any form of parliamentary debate or consultation—even when the positions expressed were not hostile to the government—as at best a waste of time, at worst a form of obstruction to be removed. Finally, while all previous governments since the Revolution had tried to limit the power of the press indirectly, by covert pressures, he felt no inhibition in exercising a direct control, censoring and suppressing publications. Unsurprisingly, the freedom of the press and of public debate would become the battleground of political opposition in the decade to come.

In *Of Present Circumstances* Staël had reluctantly come to the conclusion that the precarious conditions of the republican government in France required the control of government by a single party, strongly committed to the republic's preservation. She had also accepted the fact that the transition to the Consulate would be effected through a coup d'état, with a constitution that was enforced before it could be endorsed (as it was) by a popular referendum. But while accepting these extraconstitutional measures as necessary in a particularly difficult phase she would feel unable to subscribe in the long run to a regime that systematically violated the constitution—a constitution, moreover, that already granted extensive discretionary powers to the executive. The eviction of Constant and other "dissidents" from the Tribunat illustrated this disregard of the constitution: the deputies in question were deliberately voted out, while in principle one-fifth of the assembly—twenty out of a hundred—should have been renewed by lot, not by designation. In other words: as the regime attained a certain stability, instead of setting aside the extraordinary measures that had been necessary to secure it, it turned them into recurrent institutional practices.[19]

But in order to take the full measure of Staël's expectations and of her disillusion, it is necessary to consider more closely the book on which she was working while the directorial regime fell apart around her, the book she chose to publish in the early months of the Consulate. In the abandoned *Of Present Circum-*

stances the writer had outlined a strategy for the immediate political survival of the republic, calling on the different parties to support the government in a phase of difficult transition. Now she looked beyond this mere exercise of keeping the republic afloat to show what the new regime must achieve, in a broader historical perspective, in order to justify its existence. What exactly were the merits of the political system for which France had paid, since 1789, such high price of death and disruption? Was the mere establishment of a more or less efficient form of representative government sufficient to justify the effort?

Staël believed that the enforcement of political equality and popular sovereignty, in conformity with the principles of the Enlightenment, was the natural consequence of the progress of modern societies. But for a country like France, accustomed to centuries of royal absolutism, the transition to this new state of affairs had been too abrupt, proving traumatic and profoundly disruptive. The adoption of these new principles was not in itself a guarantee that French society would continue to progress and flourish, rather than disintegrating altogether, or possibly sinking into a kind of "democratic stagnation." For it to succeed, other conditions had to be satisfied: the adoption of rigorous standards of public morality, the promotion of intellectual and artistic excellence, the emergence of men capable of conferring on the republic a distinctive grandeur, able to match and surpass that of the old monarchy. It was against these lofty requirements that the new rule of the Consulate was now going to be measured.

REVOLUTION AND PROGRESS

With *On Literature* Staël returned, by a novel and somewhat experimental route, to the classic Enlightenment question of the progress of human societies. Using the notion of "literature" in a very broad sense—to include not just creative writing, but also scientific and philosophical works—she presented it as the measure of the advancement of European societies from antiquity to modern times. Resorting to a synoptic approach reminiscent of Montesquieu, she interpreted the literary traditions of the various nations as the product of their social and political institutions. This perspective led her in particular to emphasize the merits of the (at the time underestimated) literatures of the North—German, English, Scottish, and Scandinavian—in which she recognized the originality and creativity of "barbarous" populations strongly committed to liberty, in contrast with the more polished but submissive peoples of the South.

But the main focus of the book was, as ever, France and the consequences of the Revolution of 1789. Its main objective was to uphold the Enlightenment commitment to progress against those who took the French Revolution as the proof that men were incapable of improvement, and that history, dominated by accidental forces, unfolded without any clear direction. In this respect *On Literature* can also be considered as a belated anti-Burkean pamphlet, provocatively offered to the public after the damages caused by the Revolution had manifested themselves in full.[20] In the book's preface, she wrote, "The majority of the people, frightened by horrible political events, no longer believe in intellectual faculties, but only in hazard."[21] This reaction—she admitted—was understandable, given the traumatic character of their recent collective experience; and yet, if the French were to turn their expectations back toward intellectual and artistic achievements, this positive attitude could greatly contribute to the establishment of a safer, more stable polity. The moral and material improvement of the people was, after all, the only serious objective that any modern political regime must pursue in order to justify its existence:

> The partisans of monarchy, like those of the republic, must think that the constitution they prefer is favorable to the amelioration of society and the progress of reason; unless they were convinced of this, how could they support it in conscience?[22]

During the previous fifty years, the perfectibility of mankind had been at the center of systems of thought set forth by philosophers who lived in various countries, and under quite different political systems, such as Adam Ferguson, Immanuel Kant, Anne-Robert Turgot, and Condorcet. But while the question of progress was a common concern among other European nations, the development of French society, as illustrated by the evolution of the national literature, had followed a very distinctive pattern. Before the Revolution, and especially at the height of monarchical absolutism, under Louis XIV, France had been generally regarded as the most refined and sophisticated country in the world, and the nation's literature judged superior to any other for style and taste. However, this much-praised and admired elegance of expression concealed a fundamental superficiality and lack of substance. French writers did not confront in their works any serious moral or philosophical issues, they did not discuss religious dogmas and practices, and above all they never criticized the conduct of government. They did not avoid these subjects because they feared the repressive force of the authorities, but rather because they had so deeply embraced the feudal values and the religious prejudices of the monarchy that they had made them their own, without even realizing it. Surprisingly, perhaps, Staël cited as the only notable exception Bossuet, who alone had had the courage to spell out some uncomfortable truths, such as the equality of all men in the face of death: religious enthusiasm apparently offered a sterner resistance to tyranny than did philosophical reason.[23]

In contrast with this subservience of literature during the Grand Siècle of Louis XIV, the eighteenth century saw the beginning of that "revolution of the minds" which eventually led to a political revolution. As a matter of fact—Staël argued—the leading writers of the Enlightenment, Voltaire and Montesquieu, did not deliberately set out to destroy the French monarchy and aristocratic society; nor did they share Rousseau's critical attitude toward modern civilization. However, the adoption of a method that subjected all issues to rational analysis, the resort to irony, the identification of new objects of inquiry—all these factors led them inevitably to undermine established values. Thus if literary style did not progress beyond the achievements of the previous century, the engagement in serious philosophical issues gave to a whole generation of writers a new sentiment of independence. In particular, Staël stressed, it gave new scope to their ambitions: no longer preoccupied with "pleasing kings," they now played to a wider audience, producing work that was meant to be "useful" to the whole nation, possibly even to the whole of mankind.

The comparison between the age of Louis XIV and the eighteenth century began to give some indication of the changes that political liberty must produce in the literature of a nation. A writer who engaged in serious moral issues, who defended freedom against oppression, who pleaded for the victims against their assassins, who promoted the cause of the unfortunates—such a writer was necessarily pushed beyond himself and his selfish concerns; he could transcend his personal limitations, inspire his readers, indeed play an almost "supernatural" role. But had the Revolution actually produced this uplifting effect upon French writers and their works? And if the answer was, as one might suspect, a negative one, what were the reasons for this failure? Staël subscribed to the view that the progress of science and philosophy, on the one hand, and the development of free political institutions on the other, were interdependent. The spreading of knowledge and modern societies' higher level of education meant that the people were no longer disposed to submit without complaint to despotic rulers:

> The progress of sciences calls for the progress of politics. You need a more enlightened government, one that has more respect for public opinion, in those nations where knowledge is spreading every day; and even if you oppose the disaster of a few years to conclusions that are based upon the experience of

centuries, it is true that no nation in Europe today would stand the long sequence of base and ferocious tyrannies that oppressed the Romans.[24]

But the relation between freedom and knowledge also worked in reverse: if an advanced society called for free government, free government could not flourish while the educational level of society remained inadequate. In a country where "the citizens had a more immediate part in the action of government,"[25] the stability of free institutions depended to a large extent on the population's degree of enlightenment. In France, while the eighteenth century had seen the development of an alert and responsive public opinion, the abrupt transition to a political system based upon equality and liberty had met with some unexpected obstacles, which stood in the path of public enlightenment and the general progress of society.

The first of these obstacles came from the particular cultural climate that accompanied the Revolution. The accelerated spreading of information, the growth and circulation of the press, and the dissemination of ideas that France, like other European countries, experienced during this period were not in themselves a guarantee of intellectual and moral progress. They could lead to a higher degree of education and awareness among the people, but they could also, as they did in this case, spread prejudices and generate confusion; in some cases they could even produce "the complete abasement of societies."[26] Staël explained that most of the time, far from educating the public, the increased diffusion of information led to the repetition of superficial judgments and half-baked notions. People were bombarded by new opinions, without having the time to question them seriously: instead of forming solid beliefs about the desirable shape of political institutions, they were satisfied with hurried analysis and superficial or partial views. A crowd of journalists, pamphleteers, and other improvised leaders of opinion felt only envy toward any serious, reflective thinkers. The nation, convinced of its own newfound superiority, became blasé while remaining confused and indecisive.

The second obstacle to the progress of French society was represented by the sudden appearance on the public scene, during the Revolution, of new men who were often unprepared for their positions of power and responsibility (as unprepared, in fact, as the citizens who had elected them). The emergence of this new political class produced an effect similar to that of the invasion of the northern populations at the end of the Roman Empire; in the long run, their influence proved stimulating and beneficial, but in the short run its effect was to plunge Europe into barbarism:

> In the course of this work, I have shown how the mixing of the people of the North and those of the South had been for a time a cause of barbarism, even if subsequently it was to produce great progress for enlightenment and civilization. The introduction of a new class in the government of France was bound to produce a similar effect. This revolution can, in the long term, enlighten the mass of the people; but for several years, the vulgarity of language, manners, and opinions must cause a regression in both taste and reason.[27]

The problem was not simply the lack of refinement of the new men: after all, the great sophistication of the aristocracy under the Old Regime had offered no protection against despotism and injustice. Staël's reproach to the new political class was that they were unable or unwilling to propose themselves to the people as examples of superior qualities to imitate. Instead of trying to elevate themselves and the masses, these new demagogues mimicked the worst, least dignified attitudes of the populace, in order to win their approval. This pursuit of popular favor by the adoption of plebeian postures created a sort of vicious circle: the people chose to be represented by ignorant and vulgar men in their own image, and these men, once in power, projected back to the people the same vices and shortcomings, instead of attempting to correct them.

The incapacity of the new rulers to inspire sincere respect and admiration in the people coincided with what Staël described as "political self-conceit," an exaggerated complacency in the exercise of their power, an attitude of which, she claimed, one had seen far too many instances during the Revolution. This failure of the revolutionary political class to show a real superiority and to promote solid, convincing values, instead of pandering to popular prejudice, also meant that they had to resort to intimidation in order to preserve their authority: as they were not respected, they had to be feared; as they could not enlighten, they must oppress. "The people would be accustomed to choose ignorant and vulgar magistrates; these magistrates would destroy any enlightenment, and, by an inevitable circle, this loss of knowledge might lead to the enslavement of the people."[28] This analysis of the revolutionary experience reflected Staël's firm conviction that representative government was a system designed to promote merit, and that elected magistrates should attract popular consensus by their moral and intellectual qualities. Where under a monarchy myth and tradition were sufficient to secure obedience, in a republic rulers must be able to offer some "real qualities" in order to achieve the same result. After all, if you have been chosen by the people to occupy your position (instead of being born to it), you must be able to show that they had some reason for doing so: "A cloud of illusions and memories surrounds kings; but men who have been elected, and who rule in the name of their personal superiority, must give all the exterior marks of that superiority."[29] In a parallel to the replacement of hereditary ranks with distinctions based on merit, the new republican society should be able to establish in all domains—literature included—new standards of taste, rigor, and excellence: new, because the inspiration that writers might find in ancient classical works was no longer adequate, as these did not reflect the objects and questions proper to the modern world. These standards of excellence, sustained by the "tribunal of opinion," must be more severe under a republic than under a monarchy, to compensate for the loss of those traditional structures that held society together under the Old Regime.

The fatal error committed by the French revolutionaries was to imagine that, in order to carry the Revolution into literature, it was sufficient to abolish all existing conventional rules, "lifting those traditional barriers that preserved propriety and dignity." No doubt aristocratic society had been in some respects "too civilized": the prevalence of artificial criteria of judgment and conventional rules paralyzed innovation and creativity; envy and vanity were the dominant motives of all intellectual efforts; the fear of being exposed to ridicule could become an obstacle to the development of real talent. But this "despotism of opinion," typical of aristocratic society, was replaced during the Revolution by a "revolting vulgarity." The breaking of old rules did not contribute to the expression of those strong sentiments and "vivid beauties" one should expect from a republican culture; all it managed to produce were licentious and frivolous works, less tasteful than those written under the Old Regime, and equally superficial. Moreover, the absence of shared standards of moral and aesthetic judgment accentuated the breach between parties, failing to unite the nation, and creating a shapeless and divided opinion.

This inability to produce shared truths and credible arguments was best illustrated by the quality of political rhetoric. In a chapter devoted to "eloquence" placed at the end of *On Literature*, Staël denounced the disregard of truth, the repetition of meaningless slogans and bombastic, empty formulas that had characterized public speeches during the Revolution. To illustrate the point, she supplied some instances of the prevailing style:

> At different times in our Revolution the most revolting sophisms alone filled certain speeches; party slogans, endlessly repeated by orators, fatigued the ears and dried up the hearts of listeners. There is variety only in nature; true sentiments alone can inspire new ideas. What effects could produce that mo-

notorious violence, those terms so heated that they left the soul so cold? *It is time to reveal to you the whole truth. The nation was buried in a slumber worse than death, but the representatives of the people were there. The people has risen, etc.*[30]

In her eyes politicians' incapacity to communicate clearly and honestly with their electors, the absence of discussion and even of a common language between parties, the consequent impossibility of any constructive political debate—these were the symptoms of profound deficiencies in a system that had claimed the status of popular democracy. On the whole *On Literature* presented an ambitious vision of a future republican society in which the progress of culture—science, philosophy, literature, art—was directly linked with the quality not just of institutions, but also of public discourse and of the political class. Success in these different dimensions depended on the capacity to impose shared values and to uphold high moral and intellectual standards. To secure the loyalty and attachment of its citizens, the modern French republic needed something more than a viable constitution and material security. Order and stagnation may suit small states such as the Swiss republics. But in a large (and great) nation like France the republic must be able to promote progress in all fields, so as to surpass the achievements of the old monarchy. As Staël had observed in *Of Present Circumstances*:

> In Europe, where all states are equally civilized, small communities have no competitive spirit, no wealth, no arts, no great men, and a Frenchman would never renounce all the glories and pleasures of a large association in order to obtain in exchange perfect freedom in a small place, far away from the eyes of the world and the pleasures of wealth.[31]

In order to achieve the "glories and pleasures" of large states, the republic must advance the careers of men of genius and talent—statesmen, military commanders, philosophers, scientists, writers—dedicated to her service. Staël did not suggest that this

French vision of the modern republic as the egalitarian refashioning of the old monarchy was necessarily the best possible model of representative government. Indeed, she herself had a marked preference for the "republican" monarchy of England over the "monarchical" republic of France. But she remained convinced that *grandeur* was what the French people expected, and that they would not settle for anything less.[32]

THE RETURN OF GLORY

No other theme more effectively captures Staël's idea of a republic committed to greatness than her ongoing concern with the issue of emulation and glory. The place of glory in the modern world had been a recurrent motif in her writings, in particular in *Of the Influence of Passions*. There she had argued that one of the causes of the Old Regime's collapse had been the incapacity of aristocratic society to give full scope to individual abilities and aspirations. By eliminating aristocratic privilege, the Revolution should have opened new paths to glory; instead, for totally different reason—such as the new culture of equality, with its sentiments of social envy—postrevolutionary society seemed to be as hostile to personal distinction as the Old Regime had been. While *Of the Influence of Passions* had presented the problem without anticipating any possible solutions, *On Literature* tried to set out new prospects for the satisfaction of social aspirations. One of the reasons why the Old Regime had failed to encourage the contribution of distinguished intellectuals was that, under the monarchy, there were no opportunities for writers and thinkers to influence important decisions, and to have a significant impact on public life. "It is only in free states that it is possible to combine the genius of action with that of thought. Under the Old Regime literary talents were expected to have no political talent at all."[33] Unlike scientists—who may be satisfied with pure research—those men of genius who were interested in issues that affected the whole nation were discouraged from expressing themselves and from producing any new ideas. The monarchy restricted them to a "subordinated existence," facing them with the difficult choice between becoming open opponents of the established power or avoiding any relevant and controversial subjects. In theory the upheaval of 1789 should have changed all that, opening up opportunities for novelty and reform. But in practice the "violent spirits" who led the Revolution had no more use for original ideas than their royal predecessors had had. They exploited enlightened men for their own purposes and, whenever it suited them, made use of their doctrines to justify abuses and injustice.

Soon a climate of suspicion, jealousy, and fear discouraged the men of talent and virtue from engaging in any public cause. All things considered, such men may have been better off under the monarchy. Staël, however, rejected this conclusion, as the situation under the monarchy must be compared not with the exceptional circumstances of the Revolution, but with the opportunities that could be offered to talent by a future republican society. In other words the real comparison was that between the advantages offered by "the protection of kings" and those created by "republican emulation." Only those nations that enjoyed freedom were able to offer great men the prize that no virtuous man could refuse: fame for the present times and the hope of glory for the future.

Staël then addressed the question of the prevalence of military reputations over civil ones during the revolutionary period. She admitted that, if military power and the military spirit came to dominate a state, they could represent a threat for the enlightenment of the nation as well as for its liberty. She refused, however, to reject and stigmatize the pursuit of military glory as such, or to treat it as something that must be relegated to the past. The reason was not just that the French military had performed successfully, or that they had given proofs of loyalty in recent years. One must also consider the fact that a republican government, unstable by nature and exposed to constant dangers, required courage to defend it, as much as it needed the civic virtues and qualities of its rulers.

> The agitation that is inseparable from a republican government often puts liberty in peril; and if leaders do not offer the double guarantee of courage and enlightenment, ignorant force, or perfidious ability, will sooner or later plunge the government into despotism . . . The warrior without culture or the orator without courage is unable to capture your imagination. You will be left with feelings that he has failed to captivate, and with ideas that judge him.[34]

Military and civil qualities were complementary and equally necessary to preserve the republic. Thus great men must not be discouraged from their "devotion to glory," just as the people must not be deprived of their sentiments of admiration for them, since it is from these sentiments that "all the degrees of affection between the magistrates and the governed derive."[35]

What about the risk that a victorious commander, crowned by glory, might take the opportunity to seize power and destroy the republic? Had the time come for France to crown its Caesar or its Cromwell? Since 1789 the idea that the weakening of the monarchy might lead to a military dictatorship had been a constant theme in the comparisons between the English and French revolutions. Initially disproved by the dominance of civil leadership in the early 1790s, the expectation of the emergence of a French Cromwell had been naturally revived by Bonaparte's exploits in Italy and Egypt. Benjamin Constant was seemingly not the author of the *Apologie de Robespierre et Cromwell* (Defense of Robespierre and Cromwell), published in the *Echo des cercles patriotiques* in 1797 and originally attributed to him.[36] However, the comparison between Cromwell and Bonaparte, expressed with varying degrees of appreciation for the two characters, was sufficiently current to call for repeated refutations. Bonaparte himself provided one in his rambling speech to the Council of the Elders on the day of the coup:

Today I am already submerged by calumnies. They talk of Caesar, they talk of Cromwell, they talk of a military regime. Had I wanted a military government, would I have rushed here to give my support to the representatives of the nation?[37]

A year later, in November 1800, the new minister of the interior Lucien Bonaparte commissioned and published a pamphlet entitled *Parallèle entre César, Cromwell, Monk et Bonaparte* (Parallel between Caesar, Cromwell, Monk and Bonaparte), presenting it as the translation of an anonymous English work. Interestingly the *Parallel*, while rejecting the comparison between Bonaparte and Cromwell, was ready to accept the similarity to Caesar, on the ground of the transcendent greatness of the Roman and French consuls. The pamphlet then introduced a warning against the disastrous consequences of a repetition in Paris of the Ides of March, showing to what extent the new regime felt (and was) dependent for its survival on the person of the first consul.[38] Staël's position on the threat of a military dictatorship was that the risk existed only insofar as civil institutions were not sufficiently well established and respected. The fear of military glory was a sign of weakness on the part of the political system, rather than an indication of its strength. The republic must be able to rely upon the achievements of its citizens in all the different domains of public service. "The reputation, the approval constantly attached to those men who have honorably pursued their career in public affairs are the first means of preserving liberty. And the best way of promoting the progress of enlightenment is to mix together, as the ancients did, a career in the army, in legislation, and in philosophy."[39]

In later years Staël, like Constant, was to denounce Napoleon's politics of military conquest as a form of historical regression—an anachronism that brought back into modern Europe memories of Charlemagne's feudal empire. But in 1800 she saw Bonaparte as a rampart against the return of absolute monarchy, rather than an agent of despotism. In April 1801 she wrote to

Dupont de Nemours: "As you suspect me a little of republican enthusiasm, you will probably find my opinion suspicious. However I do believe that we are going toward the monarchy in 1801—just as we were going towards the republic in 1791—and that the only barrier standing between us and counterrevolution is Bonaparte, as then there was only Louis XVI between us and the republic."[40] The idea of a combined military, civil, and intellectual greatness expressed in *On Literature* was in no way nostalgic and regressive, a return to the tradition of ancient republicanism. On the contrary, it was an ideal that reflected the needs of a large modern nation anxious to occupy once again a prominent position in the international arena—not very far in fact from the self-image offered by the presidential Fifth Republic a century and a half later:

> But, some will object, what we must fear above all in a republic is enthusiasm for one man . . . Nothing is less philosophical, that is to say, less conducive to happiness, than the jealous system that wishes to deprive nations of their rank in history, by leveling the reputation of men. All efforts must be made to promote general instruction; but together with the great interests of the progress of enlightenment, one must leave scope for individual glory.[41]

On balance at this stage Staël was less concerned with the classical threat of a victorious dictator's emergence than with the essentially modern phenomenon of "celebrity," the meteoric rise of ephemeral reputation. Herself "condemned" (as she saw it) to celebrity, essentially for the wrong reasons—her social position, her sex, her wealth—constantly exposed to the attention of the press, often the object of slanderous allegations, she was very interested in what constituted a valid ground for durable fame. If there was anything truly personal in her relations with Bonaparte (that "monopoliser" of celebrity, as she labeled him in the *Considerations*), it was more on this front than on any other: on what conditions did anyone deserve true glory? While it would be going too far to suggest that her relations with the general were, in this respect, essentially competitive, she was acutely aware of the difficulty of maintaining the precarious balance between ambition and glory, sudden fame and well-deserved, lasting reputation.

To what extent did Staël believe that the project of a modern republic, one that promoted progress by encouraging talent, was likely to become a reality? In the preface to *On Literature* the question was deliberately left unanswered:

> Every time I speak of the improvements that can be hoped for in French literature, I always assume the existence and continuation of freedom and political equality. Does this mean that I believe in the possibility of that freedom and that equality? I am not undertaking here to solve such a problem; I am even less disposed to give up such a hope.[42]

For all her prudence, however, she was offering considerable scope and credit to the declared aspirations of the Consulate: not only did she see Bonaparte as the last hope for preserving the conquests of the Revolution, but she legitimized his ambitions and outlined a framework in which the new republic's monarchical outlook was both justified and desirable. At the same time the stakes she implicitly set, in the book, for the new regime were very high, far higher than those she had mapped out, in a logic of survival, for the directorial republic. On the one hand, the republic should match the grandeur and éclat of the old monarchy; on the other, it must avoid the temptations and risks of personal rule. As she observed in discussing Louis XIV's absolutism, if the power of one man were to prevail in contemporary France, a modern society, focused on rationality and self-interest, would be dismally ill equipped to resist against tyranny.[43]

The arguments developed in *On Literature* cannot of course be reduced to the question of the author's response to the Consulate. The book developed a variety of historical, philosophical, and aesthetic issues that went well beyond her concerns with

immediate political contingencies. There was, however, a significant continuity between the definition of the new republic's institutional framework and the reflection on the values, the language, and the culture that must be associated with it. The central
argument of the book was precisely the improvidence—and ultimate impossibility—of separating the two.

AT A CROSSROADS

On its publication *On Literature* was generally well received by
critics and the public, going rapidly through three reprints. Even
more successful, three years later, was the novel *Delphine*—a
tragic love story set at the time of the Revolution, in the fashionable genre of "émigré" narrative. Meanwhile, as the power of the
new regime was consolidated, the space for political dissent, let
alone opposition, appeared increasingly reduced. Naturally Staël
was disappointed to learn that the first consul had failed to be
impressed by *On Literature* (he allegedly confessed he had spent
about fifteen minutes reading it, and found it hard going).[44]
However, neither this setback nor Constant's dismissal from the
Tribunat would have been sufficient to convince her to leave
France for good as long as she was allowed some political space,
that is to say, the possibility of exercising some influence. The
most immediate issue was, as ever, the question of whether she
would be allowed to live in Paris—a point on which the watchful
consular government was no more lenient than the Directory.
Her extensive network of connections—which included foreign
diplomats and known political opponents, as well as members of
the government and of Bonaparte's own family—was in itself a
source of suspicion and alarm for the government.

Unexpectedly the greatest difficulty in Staël's position came
from Necker: in 1802 the former minister published his *Dernières
vues de politique et de finance offertes à la nation française* (Last views
on politics and finance offered to the French nation),[45] where he
criticized the constitution of the Year VIII (1800) on the ground of

the excessive powers it conferred on the first consul, making vague allusions to military dictatorship and Caesarism. Whatever the reasons that led Necker to abandon his customary prudence, the book provided the French government with an additional pretext for proscribing his daughter from the capital. A few months later Staël anticipated a possible improvement in her position with the likely revival of the war between France and the European coalition, after the short-lived[46] Peace of Amiens: as Bonaparte would be engaged in military operations abroad (he was then planning to invade England), she expected more favorable treatment on the part of the authorities in his absence. However, the desired conciliatory gesture did not come.

In October 1803, while she was a guest at Joseph Bonaparte's country residence of Mortfontaine, Staël hesitated between two options: either returning to Switzerland, waiting there for the tensions to dissipate as she had done on many other occasions; or undertaking a journey to Germany, a country some literary friends and correspondents encouraged her to visit. Describing her dilemma years later, she expressed her regret for not having chosen Coppet: had she done so, she might have spent with her father what turned out to be the last months of his life (he died early in April 1804). Instead, "out of pride," as she put it, on 22 October she took the road to Metz, the road to Germany and to her new life. The next day her friend Juliette Recamier simultaneously received Staël's letter announcing her departure and a message from General Jourdan, who had finally obtained from Bonaparte the reprieve they all had been hoping for—but it was too late.

The reference to a decision made "out of pride" suggests that Staël found her own position of dependence on the arbitrary decisions of the authorities, indeed of a single man, increasingly hard to bear.[47] It is less clear whether she thought at that stage that the political situation in France was truly hopeless: if the post of first consul had just been turned into a lifetime position by the constitution of the Year X (1802),[48] the likely alternatives to Bonaparte remained very unappealing, while the rapid turn-over of regimes in the previous years left open the hope of some new development in the short term. However, it is reasonable to assume that, had Staël remained in France, she would have been faced sooner or later with some other occasion of conflict with Napoleon, notwithstanding the goodwill of those who acted as intermediaries between them.

Following her chosen route, Staël met, across Europe, some of the greatest intellectual personalities of the age and produced her best-known works. In 1807 the novel *Corinne ou l'Italie* (Corinne or Italy) offered a pioneering experiment in the new literary style she herself would baptize *romantisme* (romanti-cism).[49] In 1810 the essay *De l'Allemagne* (On Germany),[50] a spin-off of her history of literature, presented to the European public the unfamiliar achievements of German philosophy and literary production, possibly becoming one of the most influential books of the nineteenth century. The brutal suppression of this work by the imperial censors, who were unable to tolerate the presenta-tion of a hostile Germany as an ethical and aesthetic model for France, consecrated Staël's role as symbol of the resistance against Napoleon's despotism.[51] But it was a difficult and thank-less part, to be played from a distance, at Coppet or in some foreign court, in the shapeless political void Europe had become. Even as she was canvassing—in Stockholm with the future king of Sweden General Bernadotte[52] or in Saint Petersburg with Tsar Alexander I—for the collapse of the empire, Staël knew very well that the end of Bonaparte's adventure would take with it, at least for the time being, all the hopes and conquests of the modern republic.

CHAPTER 9

Back to the Future

THE BOURGEOIS LIBERAL REPUBLIC

Who set fire to the powders? Were they perhaps members of the Third Estate, the archbishop of Sens, the Genevan Necker, Mirabeau, Lafayette, d'Orléans, Adrien Duport, Choderlos de Laclos, the Staëls, the La Rochefoucauld, the Beauvau, the Montmorency, the Noailles, the Lameth, the La Tour du Pin, the Lefranc de Pompignan, and so many other engines of the triumphs of 1789 over royal authority?

—Joseph Fouché, *Mémoires*

EARLY IN February 1817 Staël wrote from Paris (to which she had returned only a few months before) to Thomas Jefferson: "I am going to publish a work that I recommend to your interest. It is entitled *Considérations sur les faits principaux de la révolution de France* (*Considerations on the Principal Events of the Revolution in France*). It will appear by the end of the year and you will see there your name and the sentiments it inspires in me."[1] A few months later she was dead at the age of fifty-one; the book in question was published posthumously by her son Auguste de Staël and her son-in-law the duc de Broglie in 1818;[2] while it sold well[3] (partly no doubt out of curiosity for any personal revelations it might contain), it predictably met with a rather frosty reception in the political climate of the Restoration. Staël had been careful to preserve civil relations with the surviving members of the Bourbon family, helped in this by her reputation as Napoleon's outspoken opponent; in particular she had finally obtained from Louis XVIII restitution of the loan Necker had made to the French state before the Revolution. However, one could hardly ignore the fact that her work set forth a harsh criticism of everything the royalists had stood for since the end of the Old Regime, provoking the hostile reaction of conservative writers such as Louis de Bonald.[4] For similar (if opposed) reasons, her account of the Revolution was not designed to find favor with the die-hard Jacobins, or with the partisans of the fallen empire.

THE GHOST OF THERMIDOR

Somehow the reputation of the *Considerations* has never fully recovered from the original cross fire of its opposed ideological enemies. Even though the book represents an original and illuminating contribution to the understanding of the French Revolution, it has generally been dismissed, both by contemporary critics and by later commentators, as marginal to the Revolution's historiography: the fact that it was out of print for most of the twentieth century is a good indication of this attitude. The negative treatment of the *Considerations* has been justified on a variety of grounds. One common argument has been that the book was written "too soon" to provide a sound and balanced account, as if the very fact that Staël was a witness to, and an active participant in, some of the events she described disqualified her from providing a serious historical work. (Interestingly the fact that they were describing contemporary events is not an argument invoked to criticize Edmund Burke's or René de Chateaubriand's accounts of the Revolution.) It has also been repeatedly suggested that the *Considerations* was written as a mere biographical narrative, a set of personal recollections (comparable to the memoirs of the guillotined Girondin leader Mme Roland), of some human and historical interest, but without any substantial interpretative or theoretical content.[5] Thus in presenting the French edition of 1983 (the first to appear since 1881), the historian Jacques Godechot described it, somewhat patronizingly, as "testimonial and pamphlet."[6] More sympathetic commentators have recognized the presence in the work of a distinctive interpretative line; but the very nature of this line, generally described as a defense of liberal values and moderate government, seems to accentuate the distance, even the incompatibility, between the writer and her subject.

These critical readings contain of course some elements of truth. The *Considerations* was written not only before the cycle of events set in motion in 1789 had reached its conclusion (one could argue that it would not do so for another century), but even before the Bourbon Restoration had been sufficiently stabilized to show its true political colors. Staël was well aware of this: while she was working on the text in June 1815 she wrote to the Tory politician Lord Harrowby that she must leave "a large blank" for whatever was to follow.[7] It is also true that, when planning her work, Staël had hesitated between the mode of personal recollection and that of a detached historical narrative. If in the end she opted for the latter, substantial traces of the other approach remained in the final draft. After all it was difficult for her (as it is for the reader) to forget that she had actually watched the deputies' progress as they walked to the opening ceremony of the Estates-General on 5 May 1789, or witnessed the departure of the royal family when they were driven away from Versailles on 6 October of the same year; that she had stood by her window, on the night of 9 August 1792, listening to the bells that tolled all over Paris, calling the people to the assault of the Tuileries. It was equally natural, when discussing broader political issues, for her to evoke her unmemorable meeting in 1789 with a certain Monsieur de Robespierre, to recall an official dinner (an especially difficult one) where she was sitting between Napoleon and Sieyès, or, again, to record her conversations with Tsar Alexander

I in Saint Petersburg. Such personal anecdotes remain even today the most frequently quoted passages of the book.

More generally the *Considerations* suffers from the lack of a clear design: the work resulted in fact from the combination of several different projects that, had the author lived longer, might have been developed separately. In addition to her personal recollections, Staël had planned for a long time—since Necker's death in 1804—to write a vindication of her father's public career (she produced a separate memoir on his private life).[8] She also considered writing an anti-Bonapartist pamphlet and, following the French authorities' suppression of *On Germany* in 1810, a complementary work to be called *De l'Angleterre* (On England), an idea that is mentioned in a letter to August Wilhelm Schlegel in December 1813.[9] All these different projects are present to some extent in the final draft of the *Considerations*, adding interesting material and perspectives, but creating an unevenness of style and some imbalance in the book's structure. Thus in part 1 the narrative of the events of 1789 gives considerable space to the discussion of Necker's ministerial action and of his views on financial issues; a sweeping anti-Bonapartist rhetoric is present throughout, even when the author recalls the early years, during which she had been in fact rather favorable to Napoleon's rule; finally a whole part of the book (part 6) offers an extensive presentation of English history, society, and political institutions, which is developed beyond the scope of a simple comparison between England and France.

But what about the distinctive political approach that characterizes the *Considerations*? As François Furet pointed out in his seminal essay *Interpreting the French Revolution*, there are, politically speaking, all manner of competing histories of the Revolution—Jacobin, liberal, royalist, anarchist, and so forth—all of them authorized by the complex and controversial nature of their object.[10] Following this perspective, the *Considerations* could be simply taken to represent an early (in fact the earliest) instance of "liberal" history and could be treated accordingly as the expression of a specific political viewpoint. Instead the hostile and dismissive treatment of Staël's work goes beyond a mere ideological disagreement with her positions and has not been equally applied to the work of other "liberal" interpreters, such as Alexis de Tocqueville or François Guizot.

In the ungenerous entry devoted to the *Considerations* in the *Dictionary of the French Revolution*—produced on the occasion of the bicentenary in 1989—Marcel Gauchet presented Staël's work as an instance of "liberal discredit" of the Revolution. He also described it as marginal, heavily dependent on Necker's views on the subject, and politically too "withdrawn" when compared to *Of Present Circumstances*. Accordingly the entry in the *Dictionary* was largely dedicated to the arguments of this earlier work, rather than to the designated subject of the article. In Gauchet's words Staël's history was "the last Thermidorian peroration, which conveys the feeling of having been written by a survivor, as if it belonged to the living sphere of the Revolution."[11] Somehow, because Staël spoke as the representative of a political faction that had died out in 1792, or possibly in 1799, her "living" voice, however vivid, had no place in the serious theoretical debate that developed in the subsequent decades. It would be too easy to suggest that Gauchet's anxiety to exorcise the ghost of Thermidor proved that ghost to be still very much alive and kicking in the 1980s in the Fifth Republic of President Mitterrand.[12] More importantly, the attempt to push the *Considerations* back in time, as the echo of a spent political experience, rather than as the first tentative step of a new one, is bound to ignore some crucial elements of the book. One of these elements is the criticism the writer expressed toward the political group with whom she is generally associated, the partisans of limited monarchy or moderate republicanism. Though by 1815 Staël was indeed alone in speaking for the once large and powerful party of the Constitutionnels (other survivors having faded into obscurity or made new careers in the service of the empire), she did not produce a defense or a set of justifications for their past actions. Instead she returned to the question that had obsessed her for most of her life: why had that promising group of enlightened reformers and ambitious aristocrats proved unable to steer France out of the Old Regime, into modern representative government, without plunging the nation into anarchy and terror?

It was tempting to claim, in retrospect, that the outcome was inevitable; that given the history and circumstances of France the project of a peaceful constitutional transition similar to the Glorious Revolution of 1688 was doomed from the start. Instead Staël undertook to detail all the errors that had been committed by the French political class in general, and by her own political side in particular. In this respect the *Considerations*, far from endorsing some historical fatality as has been sometimes suggested, offered a pointed analysis of the specific choices made by particular actors at particular points in time, of good and bad politics.

> Ordinary thinkers are in the habit of believing that whatever has taken place was unavoidable: but of what use would be the reason and the liberty of man if his will were not able to prevent that which that will has so visibly accomplished?[13]

Another important feature, which is overlooked by any "retrograde" reading of the work, is the fact that Staël saw the original project of constitutional government set forth in 1789 as vindicated by subsequent events, and still valid in 1817 and for the foreseeable future. No doubt actors and circumstances had changed, but the substance of what had been attempted then was still the only viable agenda, for France as for Europe at large. The extensive comparison developed in the last part of the book between the French and English constitutional traditions was not just an attempt to settle the historical parallel between 1688 and 1789, but also a reflection on the long-term conditions for future political stability. Thus the *Considerations* was not the eulogy for a lost good cause but the confident celebration of a hard-won future victory.

"THE GREAT FORCE OF PUBLIC OPINION"

As a reflection of her own experience, Staël's account of the Revolution of 1789 was dominated by the tension between public opinion and those political powers that, at different points in time, struggled to rule it, represent it, or control it. While the theme of opinion had been central to her approach to politics from the start, the *Considerations* offered the opportunity for an overall assessment, no doubt partly intended as a warning to the newly installed power, the restored monarchy of Louis XVIII. Here as in the rest of Staël's oeuvre, the term "public opinion" was used to describe a variety of somewhat different objects: the views expressed by the elite of enlightened writers and intellectuals, the expectations and sentiments of the population at large, and their real or imagined interests; it applied equally to the short-term reactions and to the long-term disposition of the public. In the book's opening chapter Staël identified as the relevant force, within this nebulous cluster of intellectual postures and popular moods, the object of her very first political intervention of 1791, the "opinion of the majority of the nation"; here, however, she was more specific about the nature of such a majority, which consisted of "the writers, the merchants, the bankers, a great number of landholders and of persons in public employment."[14]

This sociological definition of "the majority of the nation" did not include the privileged groups at the top of French society: the nobility, the high clergy, and the members of the old *parlements*. The people who were in such position—the writer argued—could not possibly share (at least as collectives) the basic demands that the philosophers of the Enlightenment had expressed on behalf of the French people, namely, the abolition of feudality, the establishment of constitutional, nonarbitrary government, and religious toleration. On the other hand, Staël did not elaborate on the implicit exclusion from the "relevant" part of the nation of the lower orders, the propertyless laborers and peasants (her "majority of the nation" was in fact, demographically speaking, a rather large bourgeois minority). It is reasonable to infer, from what she wrote elsewhere, that she did not regard this obviously larger part of society as an autonomous component of opinion, because it had no interests or assets to protect, and because it lacked the means of well-informed political participation. For these reasons its interests were better served in the long run by the decisions of the bourgeois minority.

In her narrative of revolutionary events the mass of the people was always presented as led by primitive impulses or as the object of demagogical manipulations. The backward condition of the lower orders—the result of centuries of feudal oppression and religious superstition—was identified as the cause of the "ferocity" of revolutionary terror in France, in contrast with the more restrained behavior of the more prosperous, better-educated populations of Holland and Switzerland in similar circumstances. As to the "relevant" opinion of proprietors and the like, Staël presented it as the prime mover of 1789 and also as its terminus ad quem: it was to satisfy the legitimate aspirations of these sectors of society that the transformation of French institutions had originally been set in motion. Their demands were clear enough: no more feudal privileges, no more arbitrary government, no more violation of basic individual freedom. Significantly those aspirations did not substantially change over time: "The true public opinion, which rises superior to faction, has been the same in France for twenty-seven years; and every other direction given to it, being artificial, could have only a temporary influence."[15]

But what exactly had gone wrong in the interaction between opinion and power to make the French ruling classes lose sight of this fact? The belief that political action should be adjusted to the needs of civil society had been one of the fundamental principles for eighteenth-century reformers. The support of the public was the measure of the success of any political initiative and the only guarantee of stability for any constitutional setting. By his own account Necker had formed this conviction when he occupied "a great place in government and near the king," several years before the Revolution: "Here is what I saw. To begin with, the great force of public opinion. I was especially struck by it, and I am not saying this after any triumphs; I had in fact already come to this conclusion in my work *On the Administration of Finances*, written immediately after my resignation from the ministry in 1781."[16] Aware of her father's views, Staël recalled how he had felt bitterly hurt when his enemies had used the press to attack and denigrate him, since he looked upon public opinion with an almost religious respect:

> Next to the duties enjoined by religion, the esteem of the public was his highest concern; he sacrificed to it fortune, honours, all that the ambitious desire; and the voice of the people, not yet perverted, was to him almost divine.[17]

And yet a sequence of different regimes—beginning with an ancient, well-established monarchy, apparently well placed to preserve popular consensus—had repeatedly failed in this task of interpreting the real demands of the nation. Throughout the Revolution, and contrary to the optimistic expectations set forth by eighteenth-century writers, opinion had proved consistently elusive and opaque. The transparency of opinion was not a natural condition but the result of a long practice of liberty and open debate, which France lacked altogether. Under the Old Regime the press had been subjected to censorship, and there were no representative institutions where issues could be publicly discussed. Without a robust tradition of freedom and independence, opinion was bound to be appropriated by different groups, and to fall prey to the manipulations of those who tried to influence, deceive, or intimidate it. Before the Revolution, Necker had attempted to develop what Staël regarded as the perfect instrument to create healthy relations between government and the nation, namely, public credit. His policy of resorting to credit had been criticized as an irresponsible economic strategy, and yet

> credit is then the true modern discovery which binds a government to its people; it obliges the executive power to treat public opinion with consideration: and, in the same way that trade had the effect of civilizing nations, credit, which is the offspring of trade, had rendered the establishment of constitutional forms of some kind or another necessary to give publicity to financial transactions and guarantee contracts. How was it practicable to found credit on mistresses, favourites or ministers, who are in a course of daily change at a royal court? What father of a family would place his fortune in such a lottery?[18]

Unfortunately, the Revolution and the war had rapidly destroyed the positive effects of Necker's work, bringing back the economic instruments typical of despotic governments: forced borrowing, extraordinary contributions, and paper money. In 1789 the old practice of censorship had been replaced, without any transition, by the unrestrained freedom of the press. This necessary but too sudden emancipation, far from producing mature and responsible debate, had generated a flood of violent and slanderous publications, destroying the residual prestige of the monarchy, and undermining the authority of the new Constituent Assembly. Staël argued that the members of the assembly had been right in deciding to respect the principle of freedom of expression, even if this opened the path to the manipulations of their enemies. Unlike the Jacobins, they had not wished to establish liberty by despotic means:

> But the troubles of France were caused, it will be alleged, by the licentiousness of the press. Who does not now admit that the Constituent Assembly ought to have left seditious publications, like every other public offense, to the judgment of the courts? But if for the purpose of maintaining its power it had

silenced its adversaries, and confined the command of the press only to its adherents, the representative government would have been extinguished.[19]

Later on, by their choice to control and coerce opinion, the Jacobin and Bonapartist regimes had abandoned the path of representative government based on consensus, returning to the mode of arbitrary rule. Faced first with the clamors of partisan pamphleteers, then with the threat of repressive measures, "true" opinion had retreated into silence.

But the press was not the only means of expression of public opinion. With the advent of the constitution of 1791 the people finally had the opportunity to manifest their will through the vote. In *Of Present Circumstances* the author had stressed the phenomenon of abstention, which had divested elections of their intended role as the expression of the nation's will. This alienation of the public from political participation had been a constant pattern throughout the years of the Revolution. But what were the causes of this disaffection? How should one interpret this lack of trust in the process of selection of representatives? Staël's explanation focused on the imperfect functioning of the representative system that had taken shape in France since 1789. In her view the difficulties did not come from the faults in the various French constitutions: such faults existed but did not immediately affect the trust people placed in political institutions. They were caused instead by the absence of an adequate interaction between the citizens and their representatives.

In normal circumstances the people expressed spontaneous, disaggregated demands, which were then given shape by the parliamentary groups and debated within the legislative bodies. However, in France the practice of deliberation had not had the time to develop properly. Staël referred to the observations by Jeremy Bentham, recently edited and published by Etienne Dumont, on the functioning of the revolutionary assemblies in France, in which he analyzed their defects and advocated an appropriate regulation of parliamentary debates.[20] As Bentham explained, and as she well knew from personal observation, in the Estates-General as in the Constituent and Legislative Assemblies, deliberations had been at best chaotic, even before the radicalization of the political context: speeches could not be heard by all, minority speakers were not given the opportunity to express themselves adequately, written speeches read in the assembly were the norm. This initial confusion, essentially caused by a lack of proper experience, had subsequently given way to the use of more aggressive tactics on the part of the opposition. The presence of crowds of militants in the galleries conditioned and cowed the deputies, who became increasingly the target of threats and even of physical attacks. Organized militant minorities, by resorting to menace and intimidation, silenced the voice of the majority and dictated the resolutions to be voted by the deputies. In other words the Jacobins and the other radical factions bypassed the legal channels of political representation, imposing their decisions without any mediation or debate. Understandably the public at large could not recognize itself in a system of representation that obeyed the diktats of factious minorities.

A national representation on an imperfect plan is but an additional instrument in the hands of tyranny . . . Representatives form by no means a separate caste; they do not possess the gift of miracles; they are of importance only when supported by the nation; but as soon as that support fails them, a battalion of grenadiers is stronger than an assembly of three hundred deputies.[21]

GOOD AND BAD PARTIES

The question of the control of opinion was intimately connected with the role that the different political groups had played in the revolutionary process. Before 1789 the initiatives of those ministers, such as Necker, who wished to satisfy the public demand

for reform were impeded by the arbitrary nature of the monarchical government: the king could appoint or dismiss ministers
following his own whim, or rather, in the case of Louis XVI,
bending to the pressures of his entourage, so that the action of
government lacked continuity, coherence, and efficacy. However,
once the Constituent Assembly was established, the reforming
action was placed on firmer ground. In particular, between 14
July and 6 October 1789 the constituents "had all the power"
and were in a position to satisfy public expectations. And yet
they proved unable to consolidate their authority, rallying the
nation behind them, and securing support for their ambitious, if
hasty, legislative action.

So why exactly had they failed? For those like Staël who had
believed that the Revolution could be a peaceful constitutional
transition, this remained a crucial question. The debacle of the
Constituent Assembly had been the Pandora's box from which
all subsequent evils had emerged: not just proscriptions, terror,
and death, but also new forms of despotism. The discouraging
outcome, in 1815, of a defeated France under a restored Bourbon
monarchy, was only the last (and possibly not the worst) of a long
series of dismal consequences. One might argue that the struggle
for constitutional government supported by popular consent
had been lost in advance; that the moderate reformers, trapped
between the blind opposition of the privileged castes, on the one
hand, and the violent pressures of the radicals on the other, had
no chance to succeed. Instead even at this late stage Staël refused
to read the outcome as fated, thus exonerating her own party
from all responsibility. Events had taken a dangerous turn in
1791–92 because the constituents had been unable to take advantage of their position of unopposed control of the political space,
showing a lack of both "wisdom" and " ability," allowing power
to slide down toward the lower orders of society. The radicalization of the Revolution was not a historical necessity, but the product of wrong decisions and bad political choices on the part of
those who had been committed to a different outcome.

On Staël's account the largest share of responsibility rested with the intransigent royalists who occupied the right wing of the assembly, a group that included aristocrats and courtiers, as well as the members of the old *parlements* and of the high clergy. These ultraroyalists made no secret of the fact that they judged "the eighteenth-century discovery of the nation" as simply "ridiculous" and refused to cooperate in any way with the constitutional monarchists, even when their vote might have tipped the balance in favor of the monarchy itself. Outside the assembly, the choice of a large part of the aristocracy—including the king's own brothers—to emigrate, long before their lives were actually in danger, aggravated this desertion of the monarchy on the part of the nobility, abandoning the king and his family to their fate (a judgment that could hardly be well received by the brothers in question, the new king Louis XVIII and the future Charles X, the comte d'Artois).

If she denounced the royalists as heavily responsible, Staël did not spare the partisans of constitutional monarchy, their lack of unity and of common purpose. The difference from her earlier assessments is that now she could speak out without fear of any immediate political consequences. The "popular party" in the Constituent Assembly had consisted of several rival factions. It included a few prominent figures, such as La Fayette, Mirabeau, and Sieyès, none of whom, however, was able to fill the role of party leader. In particular there was a profound division between the mass of the moderate deputies, led by Gérard de Lally Tollendal, Pierre-Victor Malouet, and Joseph Mounier, and their dashing avant-garde represented by Adrien Duport, Antoine Barnave, and "some young men from the court."[22] These "dashing leaders of the popular party" had pursued their daring agenda with great levity, making fun of the more prudent mass of the moderates, who should have been their natural allies. This irresponsible conduct had been motivated simply by personal vanity, by the desire to be protagonists rather than serving a common cause:

The leaders of the *coté gauche*, or left side of the Assembly, would have succeeded in introducing the English constitution if they had formed a union for this purpose with M. Necker, among the ministers, and with his friends in the Assembly. But, in that case, they would have been but secondary agents in the course of events, while they wished to hold the first rank; they consequently committed the great imprudence of seeking support from the crowds out of doors, which were beginning to prepare a subterraneous explosion. They gained their ascendancy in the Assembly by ridiculing the *moderates*, as if moderation were a weakness and they the only men of energy.[23]

This lack of unity, together with the irresponsible choices made by the constitutional monarchists, had opened the path to the power of the left of the assembly, the Montagnards, with their underground network of Jacobin clubs. The main accusation addressed by Staël to her former political friends was that they never formed a proper party: they had no unity of purpose, no loyalty, no discipline, no leadership. One might see a certain contradiction in the fact that, while accusing the moderates of not acting as a party, Staël should condemn the Jacobins for their superior capacity for doing so. Her view was that the Jacobins carried their partisanship beyond the limits of normal and legal political action, conspiring, hiding their real subversive intentions, and resorting to threats and violence toward their adversaries.[24] Thus she described the network of Jacobin clubs across France as a government outside the government, a parallel organization created with subversive intentions:

> The Jacobin clubs were organized as a government more than the government itself: they passed decrees; they were connected by correspondence in the provinces with other clubs not less powerful; finally, they were to be considered a mine underground, always ready to blow up existing institutions when opportunities should offer.[25]

She also suggested that all those deputies who connived with these "illegal methods," condoning practices such as the intimidation of adversaries, in the end deserved what they got. In particular her evocation of the unhappy fate of the Girondins was notably short on compassion; although she acknowledged their individual virtues and courage, she considered them largely responsible for their own destruction, by their unforgivable choice of legitimating violence and abuse. It is easy to argue that the line Staël attempted to draw here between "good" and "bad" parties was still quite tentative. But she did draw the line, showing that France's transition to modern representative government required—among other things—a clarification of the respective roles of popular mobilization, on the one hand, and of organized parliamentary parties on the other.

DE L'ANGLETERRE

Staël's analysis of the role of factions in the Revolution is better understood in the light of the final section of the *Considerations*, dedicated to England. Like *On Germany*, the surviving fragment of what might have become *On England* provided a general overview of English history and intellectual tradition; but while Germany did not yet exist as a political entity, and could be discussed only in terms of its moral and cultural features, in the case of England the focus was inevitably on the political system. Like her favorite Anglophile writers—Montesquieu, Delolme, and Voltaire—Staël praised England's commercial achievements, its constitution, and its tradition of individual liberty, freedom of the press, and religious toleration. But what interested her above all was the functioning of English parliamentarianism and the nation's party system. All along she manifested great admiration for the Whig Party and its leaders: an admiration that was not affected by the pro-Bonapartist stand of Charles Fox's entourage, nor by the crippling divisions that wrecked the party during the French wars. Her protracted visit to England between June 1813

and May 1814, which offered her the opportunity for direct observation, did not lead her to alter her position substantially.[26]

As to the Tories, while in 1795 she had accused William Pitt
and his party of pursuing the war in order to preserve their
power, in the *Considerations* she showed greater indulgence toward them. She was ready to acknowledge England as the real
author of Napoleon's defeat, thanks to the solidity of its institutions and the strength of its economy. She also credited the English with the restoration of peace in Europe (though here the
greatest merit was attributed to the Whigs rather than to the
"ministerial party"), and she refuted the allegation that the war
had brought about an authoritarian turn in English government,
by placing excessive power in the hands of the executive:

> The enemies of the English constitution on the Continent are
> incessantly repeating that it will perish by the corruption of
> Parliament, and that ministerial influence will increase to such
> a point as to annihilate liberty: nothing of the kind is to be
> dreaded. The English Parliament always obeys national opin-
> ion, and opinion cannot be corrupted in the sense attached to
> that expression, that is, bribed.[27]

The only risk to constitutional freedom came, in England as in
France, from the popular admiration of military success, a trait
that was bound to fade away once the conflict came to an end.
While she did not exactly ignore the suggestions of her friend
Jefferson—who tried to convince her that England had sustained
the French wars only out of imperial ambition—she confined
herself to advocating a better understanding between London
and the former American colonies.[28]

For Staël the most notable feature of the English political system was the way in which popular views and demands were
transmitted and filtered through representative institutions.
Members of Parliament—she observed—had direct personal
contacts with their electors (Lord Erskine had assured her that he
had met all the voters of the constituency of Westminster at least

once);[29] the mechanisms of direct popular election forced representatives to take into account their demands and expectations. Moreover, the public was in the habit of forming associations and committees to promote and finance specific causes, and these gatherings had also to be taken into account by those who stood for election. Together the pressures of civil society, the freedom of the press, and the disciplined unfolding of parliamentary debates allowed a real confrontation between government and opposition.

The English example helped Staël to clarify her views on party loyalty. She was very eloquent in celebrating the fidelity of the Whigs who had remained in opposition, in spite of the cost to their political career, claiming that such integrity would be unthinkable in France:

> In England a man would be dishonoured if he abandoned his political friends for his own particular interest. Opinion in this respect is so strong that not long ago a man of respectable name and character shot himself, because he could not forgive himself for having accepted a post against his own party . . . even recently I have seen men of law refuse posts with 7 or 8000 *livres* of revenue, not even political posts, simply because they shared the opinions of Mr Fox's friends.

She also added that if public men behaved like that in France, their families would subject them to judicial interdiction as if they had lost their mind. But how could deputies retain their independence of judgment if they were bound by loyalty to their party? And what was the point of deliberating and discussing issues in the House if everyone had to stick to the position of his group? Her answer was that debates were essentially addressed to the mass of the deputies, who had no prominent role to play in the party, and could actually swing the majority with their vote if they were convinced by the arguments of one or the other side.

But if opinions are formed beforehand, how can truth and eloquence operate on the assembly? How can the majority change
when circumstances require it, and of what avail is discussion
if no one can vote according to his conviction? The case is not
so: what is called fidelity to your party consists in not separating your personal interest from those of your political friends,
and in your not treating separately with the men in power. But
it often happens that circumstances or arguments influence
the mass of the assembly, and that the neutral party, whose
number is considerable, that is, the men who do not take active part in politics, produce a change in the majority.[30]

The crucial point for Staël was the distinction between opinion
and interest: representatives were free to follow their own conscience, and occasionally to agree with the speakers from the opposite side in parliamentary debates, provided they acted out of
conviction, rather than because they were corrupted by the offer
of personal advantages. She assumed that a substantial number
of deputies would not be bound by party allegiances but would
simply represent local interests, without any hopes for high office: these backbenchers were the real target of debates, as they
were more disposed to take a position according to how the various issues were presented in the discussions.

In the same section Staël returned to the question of the great
power enjoyed by English heads of government, defending this
feature of the constitution against the attacks frequently set forth
by its detractors. In particular she questioned the common allegation that in England there was no real political freedom, since
the ministry was, just as it was in other countries, "the master of
everything," thanks to its power of corruption. Some claimed
that the English ministers "purchase the votes in parliament in
such a way as to obtain constantly a majority, and the whole of
this English constitution, which we hear spoken of with so much
admiration, is nothing but the art of bringing political venality
into play."[31] But this was not true: in fact the financial resources

of the executive were generally insufficient to buy parliamentary support, or to feed extensive patronage. One had only to look at the large personal debts famously left by Pitt on his death to realize that in England high office did not necessarily bring great wealth. No doubt a degree of corruption could be found in the English system as in any other, but the main motivation behind ministerial careers such as that of Pitt was political ambition, not money: reputation meant more than wealth to men like him. In any case the considerable freedom of opinion and of the press that reigned in England was the best possible guarantee against the undue influence occasionally exercised by the crown, the high nobility, or the government: the power of the minister derived from his majority in Parliament, but more crucially from the support of public opinion. Thus the occasional instances of undue influence did not alter "the nature of representative government."[32]

On the front of possible improvements to the English political system Staël advocated Catholic emancipation and a solution of compromise to the Irish question. She recognized the necessity of a reform of the electoral system to redesign constituencies, but she suggested that it should be effected gradually, disenfranchising some rotten boroughs and reallocating their seats year by year, rather than promoting a single sweeping reform. But on the whole England remained her dream model of all that France should become: a truly constitutional monarchy; a functioning representative government sustained by deliberation and debate; above all a system that obeyed the demands of opinion. The fact that "opinion ruled in England" represented for her "the true freedom of a state."[33]

THE EXAMPLE OF HENRY IV

Presenting the text of the *Considerations* in 1818, the editors warned the reader that the last two sections of the book—part 5 on the contemporary circumstances of France and part 6 on

England—had not been revised by the author. While Staël's interest in English politics was of long standing, there is no mistaking the sense of urgency in her final comparison between the two nations and her reflections on the return of the Bourbons. In order to avoid further upheavals—she argued—the restored monarchy must follow the example of the Hanovers rather than that of the Stuarts: it must make very clear that sovereignty now belonged to the nation, and that the new king would rule within the limits of the constitution.

The reason for the lasting popularity Napoleon enjoyed, making possible a fifteen-year reign and even his brief return in 1815 (Staël never forgave Constant for the support he had given to the emperor during the Hundred Days),[34] was the fact that people saw him as the enforcer and custodian of the conquests of the Revolution. This was the view of French opinion, but also of the European public at large. This continuity between Napoleon and 1789—she argued—had ceased to exist very early on in his career, and the empire had rapidly become a counterrevolutionary enterprise, modeled on the "universal monarchy" of the Middle Ages. And yet the collective imagination had continued to associate Napoleon with the cause of equality, civil rights, and modernizing reforms. No doubt his military triumphs were also a source of fascination for the French; on the other hand, many who had no interest whatever in politics appreciated the restoration of order and of the security of property he had been able to grant, after several years of chaos and instability. This sense of continuity with the best part of the revolutionary heritage made people ignore the fact that Napoleon had suppressed freedom of expression and divested representative institutions of their proper function.

Unlike Napoleon, Louis XVIII could benefit from his status as legitimate ruler, the heir to a secular dynasty. But he could not hope to rule France against the heritage of 1789, as if the last twenty-five years had simply never happened. In this respect the short-lived experience of the first return of the king in 1814 had been only partly reassuring. In particular the message conveyed by the Charte constitutionnelle (Constitutional Charter) of 1814[35] was somewhat ambiguous. Staël appreciated the use of the word "charter," which had an English ring to it, evoking the idea of the Bill of Rights. She also appreciated the fact that its content was very close to the proposal that Necker had urged Louis XVI to adopt in 1789. However, the document had been presented to the people as an *ordonnance*, a royal decree that, as such, had no permanent status and could be revoked at any time. The unavoidable analogy was with the Edict of Nantes (the document that granted religious freedom to the Protestants), issued by Henry IV in 1598, and revoked by Louis XIV in 1685, inaugurating a new wave of persecutions against the Huguenots. The formula that described the charter as a "concession" made by the king to the people, rather than a contract between him and the nation, contributed to conveying a negative impression. This halfhearted approach was unsurprising, given that Louis XVIII was surrounded and advised by die-hard ultraroyalists, who hated any form of constitutional government, and by unscrupulous opportunists, such as Staël's former friend Talleyrand.

On the positive side Staël admitted that the new monarch had undertaken no acts of personal revenge. The example that Louis XVIII should follow was not that of Charles II (with whom admittedly he had little in common), but that of his ancestor Henry IV. Staël's admiration for the first of the Bourbon kings (the only king of France she truly appreciated) was of course partly motivated by the fact that he was originally a Protestant. But she was also sensitive to other features of his personality, such as the fact that, alone among the Bourbons, he had a French mother and a French education. While Protestant ethics and Protestant attitudes toward religion were certainly relevant to Staël's political thinking, her passionate French nationalism and identification with French values were probably as important.[36] The circumstances in which Henry of Navarre had succeeded to the throne in 1594 were of course quite different from those of the 1814 Restoration. There were, however, interesting analogies. Henry had secured the crown after decades of a ferocious civil war; like Louis XVIII he was the legitimate heir but alienated from the majority of his subjects, in his case on account of his religion. His choice to convert to Catholicism, preventing any further agitation of the Huguenots, was motivated by his desire to respect the opinion of the majority of the nation, subordinating his own preferences to their will. In this way he had managed to restore peace and to stabilize the monarchy. The implication for his descendant was clear enough: just as Henry had renounced his religious beliefs to conform to those of the majority of the nation, Louis must set aside his personal convictions on the prerogatives of royalty in order to conform to the expectations of his subjects who wished for a limited monarchy.

Could things really turn out for the best for the restored monarchy? For twenty-five years every single government born of the Revolution had been "mad or bad." Why should it be different now? Staël's answer was that in a situation of foreign and domestic conflict, no good government could possibly succeed. However, with the advent of peace France could finally develop the virtues of which it was capable: "energy, patience in misfortune, audacity in enterprise, in a word, strength"; but only the establishment and preservation of free political institutions could protect the nation from further upheaval.[37] In other words the difference between France and England did not reside in the respective characters of the two nations, as was claimed by those who judged the French "unsuited to liberty." The difference was in the experience of a free and stable constitutional framework, from which England, unlike France, had been able to benefit for a long time.

THE NEW EUROPEAN ORDER

Another important issue on which the restored monarchy would be judged was the king's attitude toward the new European order created by the wars. At the beginning of the Revolution Staël's idea of Europe had not been very different from that common to most Enlightenment intellectuals: Europe was merely the geographical area within which the great powers deployed their rivalries, rivalries that were traditionally kept in check by a system of mutual threats and alliances. Seen from this perspective, a closer integration of European nations could be realized by only two means: by conquest, if a military regime were to prevail in one of the great powers; or by commerce, as the growth of the public debt and the development of international markets reduced the autonomy of individual states. Neither prospect seemed in itself very appealing. The fears of Enlightenment writers concentrated in particular on the first possibility, the emergence of a military regime that might end constitutional government on the entire continent. Many saw commerce as a more benign force, although isolated voices, such as Rousseau's, denounced its deleterious moral and political consequences upon the European populations.[38]

To these two prospects the Revolution had added a third, more appealing possibility: European nations might be united by their common choice to establish some association of free constitutional governments; but the project of a federation of "sister republics" that had briefly made its appearance in 1792 was soon crushed by the conquering ambitions of France, which had treated its "sister republics" (such as Switzerland) like occupied territories.[39] Later on Napoleon had gone even further, turning conquered Europe into the parody of a feudal empire, with his own relatives in the role of vassal monarchs:

> The re-establishment of Poland, the independence of Italy, and the deliverance of Greece were schemes that had an air of grandeur; people might have felt an interest in the revival of other peoples. But was the earth to be inundated with blood that Prince Jerome might fill the place of the Elector of Hesse; and that the Germans might be governed by French rulers

who took to themselves fiefs of which they could scarcely pronounce the titles, though they bore them, but on the revenues
of which they easily laid hold in every language?[40]

While she was eloquent in denouncing the emperor's faults,
Staël was strongly opposed to the view that once Napoleon was
out of the way, the prerevolutionary status quo could reassert
itself. For all its perverse aspects, the Napoleonic Empire had
created new cultural and political synergies among European
nations, the same synergies she had so perceptively described in
On Literature. It had also introduced, albeit by authoritarian
means, wide-ranging reforms in all the domains of the law and
public administration: this important work of modernization
could not simply be set aside to bring back the practices of the
Old Regime:

> All upright people are affected when reminded of their ances-
> tors; the idea of their fathers seems always to join itself to the
> idea of the past. But does this noble and pure feeling lead to
> the re-establishment of the torture, of the wheel, of the Inquisi-
> tion, because in remote ages abominations of this kind were
> the work of barbarous manners? Can we support what is ab-
> surd and criminal because absurdity and criminality once
> existed?[41]

The ideas that the French revolutionary armies had proclaimed
and circulated—civil rights, equality, and freedom—had not lost
their truth or their power to inspire the European peoples simply
because they had been used instrumentally and insincerely by a
part of the revolutionary elite and by Bonaparte himself.

Hurriedly drafted to keep up with the latest developments,
the conclusions of the *Considerations* show that Staël was not simply preoccupied with justifying the past. No doubt what she
wrote was partly dictated by the desire to set the record straight:
reasserting the validity of her father's policies, assigning merit
and blame to those who had determined the course of the Revo-

lution, denouncing the persecutions of which she and her friends had been victims under the Revolution and the empire. Like all other commentators, she was attempting to read the novelties created by the revolutionary experience within familiar political and historical categories, to make them more acceptable and intelligible.

However, her main purpose was the vindication of the original project of 1789, namely, the transformation of the French monarchy (which before the Revolution did not possess a proper constitution, only some fragmentary elements of one) into a functioning representative government. She was ready to recognize the mistakes committed by the partisans of that project and their responsibilities in failing to impose it. But she was anxious to show that every time the French political class had deviated from this original design—in order to protect privilege, to reassert authority, or to pursue an illusory democratic rule—the outcome had been catastrophic. Thus rather than reviving for the last time the ghost of Thermidor, Staël's account of the Revolution suggested a prefiguration of what France did eventually become two hundred years, three monarchies, and four republics later: a large bourgeois republic, with a taste for democratic rhetoric and an appetite for monarchical éclat;[42] a European nation closely bound to its neighbors by common difficulties and common aspirations.

Germaine de Staël and Modern Politics

ADMITTEDLY THE rambling perorations Bonaparte addressed to the assemblies on the occasion of the coup of Brumaire do not rank among his best oratorical performances. However, he did manage to produce a few of his distinctive lapidary formulas. Haranguing the Elders, in a tone more suited to galvanizing his troops than to ingratiating himself with a gathering of hostile legislators, he pleaded:

> Do not search the past for examples that would only delay you in your march! Nothing in history resembles the end of the eighteenth century; nothing in the end of the eighteenth century is like the present moment.[1]

What he meant in the first instance was that the deputies must disregard any rule or constraint imposed by the existing constitution. But more generally he conveyed most vividly the sense of his project's radical novelty, the myth of the tabula rasa, and of the irresistible acceleration of time, upon which he was constructing his political adventure. Staël belonged, by education and by intellectual choice, to the party of those who preferred to think of change and reform in some continuity with the past. She thought there were limits to what the magic of speed and novelty could achieve, limits inscribed within the very identity of modern commercial society: the bonds dictated by public credit and international markets, those set by the rules of limited government, and the constraints created by the emerging aspirations of European peoples to decide their own destiny. She did not fail to appreciate the cogency of Bonaparte's position: after all the claim to a radically new departure had been central to the narrative of the Enlightenment, even if at the time the form and the contours of this epochal change remained unspecified. However, the Revolution had shown her only too clearly how very wide the gap was between what the laws of progress dictated, on the one hand, and, on the other, what sheer political will (or sheer political unreason)[2] could achieve: it was a black hole into which governments and parties could disappear without trace, a gaping abyss that could wreck the lives of millions and engulf entire nations.

Representative government was not—as its most optimistic supporters believed at the beginning of the Revolution—a piece of serviceable machinery that, once jump-started, would continue to run dependably and smoothly—no more than the behavior of large populations could be predicted by scientific theories, or mapped out by skillful social engineering. Even if modern democracy was the product of the natural progress of European societies, making it work in practice was an exhausting, repetitive, and often pointless exercise, one that exposed political actors to endless frustration.

Staël's political legacy has been generally identified with the stern defense of "liberal" values—values that, with the collapse of the Old Regime, had become the pillars of modern government: civil equality, individual freedom, and the limitation of power by constitutional rules. Staël herself promoted this interpretation of her own contribution to politics. Like other intellectuals in her generation, having lived through bewildering upheavals, she longed for certainties; thus she was eager to assert the coherence of her own position, and to design a stable moral and legal framework for any future political action. In this respect the picture of the brave writer, struggling alone against tyranny in the name of timeless principles, was, before becoming a convenient historical stereotype, a sincere self-representation. It was an ideal that carried with it a sense of vindication, the belief that, in spite of the many battles lost in the short term, her position must prevail in the end.

And yet what is most interesting about Staël's career is not her loyalty to a few, relatively abstract, notions—such as liberty, progress, or moderation—but her awareness of their limited impact upon reality. She supported representative government as a regime designed to promote personal abilities and talent, while knowing that electors were far more likely to vote for the vulgar and the corrupt; she discussed the technicalities of constitutions, in the awareness that their efficacy ultimately depended on the vagaries of popular favor; she defended the freedom of the press, while contemplating with horror the flood of worthless drivel this freedom inevitably produced. All her life she argued patiently with sovereigns, ministers, and generals, affecting to ignore their lies and duplicity, hammering on regardless, in the hope that some shred of reason might filter through to them.

Staël's political experience cannot be described as being in any sense exemplary. While her intellectual background can be traced to a number of familiar traditions—the Enlightenment, the morality of sentiments, political economy, Whiggism—her personal contribution remains atypical and in the end is not "representative" of any social identity or political ideology. Like many of her political friends and enemies, like General Bonaparte himself, she had to invent a role for herself, and to improvise new strategies as she went along, taking in her stride whatever current events threw at her. Being able to extract any valuable directions from such precarious navigation was undoubtedly her greatest achievement.

How is it possible to reconcile the demand for popular participation in public decisions with the need for stable and efficient government? What is the most desirable balance between legislative and executive power? What sort of persons do we want to represent us, and what should we expect from them? Should all

beliefs and opinions be freely expressed, whatever the consequences? How can democracies respond to terrorism, when this
emerges from within their own citizenry? How sovereign can
sovereign states be in the face of global financial and economic
forces? And what exactly do we call a nation in the modern
world? These were the crucial questions Germaine de Staël
struggled with during her life. Providing convincing answers
was as difficult for her as it is for us today; but we are indebted
to her for her efforts to bring them into focus, and to give them
an intelligible shape.

Notes

INTRODUCTION. A PASSION FOR POLITICS

1. Among the most recent accounts of the life of Germaine de Staël, see Maria Fairweather, *Madame de Staël* (London: Constable & Robinson, 2005); Sergine Dixon, *Germaine de Staël, Daughter of the Enlightenment: The Writer and Her Turbulent Era* (Amherst, NY: Humanity Books, 2007); Michel Winock, *Madame de Staël* (Paris: Fayard, 2010). Among the older works, see Pierre Corday, *Madame de Staël, ou le deuil éclatant du bonheur* (Lausanne: Editions Rencontre, 1967); Ghislain de Diesbach, *Madame de Staël* (1983; Paris: Perrin, 2011); and the unsurpassed J. Christopher Herold, *Mistress to an Age: A Life of Mme de Staël* (New York: Bobbs-Merrill, 1958).

2. Staël's political activities and writings are generally discussed in her biographies; in addition to the works cited above, see, for a more specifically political approach, Simone Balayé, *Mme de Staël, lumières et liberté* (Paris: Kilncksieck, 1972); G. E. Gwynne, *Madame de Staël et la révolution française: politique, philosophie, littérature* (Paris: Nizet, 1969). Erik Egnell, *Une femme en politique, Germaine de Staël* (Paris: Editions de Fallois, 2013). See also the chapter devoted to Staël in Aurelian Craiutu, *A Virtue for Courageous Minds: Moderation in French Political Thought, 1748–1830* (Princeton, NJ: Princeton University Press, 2012), pp. 158–97.

3. See Béatrice W. Jasinski, introduction to Madame de Staël, *Correspondance générale* (hereafter *CG*), 6 vols. (1960–68; Geneva: Slatkine, 2009), 1:vii–xxxviii.

4. On the political role of salons in France, see Steven Kale, *French Salons: High Society and Political Sociability from the Old Regime to the Revolution of 1848* (Baltimore: Johns Hopkins University Press, 2004), in particular on Staël: pp. 46–76; Antoine Lilti, *Le monde des salons, sociabilité et mondanité à Paris au XVIIIème siècle* (Paris: Fayard, 2005).

5. See, for example, Henri Guillemin, *Mme de Staël et Napoléon, ou Germaine et le caïd ingrat* (1966; Paris: Seuil, 1987; Henri Grange, *Benjamin Constant amoureux et républicain, 1795–1799* (Paris: Les Belles Lettres, 2004).

6. For an overview on the position of women in society in the eighteenth-century debate, see Dena Goodman and Kathleen Wellman, eds., *The Enlightenment,* Problems in European Civilization (Boston: Wadsworth, Cengage Learning, 2004); Sarah Knott and Barbara Taylor, eds., *Women, Gender and Enlightenment* (Houndmills, Basingstoke, Hampshire: Palgrave Macmillan, 2005). On Staël and feminism, see Mona Ozouf, *Les mots des femmes: essai sur la singularité française* (Paris: Fayard, 1995).

7. See the recent study by Paul Hamilton, *Realpoetik: European Romanticism and Literary Politics* (Oxford: Oxford University Press, 2013).

8. Angelica Goodden, *Madame de Staël: The Dangerous Exile* (Oxford: Oxford University Press, 2008). See also David Glass Larg, *Madame de Staël, la seconde vie (1800–1807)* (Paris: Champion, 1928).

9. Alphonse de Lamartine, *Histoire des Girondins* (1847–48), ed. Mona Ozouf, 2 vols. (Paris: Bouquins, 2014), 1:214.

10. Jacques Necker, *Compte rendu au roy* (1781), preface by Léonard Burnand (Geneva: Slatkine Reprints, 2005). For the episode of the anonymous letter, see Jean-Denis Bredin, *Une singulière famille: Jacques Necker, Suzanne Necker et Germaine de Staël* (Paris: Fayard, 2000), p. 109.

11. On Erik-Magnus de Staël: comtesse Jean de Pange, *Monsieur de Staël* (Paris: Editions des portiques, 1931).

12. On Necker's political views and career, see Henri Grange, *Les idées de Necker* (Paris: Klincksieck, 1974); Jean Egret, *Necker, ministre de Louis XVI, 1776–1790* (Paris: Champion, 1975); Robert D. Harris, *Necker: Reform Statesman of the Ancien Régime* (Berkeley: University of California Press, 1979); Ghislain de Diesbach, *Necker ou la faillite de la vertu* (Paris: Perrin, 2004); Jean-Denis Bredin, ed., *Jacques Necker, 1732–1804, banquier, ministre, écrivain: bicentenaire de sa mort, 1804–2004, Cahiers Staëliens,* no. 55 (2005).

13. On the Estates-General and their composition, see Roland Mousnier, *Les Institutions de la France sous la monarchie absolue, 1598–1789,* 2 vols. (Paris: PUF, 2005); François Furet and Mona Ozouf, eds., *A Critical Dictionary of the French Revolution* (Cambridge, MA: Harvard University Press, 1989), pp. 45–53; Colin Lucas, ed., *The French Revolution and the Formation of Modern Political Culture* (Oxford: Pergamon Press, 1988), vol. 2, *The Political Culture of the French Revolution,* pt. 1, pp. 63–85.

14. Quoted in Comte d'Haussonville, ed., *Madame de Staël et Monsieur Necker, d'après leur correspondance inédite* (Paris: Calmann-Lévy, 1925), p. 11.

15. Among the numerous works on Constant's life, see in particular Harold Nicolson, *Benjamin Constant* (London: Constable, 1948); John Cruickshank, *Benjamin Constant* (New York: Twayne, 1974); Kurt Kloocke, *Benjamin Constant, une biographie intellectuelle* (Geneva: Droz,

1984); and Dennis Wood, *Benjamin Constant: A Biography* (London: Routledge, 1993).

16. For a general assessment of the personal and intellectual relations between Staël and Constant, see Renée Winegarten, *Germaine de Staël & Benjamin Constant: A Dual Biography* (New Haven, CT: Yale University Press, 2008). Cf. Constant's own portrait and recollection of Staël in Benjamin Constant, *Portraits, mémoires, souvenirs*, ed. Hephraïm Harpaz (Paris: Champion; Geneva, Slatkine, 1992).

17. On Constant's vision of progress, see Biancamaria Fontana, *Benjamin Constant and the Post-Revolutionary Mind* (New Haven, CT: Yale University Press, 1991), pp. 29–47; Emeric Travers, *Benjamin Constant, les principes et l'histoire*, preface by Philippe Raynaud (Paris: Champion, 2005).

18. Benjamin Constant, *De la religion, considérée dans sa source, ses formes et ses devéloppements* (1825–30), ed. Tzvetan Todorov and Etienne Hofmann (Arles: Actes Sud, 1999).

19. On the evolution of the concept of "public opinion" in the eighteenth century, see Reinhart Koselleck, *Critique and Crisis: Enlightenment and the Pathogenesis of Modern Society* (Cambridge, MA: MIT Press, 1988); Mona Ozouf, "Le concept d'opinion publique au XVIIIème siècle," in *L'Homme régénéré: essais sur la Révolution française* (Paris: Gallimard, 1989), pp. 21–53.

20. Benjamin Constant, "De la liberté des anciens comparée à celle des modernes" (1819), "The Liberty of the Ancients Compared to That of the Moderns," in *Political Writings*, ed. Biancamaria Fontana (Cambridge: Cambridge University Press, 1988), pp. 307–28.

21. On Necker and public credit, see Michael Sonenscher, *Before the Deluge: Public Debt, Inequality, and the Intellectual Origins of the French Revolution* (Princeton, NJ: Princeton University Press, 2007), pp. 302–11.

CHAPTER I. INTERPRETING THE OPINION OF THE MAJORITY OF THE NATION (1789–91)

1. "A quels signes peut-on connoître quelle est l'opinion de la majorité de la nation?" ed. Florence Lotterie, in *Mme de Staël, Oeuvres complètes* (hereafter *OCS*) (Paris: Champion, 2009), 3.1:553–66.

2. Cf. letter of 12 July 1791 to her husband, in which she mentioned having completed "a very distinguished political work" that has never been identified. *CG*, 1:458–59.

3. On the sequence of events, see Michel Vovelle, *La chute de la monarchie (1787–1792)*, Nouvelle histoire de la France contemporaine, vol. 1 (Paris: Seuil, 1972); François Furet, "La Révolution de 1789," in *La Révolution française* (Paris: Gallimard, 2007), pp. 265–327; Michel Winock,

L'échec au roi (1791–1792) (Paris: Olivier Orban, 1990); Munro Price, *The Fall of the French Monarchy: Louis XVI, Marie Antoinette and the Baron de Breteuil* (London: Macmillan, 2002).

4. On the difficulty of reading French public opinion in 1791, cf. François Furet, "Les Girondins et la guerre, les débuts de l'assemblée législative," in *La Gironde et les Girondins*, ed. François Furet and Mona Ozouf (Paris: Payot, 1991), p. 201. On the subject of public opinion, see also Keith M. Baker, *Inventing the French Revolution: Essays on French Political Culture in the Eighteenth Century* (Cambridge: Cambridge University Press, 1990).

5. On Narbonne's life and career, see Emile Dard, *Un confident de l'Empereur, le comte de Narbonne, 1755–1813* (Paris: Plon, 1943). His relation with Staël is best documented by her letters to him; see the collection *Lettres à Narbonne*, ed. Georges Solovieff (Paris: Gallimard, 1960); also *CG*, 2/1, "Lettres inédites à Louis de Narbonne."

6. On this crucial turning point, see the admirable study by Mona Ozouf, *Varennes, la mort de la royauté* (Paris: Gallimard, 2005); also Timothy Tackett, *When the King Took Flight* (Cambridge, MA: Harvard University Press, 2003).

7. On the civil constitution of the clergy, see Timothy Tackett, *Religion, Revolution, and Regional Culture in Eighteeenth-Century France: The Ecclesiastical Oath of 1791* (Princeton, NJ: Princeton University Press, 1986). On Talleyrand's career in the Church, see Emmanuel de Waresquiel, *Talleyrand, le prince immobile* (Paris: Fayard, 2003), pp. 67–78 and 110–17.

8. Gwynne, *Madame de Staël*.

9. Ozouf, "Le concept d'opinion publique au XVIIIème siècle," in *L'Homme régénéré*, pp. 21–53; Keith Baker, ed., *The Old Regime and the French Revolution* (Chicago: University of Chicago Press, 1987).

10. Léonard Burnand, *Les pamphlets contre Necker: médias et imaginaire politique au XVIIIème siècle* (Paris: Garnier, 2009).

11. *OCS*, 1.1, ed. Anne Brousteau and Florence Lotterie, pp. 17–110, Lettre IV: "Sur les ouvrages politiques de Rousseau," p. 83.

12. "From What Signs," p. 559.

13. 11 November 1786, *CG*, 1:145. On Gustav III, see Claude J. Nordmann, *Gustave III, un démocrate couronné* (Lille: Presses Universitaires de Lille, 1986).

14. 16 August 1789, *CG*, 1:325.

15. 14 November 1790, *CG*, 1:391.

16. "bannières tranquilles"; quoted in Léonard Burnand, *Necker et l'opinion publique* (Paris: Champion; Geneva: Slatkine, 2004), p. 50.

17. 21 January 1789, *CG*, 1:274.

18. Robert Mauzi, *L'idée du bonheur dans la littérature et la pensée française au XVIIIème siècle* (1979; Paris: Albin Michel, 1994).

19. Biancamaria Fontana, *Montaigne's Politics: Authority and Governance in the "Essais"* (Princeton, NJ: Princeton University Press, 2008).

20. "Comment les lois peuvent contribuer à former les moeurs, les manières et le caractère d'une nation," pt. 3, bk. 19, chap. 27 of Montesquieu, *De l'esprit des loix; The Spirit of the Laws,* ed. A. Cohler, B. Miller, and H. Stone (Cambridge: Cambridge University Press, 1989), p. 325.

21. See chapter 6 below.

22. "From What Signs," p. 560. On the concept of "repos," see also Alexandre Koyré, *Etudes newtoniennes* (Paris: Gallimard, 1968).

23. Eric Thompson, *Popular Sovereignty and the French Constituent Assembly, 1789–1791* (Manchester: Manchester University Press, 1952), in particular on the veto, pp. 37–47; Harriet B. Applewhite, *Political Alignment in the French National Assembly, 1789–1791* (Baton Rouge: Lousiana State University Press, 1993); Timothy Tackett, *Becoming a Revolutionary: The Deputies of the French National Assembly and the Emergence of Revolutionary Culture (1789–1790)* (Princeton, NJ: Princeton University Press, 1996). Also Edna H. Lemay and Alison Patrick, eds., *Revolutionaries at Work: The Constituent Assembly 1789–1791* (Oxford: Voltaire Foundation, 1996).

24. Speech of 1 September 1789, in *Orateurs de la Révolution française,* vol. 1, *Les Constituants,* ed. François Furet and Ran Halévy (Paris: Gallimard, 1989), p. 675. On Mirabeau, see also François Furet's portrait (originally written as the introduction to his speeches) republished in *La Révolution française,* pp. 797–809.

25. Speech of 7 September, in Furet and Halévi, *Orateurs de la Révolution française,* p. 1020.

26. Tackett, *Becoming a Revolutionary,* p. 193.

27. Letter to M. de Staël, 2 or 3 September 1789, *CG,* 1:330–31. Cf. Madame de la Tour du Pin, *Mémoires, 1778–1815* (Paris: Mercure de France, 1979), p. 128, on the "bad" influence Alexandre de Lameth supposedly exercised on Germaine de Staël.

28. Letter to M. de Staël, 4 September, *CG,* 1:333.

29. Tackett, *Becoming a Revolutionary,* p. 194. See also the letter from Staël to Clermont-Tonnerre in which she declined some kind of amorous proposal on his part: *CG,* 1:355–56. On Stanislas de Clermont Tonnerre (who was assassinated during the massacres of September 1792), see Charles Du Bus, *Stanislas de Clermont-Tonnerre et l'échec de la révolution monarchique (1757–1792)* (Paris: Alcan, 1931).

30. Quoted by Jasinski in *CG,* 1:334, note 4. On Barnave's assessment of the political situation, see Antoine Barnave, *De la révolution et de la Constitution,* ed. François Furet and Patrice Gueniffey (Grenoble: Presses Universitaires de Grenoble, 1988).

31. *CG,* 1:335.

32. On Mounier and his political group, Jean Egret, *La révolution des notables: Mounier et les monarchiens, 1789* (Paris: Colin, 1989).

33. G. de Staël, *Considerations on the French Revolution*, pt. 2, pp. 173–284 (French ed., pp. 175–250). See C. J. Mitchell, "Political Divisions within the Legislative Assembly of 1791," *French Historical Studies* 13, no. 3 (Spring 1984): 356–89, and *The French Legislative Assembly of 1791* (Leiden: E. J. Brill, 1988); Norman Hampson, *Prelude to Terror* (Oxford: Oxford University Press, 1988).

34. Letter to an unidentified correspondent, 17 December 1790, *CG*, 1:416.

35. Letter to the comte de Gouvernet, 16 November 1790, *CG*, 1:395. On Staël and Gouvernet, see also *Seize lettres inédites de Mme de Staël au comte de Gouvernet, 1790–1791*, ed. Charles de Pomairois (Paris: Edition du temps présent, 1913).

36. On Jacobinism, see Alphonse Aulard, *Histoire politique de la Révolution française: origines et développement de la démocratie et de la république* (Paris: Colin, 1921); Augustin Cochin, *l'Esprit du jacobinisme* (Paris: PUF, 1979); Lucas, *The French Revolution,* vol. 2, pt. 5, pp. 289–387; Lucien Jaume, *Le discours Jacobin et la démocratie* (Paris: Fayard, 1989); Tamara Kondratieva, *Bolcheviks et jacobins: itinéraire des analogies* (Paris: Payot, 1989); Bernard Manin, "Saint-Just, la logique de la terreur," *Libre*, no. 6 (1979): 165–233.

37. *CG*, 1:394. On the question of implicating the Jacobins in government, there is an obvious convergence between Staël's analysis and that offered by Mirabeau in his secret notes to the court; cf. G. Chaussinand-Nogaret, *Mirabeau* (Paris: Seuil, 1982); Barbara Luttrell, *Mirabeau* (New York: Harvester Press, 1990).

38. To Gouvernet, 21 November 1790, *CG*, 1:339.

39. "From What Signs," p. 562.

40. *Considerations*, pp. 371–74 (French ed., pp. 313–15).

41. "Oraison funèbre de M. de Mirabeau, prononcée par M. l'abbé Serutti," suivi du discours de M. l'évêque d'Autun, 4 avril 1791 (Paris: Imprimerie Labarre, 1791); cf. Fairweather, *Madame de Staël*, p. 116.

42. "From What Signs," pp. 562–63.

43. Etienne Dumont, *Souvenirs sur Mirabeau et sur les deux premières assemblées législatives* (Paris: PUF, 1951); see also J. Bénétruy, *L'atelier de Mirabeau: quatre proscrits genevois dans la tourmente révolutionnaire* (Geneva: A. Jullien, 1962).

44. See Chaussinand-Nogaret, *Mirabeau*, pp. 138–39; Gouverneur Morris, *Journal (1789–1792)*, ed. Anne Cary-Morris and Ernest Pariset (Paris: Mercure de France, 2002), pp. 105–8.

45. Roberto Martucci, *L'Ossessione costituente: forma di governo e costituzione nella rivoluzione francese* (Bologna: Il Mulino, 2001).

46. *Considerations*, pp. 266–67 (French ed., pp. 237–38).

47. "From What Signs," p. 565.

48. In May 1791 the Constituent Assembly had voted a measure, proposed by Robespierre, that declared all its members no longer eligible for the new assembly. See François Furet and Ran Halévi, *La Monarchie républicaine, La Constitution de 1791* (Paris: Fayard, 1996), pp. 227–28.

49. 1 June 1791, *CG,* 1:441.

50. "come out the winner," 16 September 1791, *CG,* 1:492–93.

51. 15 October 1791, *CG,* 1:501.

52. *Considerations,* pt. 2, pp. 173–284 (French ed., pp. 175–250).

53. Hampson, *Prelude to Terror;* Michael Sonenscher, *Sans-Culottes: An Eighteenth-Century Emblem in the French Revolution* (Princeton, NJ: Princeton University Press, 2008); Price, *The Fall of the French Monarchy.*

54. Tackett, *Becoming a Revolutionary;* Mitchell, "Political Divisions within the Legislative Assembly"; Alison Patrick, *The Men of the First French Republic: Political Arguments in the National Convention of 1792* (Baltimore: Johns Hopkins University Press, 1972); see also Daniel L. Wick, *A Conspiracy of Well-Intentioned Men: The Society of Thirty and the French Revolution* (New York: Garland Publishing, 1987), on the attempt to give some structure to the "patriot" party.

55. Later on Staël would rely on the analysis of the defects of French assemblies in the comments edited by Etienne Dumont from the manuscripts of Jeremy Bentham: Jeremy Bentham, *Tactique des assemblées législatives,* ed. Etienne Dumont (1816; Charleston, SC: Nabu Press, 2010).

CHAPTER 2. THE VIEW FROM THE EXECUTIVE (1792)

1. The Legislative Assembly was in existence from the beginning of September 1791 to 20 September 1792. See Mitchell, *The French Legislative Assembly of 1791;* Edna Lemay and Mona Ozouf, eds., *Dictionnaire des législateurs, 1791–1792* (Ferney-Voltaire: Centre international d'études du XVIIIème siècle, 2007).

2. John Isbell, "Madame de Staël, Ministre de la Guerre? Les discours de Narbonne devant l'Assemblée legislative," *Annales Historiques de la Révolution française* 307, no. 1 (1997): 93–104.

3. George Michon, *Histoire du parti feuillant: Adrien Duport* (Paris: Payot, 1924); Henri Leclercq, *Feuillants et Girondins (août 1791–20 avril 1792)* (Paris: Librairie Letouzey, 1940); Francesco Dendena, *I nostri maledetti scranni: il movimento fogliante tra la fuga di Varennes e la caduta della monarchia (1791–1792)* (Milan: Guerini e associati, 2013).

4. *Considerations,* pp. 308–9 (French ed., p. 269). On Narbonne's political and military career, see Dard, *Un confidant de l'Empereur.*

5. 11 November 1790, *CG,* 1:395.

6. On the general structure of the constitution of 1791, see Jacques

Godechot, *Les constitutions de la France depuis 1789* (Paris: Flammarion, 1979), pp. 21–32; Furet and Halévy, *La Monarchie républicaine*.

7. In Furet and Halévi, *Orateurs de la Révolution française*, pp. 575–76.

8. On elections during the Revolution, see Patrice Gueniffey, *Le nombre et la raison: la Révolution française et les élections* (Paris: Ecole des hautes études en sciences sociales, 1993); Malcolm Crook, *Elections in the French Revolution: An Apprenticeship of Democracy, 1789–1799* (Cambridge: Cambridge University Press, 2002.)

9. Quoted in Leclerq, *Feuillants et Girondins*, p. 7.

10. "notre conseil," letter of 12 December 1791, *CG*, 1:522.

11. *CG*, 1:507, note 2.

12. Morris, *Journal*, pp. 304–5.

13. On the structure of ministerial departments under Louis XVI's monarchy, see Mousnier, *Les institutions de la France*, 2:173.

14. *CG*, 1:500–528.

15. This was not just a pretext: the queen was clearly anxious to have a trustworthy man in control of the Parisian regiments; see Alma Söderhjelm, *Marie Antoinette et Barnave, Correspondance secrete (juillet 1791–janvier 1792)* (Paris: Colin, 1934), in particular the letter from the queen to Barnave of 4 December 1791, p. 200.

16. Barnave to the queen, ibid., p. 160.

17. 14 November 1791, *CG*, 1:517–18.

18. Edgar Quinet, *La révolution*, preface by Claude Lefort, 2 vols. (Paris: Belin, 1987), 1:347.

19. 14 November 91, *CG*, 1:518.

20. Letter of 7 December 1791, Söderhjelm, *Marie Antoinette et Barnave*, p. 227. On Barnave's role, see also François Furet, ed., *Terminer la Révolution: Mounier et Barnave dans la révolution française* (Grenoble: Presses de l'Université de Grenoble, 1990).

21. Letter of 18–21 November 1791, *CG*, 1:519.

22. On the transition in the running of the French army, see Albert Latreille, *L'oeuvre militaire de la révolution, l'armée et la nation à la fin de l'ancien régime: les derniers ministres de la guerre de la monarchie* (Paris: Chapelot, 1914).

23. *CG*, 1:492–96.

24. 21 December 1791, *CG*, 1:528.

25. *CG*, 1:493.

26. *Des circonstances actuelles*, in *OCS*, 3.1:420, note.

27. Price, *The Fall of the French Monarchy*, chap. 6; Michon, *Histoire du parti feuillant*.

28. *CG*, 1:518, note 5.

29. Jacques Necker, *Du pouvoir exécutif dans les grands états*, 2 vols.

(Paris, 1792); English translation *On Executive Power in Large States*, 2 vols. (London, 1792).

30. On these issues, see Michel Troper, *La séparation des pouvoirs dans l'histoire constitutionnelle française*, preface by Charles Eisenmann (Paris: Librairie générale de droit et de jurisprudence, 1973); more specifically on Necker's and Staël's position, cf. Biancamaria Fontana, "The Absent Power: The Restoration of the Executive from Necker to Constant," in *Les usages de la séparation des pouvoirs*, ed. Sandrine Baume and Biancamaria Fontana (Paris: Michel Houdiard, 2008), pp. 98–113.

31. Necker, *Du pouvoir exécutif dans les grands états*, vol. 1, chap. 11, pp. 189–205.

32. "Observations sur le ministère anglais," *Gazette de France*, 9 March 1792.

33. Ibid., p. 333.

34. *Gazette universelle*, 13 March 1792, pp. 293–94. Cf. Alain Laquièze, "Le modèle anglais et la responsabilité ministerielle selon le groupe de Coppet," in *Coppet, Creuset de l'esprit libéral*, ed. Lucien Jaume, Colloque 1998 (Aix: Presses Universitaires d'Aix-Marseille, 2000), pp. 157–76.

35. Peter Hennessy, *The Prime Minister: The Office and Its Holders since 1945* (London: Palgrave Macmillan, 2001), p. 46. On the evolution of the role of prime minister, see also Robert Blake, *The Office of Prime Minister* (London: British Academy, 1975). Cf. Walter Bagehot, *The English Constitution*, (1865–67), ed. R.H.S. Crossman (London: Fontana-Collins, 1976).

36. On the Girondins, see Albert Mathiez, *Girondins et Montagnards* (Paris: Firmin Didot, 1930); Bernardine Melchior-Bonnet, *Les Girondins* (Paris: Tallandier, 1989); Gary Kates, *The Cercle Social, the Girondins, and the French Revolution* (Princeton, NJ: Princeton University Press, 1985). Also, Marc Frayssinet, *Les idées politiques des Girondins* (Toulouse: Vialelle et Perry, 1903); Hélène Tierchant, *Hommes de la Gironde, ou la liberté éclairée* (Bordeaux: Dossiers d'Aquitaine, 1993).

37. In *Oeuvres complètes de Mme la baronne de Staël*, ed. Auguste de Staël, 17 vols. (Paris: Treuttel & Wurtz, 1820–21), 13:275–317.

38. Ibid., p. 289.

39. Cf. Biancamaria Fontana, "Les deux faces du despotisme: gloire, ambition et personnalisation de la politique chez Germaine de Staël, " in *Despotes et despotismes dans les oeuvres du Groupe de Coppet, Cahiers Staëliens*, no. 65 (November 2015).

40. The most noticeable example being Furet, "Les girondins et la guerre," in Furet and Ozouf, *La Gironde et les Girondins*, pp. 189–205. See also H.-A. Goetz-Bernstein, *La politique extérieure de Brissot et des Girondins* (Paris: Hachette, 1912).

41. See Jasinski's commentary in *CG*, 2:305–58.

42. H. Arnold Barton, *Scandinavia in the Revolutionary Era, 1760–1815*

(Minneapolis: University of Minnesota Press, 1986); Gunnar von Proschwitz, ed., *Gustav III par ses lettres* (Stockholm: Touzot, 1986).

43. 16 September 1791, *CG*, 1:492–93.

44. On Gustav III's assassination, see Alexis-François Artaud de Montor, *Histoire de l'assassinat de Gustave III, roi de Suède, par un officier polonais, témoin oculaire* (Paris: Forget, 1797).

45. 25 October 1791, *CG*, 1:508.

46. *Archives parlementaires*, 35:633.

47. 12 December 1791, *CG*, 1:523.

48. The suggestion is made by Michelet; cf. Jules Michelet, *Histoire de la révolution française*, 2 vols. (Paris: Robert Laffont, 1979), vol. 1, chap. 5, pp. 659–78.

49. 12 December 1791, *CG*, 1:524–25.

50. On Talleyrand's diplomatic mission, see Georges Pallain, ed., *Correspondance diplomatique de Talleyrand*, 4 vols. (Paris: Plon; London: Bentley; Leipzig; Brockhouse, 1889–91), vol. 1, *La mission de Talleyrand à Londres en 1792*; see also Jeremy Black, *British Foreign Policy in an Age of Revolution, 1783–1793* (Cambridge: Cambridge University Press, 1994), pp. 385–86.

51. Lady Blennerhassett, *Madame de Staël and Her Influence in Politics and Literature*, 3 vols. (London: Chapman & Hall, 1889), 2:81–86.

52. 6 March 1792, *Archives parlementaires*, 39:422. Cf. also the commentaries by Jasinski in *CG*, 2:305–58.

53. On the situation of the French army and the beginning of the war, see Samuel Scott, *The Response of the Royal Army to the French Revolution* (Oxford: Clarendon Press, 1978), pp. 151–68; T.C.W. Blanning, *The Origins of the French Revolutionary Wars* (London: Longman, 1986), chaps. 3 and 4; cf. Goetz-Bernstein, *La politique extérieure de Brissot et des Girondins*.

54. P. 50, note 12.

55. 15 October 1791, *CG*, 1:503.

CHAPTER 3. POLITICS AS PROPAGANDA:
DEFENDING THE QUEEN (1793)

1. *Réflexions sur le procès de la Reine, par une femme*, in *OCS*, 3.1, introd. by Jean-Pierre Perchellet, pp. 17–66. See also the edition by Monique Cottret (Paris: Les Editions de Paris, 2006), which includes an extensive "Postface" by the editor.

2. Cf. *CG*, 2/1:311–12. A surviving fragment of this work—*Projet d'ouvrage sur les constitutionnels*—with an introduction by Catriona Seth can be found in *OCS*, 3.1:689–94.

3. The best account of these dramatic events is the one provided by

Staël herself in the *Considerations*, pt. 3, chap. 10: "Private anecdotes," pp. 280–86 (French ed., pp. 324–32).

4. Linda Kelly, *Juniper Hall, an English Refuge from the French Revolution* (London: Weidenfeld and Nicolson, 1991).

5. On the deterioration of Staël's relations with her mother, see in particular her letter to Narbonne of 11 October 1792, *CG*, 2/1:43–45.

6. On the Swedish context, see Erik-Magnus de Staël-Holstein, *Corréspondence diplomatique* (1783–99), ed. L. Leouzon Le Duc (Paris: Hachette, 1881); *Madame de Staël et la Suède*, special issue of *Cahiers Staëliens*, no. 39 (1988).

7. Letter to Narbonne, 8 November 1793, *CG*, 2/1:203. On the reaction of the French police, see Diesbach, *Madame de Staël*, p. 138.

8. The source of these remarks is Fersen's diary, in which he also described *Reflections on the Trial* as "useless and insignificant," and he described as "ridicule" the letter Narbonne had sent him to accompany a copy of the pamphlet; quoted by Jasinski, *CG*, 2/2:468.

9. *CG*, 2/2:481–83. On Isabelle de Charrière and her relations with Staël and (especially) Benjamin Constant, see Dorothy Farnum, *The Dutch Divinity: A Biography of Madame de Charrière, 1740–1805* (London: Jarrolds, 1959); Arnold de Kerchove, *Une amie de Benjamin Constant: Belle de Charrière* (Paris: Editions de la nouvelle revue critique, 1937).

10. Letter of 16 September 1791, *CG*, 1:495. On Staël's exchanges with Rosenstein, see also Norman King, "Politique, littérature, diplomatie: lettres nouvelles de Germaine de Staël à Nils von Rosenstein," *Cahiers Staëliens*, no. 42 (1990–91): 75–107.

11. In her own words, letter to Narbonne, 5 October 1792, *CG*, 2/1:39.

12. Biancamaria Fontana, "Mon triste écrit sur la Reine: Germaine de Staël et le fantôme de la révolution," *Cahiers Staëliens*, n.s., no. 61 (2010–11): 197–208.

13. Paris: Voland, 1792; later incorporated in his work of 1796, *De la révolution française* (Paris: J. Drisonnier). *A short extract from M. Necker's pamphlet to the French nation on the trial of Louis XVI* (London, 1793) is available in an electronic version. See also Albert Soboul, ed., *Le procès de Louis XVI*, Collection archives (Paris: Gallimard-Julliard, 1973); David P. Jordan, *The King's Trial: The French Revolution vs. Louis XVI* (Berkeley: University of California Press, 1979); Michael Walzer, ed., *Regicide and Revolution: Speeches at the Trial of Louis XVI* (Cambridge: Cambridge University Press, 1974). On the queen's imprisonment and trial, see Georges Lenôtre, *La captivité et la mort de Marie-Antoinette: les Feuillants, le Temple, la conciergerie: d'après des relations des témoins oculaires et des documents inédits* (Paris: Perrin, 1928).

14. *Reflections on the Trial*, p. 33.

15. Edmund Burke, *Reflections on the Revolution in France*, ed. W. B.

Todd, introd. by Conor Cruise O'Brien (Harmondsworth: Penguin Books, 1968).

16. Cf. Germaine de Staël, *Delphine*, in *OCS*, 2.2, ed. Simone Balayé and Lucia Omacini, with the description of the "dark prison" in which Delphine and Léonce spend the last night before his execution in the concluding chapter. On the gothic novel, see Maurice Lévy, *Le roman 'gothique' anglais, 1764–1824* (Paris: Albin Michel, 1995), pp. 608–12; Annie Le Brun, *Les Châteaux de la subversion* (Paris: Gallimard, 1982); Catriona Seth, ed., *Imaginaires gothiques, aux sources du roman noir français* (Paris: Desjonquères, 2010).

17. *Jane Grey, tragédie en cinq actes*, in *Oeuvres complètes de la Baronne de Staël*, ed. Auguste de Staël, 18 vols. (Paris: Trottel & Wurtz, 1820–21), 17:128–210.

18. David J. Denby, *Sentimental Narrative and the Social Order in France, 1760–1820* (Cambridge: Cambridge University Press, 1994).

19. Letter to Narbonne, 23 October 1793, *CG*, 2/1:193–94, and in a similar tone also the letter to the same of 11 November 1793, *CG*, 2/1:205–6.

20. Burke, *Reflections on the Revolution in France*, p. 169.

21. *Reflections on the Trial*, p. 48. Staël was very interested in the subject of suicide, to which she dedicated an essay, published in 1812: it shows that she was generally against the Stoic exaltation of suicide, but (as a sincere Christian) she tried to find justifications for taking one's life, against the standard Christian arguments set forth to condemn this act. See *Refléxions sur le suicide*, ed. Florence Lotterie, in *OCS*, 1.1:339–95.

22. On Rousseau's influence on Staël and her entourage, see Florence Lotterie and Georges Poisson, eds., *Jean-Jacques Rousseau devant Coppet* (Geneva: Slatkine, 2012).

23. *Reflections on the Trial* p. 54; cf. *On the Influence of Passions*, p. 294: "A single sentiment serves as guide in all situations, it is pity: what other disposition could be more effective in sustaining others and oneself?" Cf. Denby, *Sentimental Narrative and the Social Order in France*, pp. 194–239.

24. *Reflections on the Trial*, pp. 35–36.

25. Letter to Narbonne, 24 September 1792, *CG*, 2/1:28.

26. This work is discussed in chapter 6 below.

27. Letter of 16 November 1791, *CG*, 1:494.

28. On the theme of boredom in eighteenth-century French fiction, see Biancamaria Fontana, *Du boudoir à la Révolution, Laclos et les Liaisons dangereuses dans leur siècle* (Marseilles: Agone, 2013).

29. Letter of 18–19 November 1791, *CG*, 1:519.

30. *Reflections on the Trial*, p. 43.

31. "Comment les lois peuvent contribuer à former les moeurs, les

manières et le caractère d'une nation," pt. 3, bk. 19, chap. 27 of Montesquieu, *De l'esprit des loix*; Montesquieu, *The Spirit of the Laws*, p. 325.

32. *Reflections on the Trial*, p. 44.

33. Ibid., p. 48.

34. Cf. David Hume, *Essays, Moral, Political and Literary*, ed. Eugene F. Miller (Indianapolis: Liberty Classics, 1985), "Of parties in general," pp. 54–63.

35. *Reflections on the Trial*, p. 44.

36. Ibid., p. 54.

37. Ibid., p. 49.

38. Letter of 26 January 1794, *CG*, 2/2:559.

39. *Reflections on the Trial*, p. 54.

40. See, for example, Cottret, "Postface" to *Réflexions sur le procès de la Reine, par une femme*, pp. 45–116.

41. Cf. André Castelot, *Le procès de Marie-Antoinette* (Paris: Perrin, 1993), pp. 125–29, and p. 214 for bibliographical references to Lord Grenville's intelligence sources.

42. Hébert was actually guillotined in 1794; Cambon died in exile in Brussels after the Restoration. On the individual destiny of the members of the committee, see R. R. Palmer, *Twelve Who Ruled: The Year of the Terror* (1941), introd. by Isser Woloch (Princeton, NJ: Princeton University Press, 2005); on the attitude toward death of revolutionary militants, see Michel Biard, *La liberté ou la mort: mourir en député, 1792–1795* (Paris: Tallandier, 2015).

43. *Reflections on the Trial*, p. 54.

44. *CG*, 2/2:622.

45. Biancamaria Fontana, "Democracy and the French Revolution," in *Democracy: The Unfinished Journey, 508 BC to 1993 AD*, ed. John Dunn (Oxford: Oxford University Press, 1992), pp. 107–24; Lucas, *The French Revolution*, vol. 2, pt. 5, pp. 289–387; Jaume, *Le discours Jacobin*.

CHAPTER 4. ADDRESSING WILLIAM PITT (1794)

1. *Considerations*, p. 375 (French ed., p. 316).

2. On Adolphe Ribbing, in addition to the letters in the *CG*, see Madame de Staël, *Lettres à Ribbing*, preface by the comtesse Jean de Pange, ed. Simone Balayé (Paris: Gallimard, 1960); see also Germaine de Staël, "Conclusion proposée aux mémoires de Ribbing," ed. Catriona Seth, in *OCS*, 3.1:611–20. See also Robert Nisbet Bain, *Gustav III and His Contemporaries (1742–1792), an Overlooked Chapter in 18th Century History* (New York: Bergman, 1970).

3. Richmond Laurin Hawkins, *Madame de Staël and the United States* (1930; New York: Kraus Reprints, 1966).

4. *Réflexions sur la paix, addressées à M. Pitt et aux Français*, ed. Lucien Jaume, in *OCS*, 3.1:67–119.

5. Jean Tulard, *Les Thermidoriens* (Paris: Fayard, 2005), pp. 248–49.

6. Letter of 4 August 1794, *CG*, 3/1:80–83.

7. Maximilien de Robespierre, *Discours et rapports à la Convention*, ed. Marc Bouloiseau (Paris: Union générale d'éditions, 1988).

8. Letter to Ribbing, 1–2 September 1794, *CG*, 3/1:103. On the 1792 revolution in Geneva, see Louis Binz, ed., *Regards sur la Révolution genevoise, 1792–1798* (Geneva: Droz; Paris: Champion, 1992).

9. 8 October 1794, *CG*, 3/1:148–49.

10. 2 December 1794, *CG*, 3/1:191.

11. On the issue of counterrevolution, see Jean Tulard, ed., *La Contrerévolution, origines, histoire, postérité* (Paris: Perrin, 1990).

12. Staël's assessment coincides with that of another writer, Choderlos de Laclos, who used the same argument to claim that France must pursue the war in order to save the Revolution: Pierre-Ambroise Choderlos de Laclos, "De la guerre et de la paix," in *Oeuvres complétes*, ed. Laurent Versini (Paris: Gallimard, 1979), pp. 701–18; see also Fontana, *Du boudoir à la Révolution*, pp. 69–72.

13. Ghislain de Diesbach, *Histoire de l'émigration: 1789–1814* (Paris: Perrin, 2007).

14. *Reflections on Peace*, pp. 90–93.

15. Ibid., p. 85.

16. Ibid., p. 87.

17. Ibid.

18. *Considerations*, p. 372 (French ed., pp. 313–14).

19. *Reflections on Peace*, p. 88. On Robespierre, see Ruth Scurr, *Fatal Purity: Robespierre and the French Revolution* (New York: Henry Holt, 2006); Colin Haydon and William Doyle, eds., *Robespierre* (Cambridge: Cambridge University Press, 2006).

20. *Reflections on Peace*, p. 87.

21. Ibid., p. 91.

22. Ibid., p. 89.

23. Ibid., p. 88.

24. Ibid., p. 89.

25. Ibid., p. 67.

26. Ibid., p. 85.

27. 23 April 1793, *CG*, 2/2:429.

28. On the actual circumstances of the Whig Party at the time, see Francis O'Gorman, *The Whig Party and the French Revolution* (London: Macmillan, 1967); L. G. Mitchell, *Charles James Fox and the Disintegration of the Whig Party: 1782–1794* (London: Oxford University Press, 1971); Stanley Ayling, *Fox: The Life of Charles James Fox* (London: John Murray,

1991), pp. 185–222; Kathryn Chittick, *The Language of Whiggism, Liberty and Patriotism* (London: Pickering and Chatto, 2010).

29. On this marriage plan, cf. Bredin, *Une singulière famille*, pp. 156–57; Fairweather, *Madame de Staël*, p. 46; and Staël's letter of 11 May 1787, *CG*, 1:163–69.

30. John Ehrman, *The Younger Pitt* (1969; London, Constable, 1996); Eric J. Evans, *William Pitt the Younger* (London: Routledge, 1999); Michael Duffy, *The Younger Pitt* (Harlow, UK: Longman, 2000); William Hague, *William Pitt the Younger, a Biography* (London: Harper, 2005).

31. William Pitt (1759–1806), *The War Speeches of William Pitt the Younger*, ed. R. Coupland (Oxford: Clarendon Press, 1940); Jennifer Mori, *William Pitt and the French Revolution, 1785–1795* (Edinburgh: Keele University Press, 1997).

32. *Reflections on Peace*, p. 105.

33. Peter Jupp, *Lord Grenville: 1759–1834* (Oxford: Clarendon Press, 1985).

34. 25 April 1793, *CG*, 2/2:424.

35. 23 December 1793, *CG*, 2/2:538.

36. 6 February 1793, *CG*, 2/2:563; Staël noted that after the opening of Parliament the opposition had 44 votes to 270; in January 1794, 59 to 277.

37. Speech of June 1794, cf. Mitchell, *Charles James Fox and the Disintegration of the Whig Party, 1782–1794*, p. 235.

38. See chapter 9 below.

39. *Reflections on Peace*, pp. 100–101.

40. Ibid., p. 107.

41. Ibid., p. 103.

42. Ibid., p. 102.

43. Ibid., p. 105.

44. Peter Douglas Brown, *William Pitt, Earl of Chatham: The Great Commoner* (London: Allen and Unwin, 1978).

45. *Morning Chronicle*, 8 July 1794, p. 211.

46. Letter of 18 August 1794, Quoted in O'Gorman, *The Whig Party and the French Revolution*, p. 212.

47. Both Charles Fox and Lord Lansdowne wrote to Staël praising her text: cf. her letters to Erik-Magnus de Staël of 8 May 1795, *CG*, 3/1:322–24, and to Adolphe Ribbing, 15 May 1795, *CG*, 3/1:330–31.

48. Otto Karmin, *Sir Francis d'Ivernois: 1757–1842: sa vie, son oeuvre et son temps* (Geneva: Revue historique de la révolution française et de l'Empire, 1820); see also Otto Karmin, ed., "Une lettre inédite de Sir Francis d'Ivernois sur Mme de Staël," *Bulletin de l'Institut national genevois* 42 (1914).

49. Francis d'Ivernois, *Reflections on the War. In Response to the Reflections on Peace addressed to Mr Pitt and the French Nation* (trans. from the

original French), (London, June 1795), p. 9. See also Edmund Burke, *Letters on a Regicide Peace* (London: E. J. Paine, 1795).

50. 8 November 1794, *CG*, 3/1:178.

51. Fairweather, *Madame de Staël*, p. 207.

52. 3 May 1795, *CG*, 3/1:317.

53. 5 May 1795, *CG*, 3/1:318–22.

CHAPTER 5. THE ADVENT OF MODERN LIBERTY (1795)

1. *CG*, 3/2:2–3.

2. 26 May 1795, *CG*, 3/2:4–5.

3. Quoted in Kloocke, *Benjamin Constant*, p. 61.

4. See the description Constant provided of the different "tribes" that crowded Staël's salon, in Benjamin Constant, *Ecrits et discours politiques*, ed. Olivier Pozzo di Borgo, 2 vols. (Paris: Pauvert, 1964–65), 1:8–9; On the role of Staël's salon at this particular time, see Bronislaw Baczko, "Utopie salonnière et réalisme politique," in *Politiques de la Révolution française* (Paris: Gallimard, 2008), pp. 341–491.

5. *Réflexions sur la paix intérieure*, ed. Lucien Jaume, in *OCS,*, 3.1.121–82.

6. Staël considered that those who had emigrated before the massacres of September 1792, i.e., before the Revolution took a violent turn, had deliberately chosen to exclude themselves from their own country.

7. *Reflections on Domestic Peace*, p. 139.

8. Ibid., p. 148.

9. Ibid., p. 155.

10. Ibid., p. 158.

11. Ibid., p. 135.

12. Ibid., p. 137.

13. Ibid., p. 168.

14. Ibid.

15. Ibid., p. 169.

16. Ibid., p. 172.

17. On Sieyès's views on representation, see Jean-Denis Bredin, *Sieyès, la clé de la révolution française* (Paris: Flammarion, 1988); Paul Bastid, *Sieyès et sa pensée* (Geneva: Slatkine, 1978); Pasquale Pasquino, *Sieyès et l'invention de la constitution en France* (Paris: O. Jacob, 1998); also, Paul Bastide, ed., *Les discours de Sieyès dans les débats constitutionnels de l'an III:2 et 18 thermidor* (Paris: Hachette, 1939).

18. On the vast debate on modern liberty, Isaiah Berlin, "Two Concepts of Liberty," in *Four Essays on Liberty* (Oxford: Oxford University Press, 1969); Stephen Holmes, *Benjamin Constant and the Making of Modern Liberalism* (New Haven, CT: Yale University Press, 1984); Quentin Skinner, *Liberty before Liberalism* (Cambridge: Cambridge University

Press, 1998); Samuel Fleischacker, *A Third Concept of Liberty: Judgment and Freedom in Kant and Adam Smith* (Princeton, NJ: Princeton University Press, 1999); Philip Pettit, *Republicanism: A Theory of Freedom and Government* (Oxford: Oxford University Press, 1999); see also Biancamaria Fontana, introduction to Constant, *Political Writings*.

19. *Reflections on Domestic Peace*, p. 154.

20. Ibid., pp. 164–65.

21. Ibid., p. 167.

22. See in particular for a summary of Necker's views, Jacques Necker, *Réflexions philosophiques sur l'égalité*, ed. Jean-Fabien Spitz (Paris: Les Belles Lettres, 2005).

23. In a letter to François de Pange, Staël described the reluctance of people living outside Paris to accept any form of payment in "new" money, not just the assignats, but also the new coinage: "Everything is easily arranged in the mind of the people: they are all ready to buy the properties of the émigrés, but they refuse republican coins as they believe they were made by melting down the Church's plate." 27 December 1795, *CG*, 3/2:91–93.

24. *Reflections on Domestic Peace*, p. 169.

25. Ibid., p. 176.

26. 12 September 1795, *CG*, 3/2:51.

27. Michel Troper, *Terminer la Révolution: la Constitution de 1795* (Paris: Fayard, 2006), pp. 11–90.

28. Gérard Cornac and Jean-Pierre Machelon, eds., *La Constitution de l'an III: Boissy d'Anglas et la naissance du libéralisme constitutionnel* (Paris: PUF, 1999).

29. 5 May 1795, *CG*, 3/1:321.

30. Cf. Sieyès's speech to the Convention: "Since its acceptance [of the constitution of 1793] has not been made in this room, but in the people's assemblies, it is respectable and cannot be attacked." Quoted in Bredin, *Sieyès, la clé de la révolution française*, pp. 357–58, See also Troper, *Terminer la Révolution*, pp. 23–42.

31. *Idées pour une déclaration des droits*, ed. Lucien Jaume, *OCS*, 3.1:629–44.

32. Ibid., p. 641.

33. *Reflections on Domestic Peace*, p. 147.

34. 5 June 1795, *CG*, 3/2:12–13.

35. *Reflections on Peace*, p. 163.

36. See Ruth Scurr, "The Doctrine of the Separation of Powers in Pierre-Louis Roederer's 'Cours d'organisation sociale' (1793) and 'Du Gouvernement' (1795)," in Baume and Fontana, *Les usages de la séparation des pouvoirs*, pp. 83–97.

37. 9 June 1795, *CG*, 3/2:14–17.

38. 24 November 1796, *CG*, 3/2:274–75; for a very similar formulation, see *De l'Influence des passions*, in *OCS*, 3.1:275.

39. *Considerations*, p. 380 (French ed., p. 319).

40. On Staël and the 1795 constitution, see Basil Munteanu, *Les idées politiques de Madame de Staël et la constitution de l'an III* (Paris: Les Belles Lettres, 1931); Jaume, *Coppet, creuset de l'esprit libéral*; Aurelian Craiutu, "Faces of Moderation: Mme de Staël's politics during the Directory," *Jus Politicum*, no. 6 (2008). Cf. also Staël's commentary on Necker's views on the subject, "Examen de la Constitution de l'an III, Extrait du dernier Ouvrage de M.Necker," ed. Léonard Burnand, in *OCS*, 3.1:657–64.

41. *CG*, 32:73.

42. 10 October 1795, *CG*, 3/2:78.

43. 31 May–2 June 1795, *CG*, 3/2:6–8; republished in *OCS*, 3.1:627–28; the writer was in fact twenty-nine.

44. 26 September 1795, *CG*, 3/2:69.

45. Charles de Lacretelle, *Dix années d'épreuves pendant la Révolution, mémoires* (Paris: Tallandier, 2011), p. 152.

46. Henri Guillemin, *Benjamin Constant muscadin: 1795–1798* (Paris: Gallimard, 1958).

47. 24 October 1795, *CG*, 3/2:86–87.

CHAPTER 6. CONDEMNED TO CELEBRITY: THE INFLUENCE OF PASSIONS (1796)

1. *De la force du gouvernment actuel de la France, et de la nécessité de s'y rallier*, ed. Philippe Raynaud (Paris: Flammarion, 1988), pp. 27–89.

2. On Staël's complex relation to future projects and expectations, see George Poulet, "Madame de Staël," in *Etudes sur le temps humain/4* (Paris: Plon, 1964), pp. 193–212.

3. *De l'Influence des passions sur le bonheur des individus et des nations*, in *OCS*, 1.1:111–302. See also the pocket edition with a preface by Chantal Thomas (Paris: Payot Rivages, 2000). An anonymous English translation was published in London in 1798 with the title *A Treatise on the influence of the passions, upon the happiness of individuals and of nations, Illustrated by striking references to the Principal Events and Characters that have Distinguished the French Revolution* (London, George Cawthorn); this translation is available in electronic format.

4. On the notion of celebrity in the eighteenth-century debate, see George Minois, *Histoire de la célébrité, les trompettes de la renommée* (Paris: Perrin, 2012), and Antoine Lilti, *Figures publiques: l'invention de la célébrité, 1750–1850* (Paris: Fayard, 2014).

5. Biancamaria Fontana, "Madame de Staël, le gouvernement des passions et la Révolution française," in *Actes du IV Colloque de Coppet* (Lausanne: Jean Touzot, 1988), pp. 175–81; Tili Boon Cuillé and Karyna

Szmurlo, eds., *Staël's Philosophy of the Passions: Sensibility, Society, and the Sister Arts* (Lewisburg, PA: Bucknell University Press, 2013); the work is discussed in a number of general studies on the subject of emotions and the morality of sentiments; see: Denby, *Sentimental Narrative and Social Order in France*, pp. 194–239; Martin S. Staum, *Minerva's Message: Stabilizing the French Revolution* (Montreal: McGill-Queen's University Press, 1996), pp. 95–153; William M. Reddy, *The Navigation of Feeling: A Framework for the History of Emotions* (Cambridge: Cambridge University Press, 2001), pp. 142–210.

6. On the eighteenth-century French background, see Mauzi, *L'idée du bonheur dans la littérature et la pensée française au XVIIIème siècle*; Jacques Domenech, *L'Ethique des lumières, les fondements de la morale dans la philosophie française du XVIIIème siècle* (Paris: Vrin, 1989); Michel Meyer, *Le philosophe et les passions* (Paris: Livre de poche, 1991).

7. Adam Smith, *The Theory of Moral Sentiments* (1759), ed. D. D. Raphael and A. L. Macfie (Oxford: Clarendon Press, 1991). See also John Reeder, ed., *On Moral Sentiments: Contemporary Responses to Adam Smith* (Bristol: Thoemmes Press, 1997). In an undated letter (probably written in the early months of 1796), Staël asked one of the professors at the Académie of Lausanne for a copy of the French translation, *Théorie des sentiments moraux*; see *CG*, 3/2:148–49 (possibly one of the earlier ones published in the 1760s and 1770s; the one by Sophie Grouchy de Condorcet was published only in 1798).

8. *Of the Influence of Passions*, p. 134.

9. Ibid., p. 135.

10. Ibid., p. 136.

11. It has been suggested that Staël's unpublished work of 1798, *Des Circonstances actuelles*, might be this missing second part, but this seems unlikely: see Florence Lotterie, "Note sur l'histoire de l'ouvrage," in *OCS*, 1.1:113–30; and Lucia Omacini's introduction to *Des Circonstances actuelles* in *OCS*, 3.1:277–84.

12. Hume, *Essays, Moral, Political and Literary*, pp. 14–31; Staël did not cite Hume, but his influence is apparent in different parts of her text.

13. *Of the Influence of Passions*, p. 137.

14. Ibid., pp. 137–38.

15. Emmanuel Naya and Anne-Pascale Pouey, eds., *Eloge de la médiocrité: le juste milieu à la Renaissance* (Paris: Editions Rue d'Ulm, 2005).

16. On the notion of moderation, see Craiutu, *A Virtue for Courageous Minds*.

17. *Of the Influence of Passions*, p. 138.

18. "Nobody imagined, in 1789, that vehement passions lurked under this apparent tranquillity," *Considerations*, p. 222 (French ed., p. 207).

19. Robert Morrissey, *Napoléon et l'heritage de la gloire* (Paris: PUF, 2010).

20. See above, chap. 2, note 53.
21. *Of the Influence of Passions*, p. 163.
22. This portrait of the ambitious man is recognizable in a series of later accounts of Bonaparte's personality. See, for example, *Considerations*, p. 442 (French ed., p. 365).
23. *Of the Influence of Passions*, pp. 179–80.
24. Ibid., p. 180.
25. Ibid., p. 193.
26. Ibid.
27. Ibid., p. 182.
28. Ibid., p. 221.
29. On Condorcet's politics, see Franck Alengry, *Condorcet: guide de la révolution française: théoricien du droit constitutionnel et précurseur de la science sociale* (1904; Geneva: Slatkine, 1971); Keith Michael Baker, *Condorcet: From Natural Philosophy to Social Mathematics* (Chicago: University of Chicago Press, 1975); cf. *Condorcet: Political Writings*, ed. Steven Lukes (Cambridge: Cambridge University Press, 2012).
30. Marie-Jean Antoine Caritat de Condorcet, *Rapport sur l'instruction publique*, ed. Charles Coutel (Paris: Edilig, 1989); *Cinque mémoires sur l'instruction publique*, ed. C. Coutel and Catherine Kinzler (Paris: Flammarion, 1996); C. Hippeau and Bernard Jolibet, eds., *L'instruction publique en France pendant la révolution: discours et rapports de Mirabeau, Talleyrand-Perigord, Condorcet, Lanthenas, Romme, Le Peletier de Saint-Fargeau, Cales, Lakanal, Daunou et Fourcroy* (Paris: Klincksieck, 1990). Also, Charles Coutel, *Condorcet, Instituer le citoyen* (Paris: Editions Michalon, 1999).
31. Cf. Jasinski's comments in *CG*, 1:486–87.
32. On Staël and the *Décade*, see Sergio Moravia, *Il tramonto dell'Illuminismo* (Bari: Laterza, 1968; reprint, 1986), pp. 233–47. See also Andrew Jainchill, *Reimagining Politics after Terror: The Republican Origins of French Liberalism* (Ithaca, NY: Cornell University Press, 2008).
33. *Of the Influence of Passions*, p. 221.
34. "When men act in a faction, they are apt, without shame or remorse, to neglect all the ties of honour and morality, in order to serve their party"; David Hume, "Of the First Principles of Government," in *Essays, Moral, Political and Literary*, pp. 32–36, p. 33.
35. *Of the Influence of Passions*, p. 298.
36. Ibid., p. 296.
37. Ibid., pp. 294–95, note.
38. Ibid., pp. 295–96.
39. Ibid., p. 161.
40. Here Staël used the word "democracy" to indicate the political system created by the Revolution; she admitted, however, that the term

was ambiguous and possibly best avoided; in a footnote, explaining her own use of the expression "demagogical constitution," she wrote: "I mean by demagogical constitution the one that puts people in a state of fermentation, while confusing all powers, in short, the constitution of 1793. Since the word democracy is taken, in our time, as having different meanings, it would not render with sufficient precision what I wish to express" (see p. 143, note).

41. *Of the Influence of Passions*, p. 146.

42. Ibid., pp. 146–47.

43. Ibid., pp. 142–43.

44. On this formulation, see Bronislaw Baczko, "Opinions des vainqueurs, sentiments des vaincus," introduction to *Des Circonstances actuelles*, in *OCS*, 3.1:183–275.

45. *Of the Influence of Passions*, p. 299.

46. Ibid., p. 300.

47. The term "Great Nation" had been already used by Staël in 1788 in her *Lettres sur J.-J. Rousseau*, in *OCS*, 1.1:83.

48. *Of the Influence of Passions*, p. 149.

49. See also the reviews by Amaury Duval in the *Décade philosophique* (nos. 75 and 76, 19–29 May 1796) and by Dupont de Nemours and Pierre Samuel in *L'Historien* (no. 158, 27 April 1796).

50. Benjamin Constant, "De la restitution des droits politiques aux descendants des religionnaires fugitifs," *Le Moniteur*, 26 August 1796.

51. Grange, *Benjamin Constant*, p. 151; Paul Bastid, *Benjamin Constant et sa doctrine*, 2 vols. (Paris: Colin, 1966), 1:121.

52. Béatrice W. Jasinski, *L'engagement de Benjamin Constant, amour et politique (1794–1796)* (Paris: Minard, 1971).

53. 17 July 1796, *CG*, 3/2:217–19.

54. 1 October 1796, *CG*, 3/2:244–50.

55. *Essai sur les fictions*, ed. Stéphanie Genand, in *OCS*, 1.2:39–65. See also the old edition by Simone Balayé and John Isbell, in Madame de Staël, *Oeuvres de Jeunesse* (Paris: Desjonquères, 1997), pp. 131–56. This text was particularly appreciated by Goethe, who edited a German translation the following year.

56. *Essai sur les Fictions*, in *OCS*, 1.2:57.

CHAPTER 7. THE REPUBLIC IN THEORY AND PRACTICE (1797–99)

1. 1 October 1796, *CG*, 3/2:249.

2. September or October 1799, *CG*, 4/1:240–41.

3. Necker's properties in France had been confiscated on the basis of the revolutionary legislation against the émigrés, a definition that could

not possibly apply to him: the former minister was in fact a foreign citizen, who had left France, after his resignation in 1790, with the permission of the government.

4. Simone Balayé, *La nationalité de Madame de Staël, textes inédits de Mme de Staël et de Benjamin Constant* (Paris: Hermann, 1968).

5. See in particular his speeches "Discours prononcé au Cercle constitutionnel le 30 fructidor an V" (Paris: Lemaire, 1797); and "Discours prononcé au Cercle constitutionnel le 9 ventose an VI" (Paris: Veuve Galletti, 1798).

6. Paul-Jean-François Nicolas Barras, *Mémoires de Barras, membre du Directoire*, ed. Georges Duruy, 4 vols. (Paris: Hachette, 1895–96), vol. 2; also the edition by Jean-Pierre Thomas, *Mémoires de Barras* (Paris: Mercure de France, 2005).

7. *Des circonstances actuelles qui peuvent terminer la révolution et des principes qui doivent fonder la république en France*, in *OCS*, 3.1:277–549, ed. Lucia Omacini, introd. by Bronislaw Baczko. This latest (2009) study by Lucia Omacini on the text leaves open for lack of evidence a series of question concerning the composition and structure of the work; cf. her previous critical edition of the same work published in 1979 (Geneva: Droz). On the interpretation of this work, see also Biancamaria Fontana, "The Thermidorian Republic and Its Principles," in *The Invention of the Modern Republic*, ed. B. Fontana (Cambridge: Cambridge University Press, 1994), pp. 118–38.

8. *Of Present Circumstances*, pp. 288–89.

9. Ibid., p. 289.

10. Ibid., p. 308.

11. Pierre Serna, "Le retour du refoulé, ou l'histoire de la révolution anglaise à l'ordre du jour de la crise du Directoire," in *La Révolution, 1789–1871*, ed. Philippe Bourdin (Clermont Ferrant: Université Blaise Pascal, 2008), pp. 213–40.

12. *Of Present Circumstances* p. 345.

13. On Gracchus Babeuf and his attempted insurrection of 1797, see Philippe Buonarroti, *Conspiration pour l'égalité, dite de Babeuf*, ed. Jean-Marc Schiappa and Jean-Numa Ducange (Montreuil: La Ville Brule, 2014). See also Maurice Dommanget, *Babeuf et la conjuration des Egaux* (Paris: Lefevre, 1972); Robert Barrie Rose, *Gracchus Babeuf: The First Revolutionary Communist* (London: Arnold, 1978).

14. *Of Present Circumstances*, pp. 293–94.

15. Ibid.

16. Necker, *Refléxions philosophiques sur l'égalité*.

17. Necker, *Du pouvoir exécutif dans les grands états*.

18. *Philosophical Reflections on Equality*, p. 35.

19. Ibid., pp. 35–36.

20. Cf. Michael *Sans-Culottes*, chap. 5, "The Entitlements of Merit," pp. 283–361.

21. *Of Present Circumstances*, pp. 295–96.

22. Ibid., pp. 298–300.

23. Ibid., p. 299.

24. Ibid., p. 301.

25. Ibid., p. 373.

26. Ibid., p. 353.

27. Gueniffey, *Le nombre et la raison*; Crook, *Elections in the French Revolution*.

28. Cf. the letter to Gouvernet of 16 November 1790, *CG*, 1:394–95.

29. *Of Present Circumstances*, p. 319.

30. Cf. Adrien Lezay-Marnesia, *Lettre à un suisse sur la nouvelle constitution helvétique: précédée de cette constitution* (Paris: Impr. Roederer, an VI [1798]). There are very few comprehensive studies on the République helvétique, as most of the literature is focused on individual regions or cantons. See Anton von Tillier, *Histoire de la république helvétique: depuis sa fondation en 1798 jusqu'à sa dissolution en 1803*, trans. from the German (Paris: A. Cherbuliez, 1846); Emile Dunant, ed., *Les relations diplomatiques de la France et de la République helvétique* (Basel: A. Geering, 1901); also, Gustave Gautherot, *Les relations franco-helvétiques de 1789 à 1792* (Paris: Champion, 1908).

31. Letter of 21 January 1798, *CG.*, 4/1:110.

32. 8 February 1798, *CG*, 4/1:121. On Staël's views on the "sister republics," see Biancamaria Fontana, "The Political Passions of Other Nations, National Choices and the European Order in the Writings of Germaine de Staël," in *The Political Culture of the Sister Republics, 1794–1806: France, the Netherlands, Switzerland and Italy*, ed. J. Oddens, M. Rutjes, and E. Jacobs (Amsterdam: Amsterdam University Press, 2015), pp. 33–40.

33. *CG*, 4/1:128 ff.

34. 22 January 1798, *CG*, 4/1:111.

35. On subsequent developments, see Alain-Jacques Czouz-Tornare, ed., *Quand Napoléon Bonaparte créa la Suisse, La genèse et mise en oeuvre de l'Acte de Mediation*, Société d'études robespierristes no. 7 (Paris, 2005).

36. *Of Present Circumstances*, p. 355.

37. Ibid., pp. 357–59.

38. Ibid., p. 364.

39. Ibid., p. 346.

40. *De la littérature considérée dans ses rapports avec les institutions sociales*, ed. Jean Goldzink, in *OCS*, 1.2:99–388.

41. *Considerations*, pp. 384–88 (French ed., pp. 329–33).

42. See, for example, François Furet, *La Révolution, de Turgot à Jules*

Ferry, in *La Révolution française*, pp. 381–409; Tulard, *Les Thermidoriens*, pp. 127–65.

43. Albert Vandal, *L'avènement de Bonaparte*, 2 vols. (Paris: Plon-Nourrit, 1902), vol. 1; Thierry Lentz, *Le 18 brumaire: les coups d'état de Napoléon Bonaparte (novembre–décembre 1799)* (Paris: Picollec, 1997); Patrice Gueniffey, *Le dix-huit brumaire: l'épilogue de la révolution française, 9–10 novembre 1799* (Paris: Gallimard, 2008).

44. *Considerations*, p. 421–22 (French ed., pp. 356–56); *Dix annés d' exil*, ed. Simone Balayé and Mariella Vianello Bonifacio (Paris: Fayard, 1996), p. 68.

45. *CG*, 24 September 1799 (?), 4/1:237.

46. On the general tendency in French politics to gravitate toward the center and to support a single-party regime, see Pierre Serna, *La République des girouettes, 1789–1815 et au delà: une anomalie politique, la France de l'extrême centre* (Seyssel: Champ Vallon, 2005), in particular on Staël, pp. 469–76.

CHAPTER 8. RAISING THE STAKES: THE MEASURE OF AMBITION (1800)

1. *De la littérature considérée dans ses rapports avec les institutions sociales*, ed. Jean Goldzink, in *OCS*, 1.2:99–388.

2. For a recent reformulation of this view, see Patrice Gueniffey, *Bonaparte: (1769–1802)* (Paris: Gallimard, 2013), pp. 318–21.

3. More generally on the rallying of the French political class to Bonaparte, see Jainchill, *Reimagining Politics after Terror*.

4. "The Constitution? How can you appeal to it? And does it still represent a guarantee for the French people? You have violated it on the 18 *fructidor*, you violated it on the 22 *floréal*, you violated it on the 30 *prarial*. The Constitution? It is invoked by all factions and has been violated by all of them"; quoted in Gueniffey, *Bonaparte*, p. 482. See also Steven Englund, *Napoleon: A Political Life* (Cambridge, MA: Harvard University Press, 2005), and Luigi Mascelli Migliorini, *Napoléon* (Paris: Perrin, 2001).

5. On the *idéologues*, see François Picavet, *Les idéologues: essai sur l'histoire des idées et des théories scientifiques, philosophiques, religieuses etc. en France depuis 1789* (Paris: Alcan, 1891); Sergio Moravia, *Il pensiero degli idéologues (1780–1815)* (Florence: La Nuova Italia, 1974); Georges Gusdorf, *La conscience révolutionnaire: les idéologues* (Paris: Payot, 1978); Cheryl B. Welch, *Liberty and Utility: The French Ideologues and the Transformation of Liberalism* (New York: Columbia University Press, 1984); Mario Matucci, ed., *Gli 'idéologues' e la rivoluzione: Atti del Colloquio Internazionale di Grosseto, 1989* (Pisa: Pacini, 1991); François Azouvi, ed.,

L'institution de la raison: la révolution culturelle des idéologues (Paris: Vrin, 1992).

6. There are some apparent analogies between Staël's views on the promotion of talents and the scientific study of social movements, and the position of the idéologues. However, with the exception of Roederer, she was not personally close to any of them; there were also important ideological differences, as she did not share the atheist materialism and determinism characteristic of the group. The fact that some of them (in particular Roederer) rallied to Bonaparte and accepted posts in the administration or scientific institutions of the empire accentuated their distance. Cf. Chinatsu Takeda, ed., *Les idéologues et le groupe de Coppet* (Paris: Picard, 2003).

7. Cf. on this Biancamaria Fontana, "The Thermidorian Republic and Its Principles," in *The Invention of the Modern Republic.*

8. Godechot, *Les constitutions de la France*, pp. 143–50.

9. Bredin, *Sieyès, la clé de la révolution française*, p. 468.

10. Jean Tulard, *Le 18 Brumaire. Comment Terminer la Révolution* (Paris: Perrin 1999); Mona Ozouf, "De Thermidor à Brumaire: le discours de la Révolution sur elle-même," *Revue historique*, no. 243 (1970): 31–66.

11. *Considerations*, p. 430 (French ed., p. 357).

12. For some recent examples of the continuing controversy on the nature of Napoleon's regime, see Natalie Petitau, *Napoléon Bonaparte, la nation incarnée* (Paris: Colin, 2015); Gérard Grunberg, *Napoléon Bonaparte, le noir génie* (Paris: Editions du CNRS, 2015); Xavier Mauduit, *L'Homme qui voulait tout: Napoléon, le faste et la propagande* (Paris: Editions Autrement, 2015).

13. Gueniffey, *Le dix-huit brumaire*, p. 265.

14. Englund, *Napoleon*, p. 159.

15. 28 December 1800, *CG*, 4/2:343. For other instances of Staël's admiration for Bonaparte, see her letters to Henri Meister of 15 October 1799 (*CG*, 4/1:243) and to Pictet de Rochemont, 24 October 1799 (*CG*, 4/2:245).

16. *Considerations*, p. 408 (French ed., p. 337).

17. The 1800 constitution, in which the three consuls were mentioned by name, replaced them with Cambacérès and Lebrun. See Godechot, *Les constitutions de la France*, "La Constitution de l'an VIII," titre IV, art. 39, p. 155.

18. To Pictet-Diodati, 25 May 1799, *CG*, 4/1:208. See also the letter to Henri Meister of 27 August 1799, where Sieyès is identified with the "true republic," *CG*, 4/1:229. Sieyès had already been elected to the Directory in 1795 but had refused the appointment; cf. Tulard, *Les Thermidoriens*, pp. 117–18.

19. The 1800 constitution did not specify how the fifth of the members

of the Tribunat (20 out of 100) that were replaced should be selected: see titre III, art. 27 (Godechot, *Les constitutions de la France*, p. 154).

20. Constant's planned refutation of Burke was never written; but see the one produced by his and Staël's friend James Mackintosh, *Vindiciae Gallicae: defence of the French Revolution* (1791), critical edition (London: Palgrave/MacMillan, 2008). See also Norman King, "Lettres de Madame de Staël à Sir James Mackintosh," *Cahiers Staëliens*, no. 10 (1970): 27–57.

21. *On Literature*, p. 118.

22. Ibid., pp. 109–10.

23. Faithful to her Protestant education, Staël was generally hostile to those aspects of Catholicism she associated with the corruption of the French monarchy: superstition, bigotry, and intolerance. On the other hand, she recognized the positive role that sincere religious sentiment and Christian values could play in shaping private and public morality. See Maurice Souriau, *Les idées morales de Madame de Staël* (Paris: Bloud, 1910); Henri Perrochon, *Les sources suisses de la religion de Madame de Staël* (Paris: Klincksieck, 1970). On the Protestant roots of French liberalism, see Helena Rosenblatt, *Liberal Values, Benjamin Constant and the Politics of Religion* (Cambridge: Cambridge University Press, 2008); Patrick Cabanel, *Les Protestants et la République* (Paris: Editions Complexe, 2000).

24. *On Literature*, pp. 111–12.

25. Ibid., p. 121.

26. Ibid., p. 120.

27. Ibid., pp. 285–86.

28. Ibid., p. 122.

29. Ibid., p. 292.

30. Ibid., p. 356.

31. *Of Present Circumstances*, p. 373.

32. On the French cult of great men, see Mona Ozouf, "Le Panthéon," in *Les lieux de mémoire*, ed. Pierre Nora (Paris: Gallimard, 1984), 1:139–66; Marc Fumaroli, *L'Etat culturel, une religion moderne* (Paris: Editions de Fallois, 1995). On the notion of genius in the French tradition, see Ann Jefferson, *Genius in France: An Idea and Its Uses* (Princeton, NJ: Princeton University Press, 2014).

33. *On Literature*, p. 305.

34. Ibid., p. 307.

35. Ibid., p. 308.

36. Cf. Etienne Hofmann, *Les Principes de Politique de Benjamin Constant, la genèse d'une oeuvre*, 2 vols. (Geneva: Droz, 1980), 1:155–58; see also Constant's essay comparing the consequences of the English and the French revolutions: *Des suites de la contre-révolution de 1660 en Angleterre* (Paris: F. Buisson, 1798–99).

37. Quoted in Lentz, *Le 18 brumaire*, p. 307.

38. Bronislaw Baczko, "Un Washington manqué: Napoléon Bonaparte," in *Politiques de la Révolution française*, pp. 535–693.

39. *On Literature*, p. 309.

40. 20 April 1801, *CG*, 4/2:367.

41. *On Literature*, p. 307.

42. Ibid., p. 285.

43. Ibid., pp. 274–75.

44. For a recent reassessment of the relations between Staël and Napoleon, see Léonard Burnand, "Madame de Staël et Napoléon, mythes et réalité d'un duel," in *Germaine de Staël, retour d'exile*, ed. Léonard Burnand et al. (Geneva: Editions Zoe, 2015), pp. 45–77.

45. *Dernières vues de politique et de finance offertes à la nation française* (Paris, An X [1802]). On the consequences for Staël's position, see Bastid, *Benjamin Constant et sa doctrine*, 1:175.

46. From March 1802 to May 1803.

47. Cf. the letter she addressed to Bonaparte on 7–8 October 1803, in which she accused him of "persecuting a woman and her children" and "causing great pain to a defenseless person," in the same self-victimizing style she had used pleading with the previous regimes. *CG*, 4/1:54–55.

48. The decision to be submitted to a popular vote or *plébiscite*: cf. Godechot, *Les constitutions de la France*, pp. 163–66.

49. *Corinne ou l'Italie*, in *OCS*, 2.3, ed. Simone Balayé (Paris: Champion; Geneva: Slatkine, 2000).

50. *De l'Allemagne*, ed. Simone Balayé, 2 vols. (Paris: Flammarion, 2006–7). On the content and fortunes of this work, see Ian Allan Henning, *L'Allemagne de Mme de Staël et la polémique romantique: première fortune de l'ouvrage en France et en Allemagne, 1814–1830* (Geneva: Slatkine, 1975); Katherine Elisabeth Laros, *Madame de Staël as a Critic of Goethe and Schiller* (Whitefish, MT: Kessinger Publishing, 2008).

51. Simone Balayé, *Madame de Staël et le gouvernement impérial en 1810: le dossier de la suppression de l'Allemagne* (Paris: Attinger 1974).

52. The pamphlet *An appeal to the nations of Europe against the continental system published in Stockholm by the authority of Bernadotte (March 1813) by Madame de Staël Holstein* (London: J. M. Richardson, 1813) was in fact written by A. W. von Schlegel. See also Benjamin Constant, *Lettres à Bernadotte* (Geneva: Droz, 1952); Frank Favier, *Bernadotte, un maréchal de l'empire sur le trône de Suède* (Paris: Ellipses, 2010).

CHAPTER 9. BACK TO THE FUTURE:
THE BOURGEOIS LIBERAL REPUBLIC

1. Letter of 2 February 1817, in *Madame de Staël, ses amis, ses correspondants. Choix de lettres (1778–1817)*, ed. Georges Solovieff (Paris: Klincks-

ieck, 1970). See also Gilbert Chinard, "La correspondance de Mme de Staël avec Jefferson," *Revue de littérature comparée*, no. 2 (1922).

2. *Considérations sur les principaux événements de la Révolution française, ouvrage posthume de Mme la baronne de Staël, publié par le duc de Broglie et le baron de Staël*, 3 vols. (London: Baldwin, Cradock and Joy, 1818).

3. It went through several editions and, according to Jacques Godechot, sold about sixty thousand copies; see his introduction to *Considérations*, pp. 7–48.

4. Louis de Bonald, *La vraie revolution: réponse à Mme de Staël* (1818), ed. Michel Toda (Etampes: Clovis, 1997); see also Jacques-Charles Bailleul, *Examen critique de l'ouvrage posthume de Mme la baronne de Staël* (Paris: A. Bailleul, 1818); Aristarque-Marie Tardieu de Maleissye, *Observations sur l'ouvrage de Mme de Staël intitulé: Considérations sur la Révolution* (Paris: Fonvielle, 1822).

5. Manon Roland, *Mémoires de Mme Roland*, ed. Paul de Roux (Paris: Mercure de France, 1966, reprint, 1986); the comparison is made, for example, in Béatrice Didier, *Ecrire la Révolution (1789–1799)* (Paris: PUF, 1989).

6. Introduction to *Considérations*.

7. Quoted in Béatrice Jasinski, "Madame de Staël, l'Angleterre de 1813–1814 et les 'Considérations sur la Révolution française'," *Revue d'Histoire littéraire de la France*, no. 1 (January–March 1966): 12–24.

8. "Du caractère de M. Necker et de sa vie privée," in *Oeuvres complètes*, ed. Auguste de Staël, (1820–21), 17:1–127.

9. Letter of 13 December 1813; see comtesse Jean de Pange, *Auguste-Guillaume Schlegel et Madame de Staël* (Paris: Editions Albert, 1938).

10. François Furet, *Penser la Révolution française* (Paris: Gallimard, 1977), p. 23.

11. Marcel Gauchet, "Madame de Staël," in *Dictionnaire critique de la Révolution française*, ed. François Furet and Mona Ozouf (Paris: Flammarion, 1988), pp. 1053–60; English translation, *A Critical Dictionary of the French Revolution* (Cambridge, MA: Harvard University Press, 1989).

12. For a long-term perspective on the aftermath of the Revolution, see Robert Tombs, *France, 1814–1914* (London: Longman, 1996); Robert Gildea, *Children of the Revolution: The French 1799–1914* (London: Penguin, 2009); Jeremy Jenkins, *Revolution and the Republic: A History of Political Thought in France since the Eighteenth Century* (Oxford: Oxford University Press, 2011).

13. *Considerations*, p. 203 (French ed., p. 195).

14. Ibid., p. 47 (French ed., p. 83).

15. Ibid., p. 144 (French ed., p. 148).

16. Jacques Necker, *De la révolution française*, 4 vols. (Paris: J. Drisonnier, 1796), 1:6–7.

17. *Considerations*, p. 78 (French ed., p. 104).

18. Ibid., p. 59 (French ed., p. 90).

19. Ibid., p. 196 (French ed., p. 190).

20. Jeremy Bentham, *Tactique des assemblées législatives*, ed. Etienne Dumont (1816; Charleston, SC: Nabu Press, 2010).

21. *Considerations*, p. 196 (French ed., p. 190).

22. Possibly her personal friends, the brothers Alexandre and Charles de Lameth.

23. *Considerations*, p. 202 (French ed., p. 194).

24. On the interpretation of the role of the Jacobins in terms of "conspiracy," the leading reference is Augustin Barruel, *Mémoires pour servir à l'histoire du jacobinisme* (1818), ed. Christian Lagrave (Chiré-en-Montreuil: Editions de Chiré, 2005).

25. *Considerations*, p. 262 (French ed., p. 235).

26. On the situation of the Whig Party after Charles Fox's death, see Michael Roberts, *The Whig Party, 1807–1812* (London: Cass, 1965).

27. *Considerations*, p. 718 (French ed., p. 577).

28. Solovieff, *Madame de Staël, ses amis, ses correspondants*.

29. Leslie Mitchell, *The Whig World, 1760–1837* (London:, Hambeldon Continuum, 2005), p. 140.

30. *Considerations*, pp. 667–68 (French ed., p. 537).

31. Ibid., p. 665 (French ed., p. 536).

32. Ibid., p. 669 (French ed., pp. 538–39).

33. Ibid.

34. For Constant's viewpoint on this episode, see Benjamin Constant, *Mémoires sur les Cent-Jours* (1820–22), ed. K. Kloocke and A. Cabanis, In *Oeuvres complètes de Benjamin Constant* (Tübingen: Niemeyer, 1993), vol.14.

35. On the 1814 constitution, see Pierre Rosanvallon, *La Monarchie impossible: Les Chartes de 1814 et 1830* (Paris: Fayard, 1994).

36. On the relevance of Protestantism in Constant's and Staël's theory, see Rosenblatt, *Liberal Values*.

37. *Considerations*, pp. 629–33 (French ed., pp. 509–12).

38. On these debates, see Istvan Hont, *Jealousy of Trade: International Competition and the Nation-State in Historical Perspective* (Cambridge, MA: Belknap Press of Harvard University Press, 2005).

39. See Fontana, "The Political Passions of Other Nations."

40. *Considerations*, p. 492 (French ed., pp. 401–2). On French conquest and the empire, see Jacques Godechot, *La grande nation* (Paris: Flammarion 1983); Jean Tulard, *Le grand empire, 1804–1815* (1982; Paris: Albin Michel, 2009); Stuart Woolf, *Napoleon's Integration of Europe* (London, Routledge, 1991); Paul W. Schroeder, *The Transformation of European Politics, 1763–1848* (Oxford: Clarendon Press, 1994); Thierry Lentz, ed., *Napoléon et l'Europe: regards sur une politique* (Paris: Fayard, 2005) and *Le*

congrès de Vienne, une refondation de l'Europe 1814–1815 (Paris: Perrin, 2013); on the views of Staël's circle, see Simone Balayé and Kurt Klocke, eds., *Le Groupe de Coppet et l'Europe, 1789–1830* (Lausanne: Institut Benjamin Constant, 1994).

41. *Considerations*, p. 746 (French ed., pp. 599–600).

42. John Dunn, "The Identity of the Bourgeois Liberal Republic," in Fontana, *The Invention of the Modern Republic*, pp. 206–25.

CONCLUSION. GERMAINE DE STAËL AND MODERN POLITICS

1. "Qu'on ne cherche pas dans le passé des exemples qui pourraient retarder votre marche! Rien dans l'histoire ne ressemble à la fin du dix-huitième siècle; rien dans la fin du dix-huitième siècle ne ressemble au moment actuel." Quoted in Gueniffey, *Le dix-huit brumaire*, p. 27. There is no official record of the speech, only reports by witnesses, as the constitution did not formally allow Bonaparte to address the assemblies: he was admitted inside the room during a break in the meeting, allegedly to convey an urgent message about national security.

2. I am borrowing this term from John Dunn, *The Cunning of Unreason: Making Sense of Politics* (London: Harper Collins, 2000).

Bibliography

EDITIONS AND TRANSLATIONS OF
GERMAINE DE STAËL'S WORKS AND CORRESPONDENCE

Works

A new French edition of Germaine de Staël's collected works (the first one to appear since the nineteenth century), based on her manuscripts at the château of Coppet, is presently in the course of publication; I have used the volumes that have been published thus far (they are indicated in the notes as *OCS*):

Corinne ou l'Italie, ed. Simone Balayé. *Oeuvres complètes*, ser. 2, *Oeuvres littéraires*, vol. 3. Paris:, Champion; Geneva: Slatkine, 2000.

Delphine. ed. Simone Balayé and Lucia Omacini. *Oeuvres complètes*, ser. 2, *Oeuvres littéraires*, vol. 2. Paris: Champion; Geneva: Slatkine, 2004.

Lettres sur les écrits et le caractère de J.-J. Rousseau; De l'influence des passions sur le bonheur des individus et des nations (see also the pocket edition with a preface by Chantal Thomas, Paris: Payot Rivages, 2000); *De l'éducation de l'âme par la vie; Réflexions sur le suicide*. *Oeuvres complètes*, ser. 1, *Oeuvres critiques*, vol. 1, ed. Anne Brousteau and Florence Lotterie. Paris: Champion; Geneva: Slatkine, 2008.

Des circonstances actuelles et autres essais politiques sous la Révolution, ed. Lucia Omacini, Bronislaw Baczko, et al. *Oeuvres complètes*, ser. 3, *Oeuvres Historiques*, vol. 1. Paris: Champion; Geneva: Slatkine, 2009.

De la littérature; et autres essais littéraires, ed. Stéphanie Genand. *Oeuvres complètes*, ser. 1, *Oeuvres critiques*, vol. 2. Paris: Champion; Geneva: Slatkine, 2013.

See also (for works that have not yet appeared in the new *Oeuvres complètes*) the first edition of the collected works published by Auguste de Staël after his mother's death:

Oeuvres complètes de Mme la baronne de Staël, publiées par son fils; précédées d'une Notice sur le caractère et les écrits de Mme de Staël par Mme Necker de Saussure. Paris: Treuttel et Würtz, 1820–21.

A reprint of the 1861 edition of the *Oeuvres complètes* has appeared recently:

Oeuvres complètes de la baronne de Staël-Holstein. 2 vols. Geneva: Slatkine, 2014.

Whenever I refer to separate editions of single works of Staël, these will be indicated in the notes. In particular I have cited the following:

Oeuvres de Jeunesse de Madame de Staël, ed. Simone Balayé and John Isbell. Paris: Desjonquères, 1997.

Réflexions sur le procès de la Reine, ed. with a "Postface" by Monique Cottret. Paris: Les Editions de Paris, 2006.

De l'Allemagne, ed. Simone Balayé. 2 vols. Paris: Flammarion, 2006–7.

Correspondence

For the correspondence, references in the book are to the invaluable Madame de Staël, *Correspondance générale,* ed. Béatrice W. Jasinski and (for vol.7) Othenin d'Haussonville, 7 vols. (Geneva: Slatkine, 2009). (This is a reprint of the original edition of 1960–68; some volumes combine what were two separate volumes in the old edition.) In the notes this edition is indicated as *CG.*

References to other collections of correspondence (the Jasinski edition stops at 1812) are given separately, in particular the following:

Seize lettres inédites de Mme de Staël au comte de Gouvernet, 1790–1791, ed. Charles de Pomairois. Paris: Edition du temps présent, 1913.

Lettres à Narbonne, ed. Georges Solovieff. Paris: Gallimard, 1960.

Lettres à Ribbing, preface by the comtesse Jean de Pange, ed. Simone Balayé. Paris: Gallimard, 1960.

Madame de Staël ses amis, ses correspondants. Choix de lettres (1778–1817), ed. Georges Solovieff. Paris: Kincksieck, 1970.

King, Norman, ed. "Lettres de Madame de Staël à Sir James Mackintosh." *Cahiers Staëliens,* no. 10 (1970): 27–57.

———. "Politique, littérature, diplomatie: lettres nouvelles de Germaine de Staël à Nils von Rosenstein." *Cahiers Staëliens,* no. 42 (1990–91): pp. 75–107.

Chinard, Gilbert. "La correspondance de Mme de Staël avec Jefferson." *Revue de littérature comparée,* no. 2 (1922).

In English: *Selected Correspondence,* ed. Georges Solovieff, trans. Kathleen Jameson-Cemper. Dordrecht: Kluwer Academic Publishing, 2000.

Since the 1960s the bulk of studies and contributions on Germaine de Staël and her circle are collected in the review *Cahiers Staëliens.*

All translations from Staël's works and correspondence are my own, with the exception of the quotations from the *Considérations sur la revo-*

lution française, the only one of the works I discuss extensively that is available in a current English translation: Germaine de Staël, *Considerations on the Principal Events of the French Revolution*, ed. Aurelian Craiutu (Indianapolis, IN: Liberty Fund, 2008). In the notes I indicate the page numbers of the current French edition (as this work has not yet appeared in the *Oeuvres complètes*): *Considérations sur la Révolution française*, ed. Jacques Godechot (Paris: Tallandier, 1983).

See also the original edition: *Considérations sur les principaux événements de la Révolution française, ouvrage posthume de Mme la baronne de Staël, publié par le duc de Broglie et le baron de Staël*, 3 vols. (London: Baldwin, Cradock and Joy, 1818).

Other relevant works by Staël available in English are *Ten Years of Exile*, trans. Avriel H. Goldberger (DeKalb: Northern Illinois University Press, 2000) (French edition: *Dix années d'exil*, ed. Simone Balayé and Mariella Vianello Bonifacio [Paris: Fayard, 1996]); and the anthology *Politics, Literature and National Character*, trans. Monroe Berger (New Brunswick, NJ: Transaction Publishers, 2000). The English 1798 translation of *De l'influence des passions* is available in an electronic version.

SECONDARY SOURCES

Alengry, Franck. *Condorcet: guide de la révolution française: théoricien du droit constitutionnel et précurseur de la science sociale*. 1904. Geneva: Slatkine, 1971.

Andrews, Wayne. *Germaine: A Portrait of Madame de Staël*. London: Gollanz, 1964.

Ansart-Dourien, Michèle. *L'action politique des personnalités et l'idéologie jacobine: rationalisme et passions révolutionnaires*. Paris: l'Harmattan, 1998.

Applewhite, Harriet B. *Political Alignment in the French National Assembly, 1789–1791*. Baton Rouge: Lousiana State University Press, 1993.

Artaud de Montor, Alexis François. *Histoire de l'assassinat de Gustave III, roi de Suède, par un officier polonais, témoin oculaire*. Paris: Forget, 1797.

Aulard, Alphonse. *Histoire politique de la Révolution française: origines et développement de la démocratie et de la république*. Paris: Colin, 1921.

Ayling, Stanley. *Fox: The Life of Charles James Fox*. London: John Murray, 1991.

Azouvi, François, ed. *L'institution de la raison: la révolution culturelle des idéologues*. Paris: Vrin, 1992.

Baczko, Bronislaw. *Politiques de la Révolution française*. Paris: Gallimard, 2008.

Bagehot, Walter. *The English Constitution*. 1865–67. Ed. R.H.S. Crossman. London, Fontana-Collins, 1976.

Bailleul, Jacques-Charles. *Examen critique de l'ouvrage posthume de Mme la baronne de Staël*. Paris: A. Bailleul, 1818.

Bain, Robert Nisbet. *Gustav III and His Contemporaries (1742–1792), an Overlooked Chapter in 18th Century History*. New York: Bergman, 1970.

Baker, Keith Michael. *Condorcet: From Natural Philosophy to Social Mathematics*. Chicago: University of Chicago Press, 1975.

———. *Inventing the French Revolution: Essays on French Political Culture in the Eighteenth Century*. Cambridge: Cambridge University Press, 1990.

———. *The Old Regime and the French Revolution*. Chicago: University of Chicago Press, 1987.

Balayé, Simone. *Madame de Staël et le gouvernement impérial en 1810: le dossier de la suppression de l'Allemagne*. Paris: Attinger, 1974.

———. *Mme de Staël, lumières et liberté*. Paris: Kilncksieck, 1972.

———. *La nationalité de Madame de Staël, textes inédits de Mme de Staël et de Benjamin Constant*. Paris: Hermann, 1968.

Balayé, Simone, and Kurt Kloocke, eds. *Le Groupe de Coppet et l'Europe, 1789–1830*. Lausanne: Institut Benjamin Constant, 1994.

Barnave, Antoine. *De la révolution et de la Constitution*. Ed. François Furet and Patrice Gueniffey. Grenoble: Presses Universitaires de Grenoble, 1988.

Barras, Paul-Jean-François Nicolas. *Mémoires de Barras*. Ed. Jean Pierre Thomas. Paris: Mercure de France, 2005.

———. *Mémoires de Barras, membre du Directoire*. Ed. Georges Duruy. 4 vols. Paris: Hachette, 1895–96.

Barruel, Augustin. *Mémoires pour servir à l'histoire du jacobinisme*. 1818. Ed. Christian Lagrave. Chiré-en-Montreuil: Editions de Chiré, 2005.

Barton, H. Arnold. *Scandinavia in the Revolutionary Era, 1760–1815*, Minneapolis: University of Minnesota Press, 1986.

Bastide, Paul. *Benjamin Constant et sa doctrine*. 2 vols. Paris: Colin, 1966.

———, ed. *Les discours de Sieyès dans les débats constitutionnels de l'an III:2 et 18 thermidor*. Paris: Hachette, 1939.

———. *Sieyès et sa pensée*. Geneva: Slatkine, 1978.

Baume, Sandrine, and Biancamaria Fontana, eds. *Les usages de la séparation des pouvoirs*. Paris: Michel Houdiard, 2008.

Bénétruy, J. *L'atelier de Mirabeau: quatre proscrits genevois dans la tourmente révolutionnaire*. Geneva: A. Jullien. 1962.

Bentham, Jeremy. *Tactique des assemblées législatives*. Ed. Etienne Dumont. 1816. Charleston, SC: Nabu Press, 2010.

Berlin, Isaiah. *Four Essays on Liberty*. Oxford: Oxford University Press, 1969.

Biard, Michel. *La liberté ou la mort: mourir en député, 1792–1795*. Paris: Tallandier, 2015.

Binz, Louis, ed. *Regards sur la Révolution genevoise, 1792–1798.* Geneva: Droz; Paris: Champion, 1992.

Black, Jeremy. *British Foreign Policy in an Age of Revolution, 1783–1793.* Cambridge: Cambridge University Press, 1994.

Blake, Robert. *The Office of Prime Minister.* London: British Academy, 1975.

Blanning, T.C.W. *The Origins of the French Revolutionary Wars.* London: Longman, 1986.

Blennerhassett, Lady. *Madame de Staël and Her Influence in Politics and Literature.* 3 vols. London: Chapman & Hall, 1889.

Bonald, Louis de. *La vraie revolution: réponse à Mme de Staël.* 1818. Ed. Michel Toda. Etampes: Clovis, 1997.

Bredin Jean-Denis, ed. *Jacques Necker, 1732–1804, banquier, ministre, écrivain: bicentenaire de sa mort, 1804–2004. Cahiers Staëliens,* no. 55 (2005).

———. *Sieyès, la clé de la révolution française.* Paris: Flammarion, 1988.

———. *Une singulière famille: Jacques Necker, Suzanne Necker et Germaine de Staël.* Paris: Fayard, 2000.

Brown, Peter Douglas. *William Pitt, Earl of Chatham: The Great Commoner.* London: Allen and Unwin, 1978.

Buonarroti, Philippe. *Conspiration pour l'égalité, dite de Babeuf.* Ed. Jean-Marc Schiappa and Jean-Numa Ducange. Montreuil: La Ville Brule, 2014.

Burke, Edmund. *Letters on a Regicide Peace.* London: E. J. Paine, 1795.

———. *Reflections on the Revolution in France.* Ed. W. B. Todd. Introd. Conor Cruise O'Brien. Harmondsworth, Penguin Books, 1968.

Burnand, Léonard. "Madame de Staël et Napoléon, mythes et réalité d'un duel." In *Germaine de Staël, retour d'exile,* ed. Léonard Burnand et al., pp. 45–77. Geneva: Editions Zoe, 2015.

———. *Necker et l'opinion publique.* Paris: Champion; Geneva: Slatkine, 2004.

———. *Les pamphlets contre Necker: médias et imaginaire politique au XVIIIème siècle.* Paris: Garnier, 2009.

Cabanel, Patrick. *Les Protestants et la République.* Paris: Editions Complexe, 2000.

Castelot, André. *Le procès de Marie-Antoinette.* Paris: Perrin, 1993.

Chaussinand-Nogaret, G. *Mirabeau.* Paris: Seuil, 1982.

Chittick, Kathryn. *The Language of Whiggism, Liberty and Patriotism.* London: Pickering and Chatto, 2010.

Choderlos de Laclos, Pierre Ambroise. "De la guerre et de la paix." In *Oeuvres complétes,* ed. Laurent Versini. Paris: Gallimard, 1979.

Cochin, Augustin. *l'Esprit du jacobinisme.* Paris: PUF, 1979.

Condorcet, Marie-Jean Antoine Caritat de. *Cinque mémoires sur l'instruction publique.* Ed. C. Coutel and Catherine Kinzler. Paris: Flammarion, 1996.

———. *Political Writings.* Ed. Steven Lukes. Cambridge: Cambridge University Press, 2012.

———. *Rapport sur l'instruction publique.* Ed. Charles Coutel. Paris: Edilig, 1989.

Constant, Benjamin. *De la force du gouvernment actuel de la France, et de la nécessité de s'y rallier.* Ed. Philippe Raynaud. Paris: Flammarion, 1988.

———. *De la religion, considérée dans sa source, ses formes et ses développements.* 1825–30. Ed. Tzvetan Todorov and Etienne Hofmann. Arles: Actes Sud, 1999.

———. "De la restitution des droits politiques aux descendants des religionnaires fugitifs." *Le Moniteur,* 26 August 1796.

———. *Ecrits et discours politiques.* Ed. Olivier Pozzo di Borgo. 2 vols. Paris: Pauvert, 1964–65.

———. *Lettres à Bernadotte.* Geneva: Droz, 1952.

———. *Mémoires sur les Cent-Jours.* 1820–22. Ed. K. Kloocke and A. Cabanis, in *Oeuvres complètes de Benjamin Constant,* vol. 14. Tübingen: Niemeyer, 1993.

———. *Political Writings.* Ed. Biancamaria Fontana. Cambridge: Cambridge University Press, 1988.

———. *Portraits, mémoires, souvenirs.* Ed. Hephraïm Harpaz. Paris: Champion; Geneva: Slatkine, 1992.

———. *Des suites de la contre-révolution de 1660 en Angleterre.* Paris: F. Buisson, 1798–99.

Corday, Pierre. *Madame de Staël, ou le deuil éclatant du bonheur.* Lausanne: Editions Rencontre, 1967.

Cornac, Gérard, and Jean-Pierre Machelon, eds. *La Constitution de l'an III: Boissy d'Anglas et la naissance du libéralisme constitutionnel.* Paris: PUF, 1999.

Coutel, Charles. *Condorcet, Instituer le citoyen.* Paris: Editions Michalon, 1999.

Craiutu, Aurelian. "Faces of Moderation: Mme de Staël's Politics during the Directory." *Jus Politicum,* no. 6 (2008).

———. *A Virtue for Courageous Minds: Moderation in French Political Thought, 1748–1830.* Princeton, NJ: Princeton University Press, 2012.

Crook, Malcolm. *Elections in the French Revolution: An Apprenticeship of Democracy, 1789–1799.* Cambridge: Cambridge University Press, 2002.

Cruickshank, John. *Benjamin Constant.* New York:, Twayne, 1974.

Cuillé, Tili Boon, and Karyna Szmurlo, eds. *Staël's Philosophy of the Passions: Sensibility, Society, and the Sister Arts.* Lewisburg, PA: Bucknell University Press, 2013.

Czouz-Tornare, Alain Jacques, ed. *Quand Napoléon Bonaparte créa la Su-*

isse, La genèse et mise en oeuvre de l'Acte de Mediation. Société d'études robespierristes no. 7. Paris: 2005.

Dard, Emile. *Un confident de l'Empereur, le comte de Narbonne, 1755–1813*. Paris: Plon, 1943.

Denby, David, J. *Sentimental Narrative and the Social Order in France, 1760–1820*. Cambridge: Cambridge University Press, 1994.

Dendena, Francesco. *I nostri maledetti scranni: il movimento fogliante tra la fuga di Varennes e la caduta della monarchia (1791–1792)*. Milan: Guerini e associati, 2013.

Didier, Béatrice. *Ecrire la Révolution (1789–1799)*. Paris: PUF, 1989.

Diesbach, Ghislain de. *Histoire de l'émigration: 1789–1814*. Paris: Perrin, 2007.

———. *Madame de Staël*. 1983. Paris: Perrin, 2011.

———. *Necker ou la faillite de la vertu*. Paris: Perrin, 2004.

Dixon, Sergine. *Germaine de Staël, Daughter of the Enlightenment: The Writer and Her Turbulent Era*. Amherst, NY: Humanity Books, 2007.

Domenech, Jacques. *L'Ethique des lumières, les fondements de la morale dans la philosophie française du XVIIIème siècle*. Paris: Vrin, 1989.

Dommanget, Maurice. *Babeuf et la conjuration des Egaux*. Paris: Lefevre, 1972.

Du Bus, Charles. *Stanislas de Clermont-Tonnerre et l'échec de la révolution monarchique, (1757–1792)*. Paris: Alcan, 1931.

Duffy, Michael. *The Younger Pitt*. Harlow, UK: Longman, 2000.

Dumont, Etienne. *Souvenirs sur Mirabeau et sur les deux premières assemblées législatives*. Paris: PUF, 1951.

Dunant, Emile, ed. *Les relations diplomatiques de la France et de la République helvétique*. Basel: A. Geering, 1901.

Dunn, John. *The Cunning of Unreason: Making Sense of Politics*. London: Harper Collins, 2000.

———, ed. *Democracy: The Unfinished Journey, 508 BC to 1993 AD*. Oxford: Oxford University Press, 1992.

Egnell, Erik. *Une femme en politique, Germaine de Staël*. Paris: Editions de Fallois, 2013.

Egret, Jean. *Necker, ministre de Louis XVI, (1776–1790)*. Paris: Champion, 1975.

———. *La pré-révolution française, (1787–1788)*. Paris: PUF, 1962.

———. *La révolution des notables: Mounier et les monarchiens, 1789*. Paris: Colin, 1950.

Ehrman, John. *The Younger Pitt*. 1969. London: Constable, 1996.

Englund, Steven. *Napoleon: A Political Life*. Cambridge, MA: Harvard University Press, 2005.

Escarpit, Robert. *L'Angleterre dans l'oeuvre de Mme de Staël*. Paris: Didier, 1954.

Evans, Eric J. *William Pitt the Younger*. London: Routledge, 1999.

Fairweather, Maria. *Madame de Staël*. London: Constable & Robinson, 2005.

Farnum, Dorothy. *The Dutch Divinity: A Biography of Madame de Charrière, 1740–1805*. London: Jarrolds, 1959.

Favier, Frank. *Bernadotte, un maréchal de l'empire sur le thrône de Suède*. Paris: Ellipses, 2010.

Fleischacker, Samuel. *A Third Concept of Liberty: Judgment and Freedom in Kant and Adam Smith*. Princeton, NJ: Princeton University Press, 1999.

Fontana, Biancamaria. *Benjamin Constant and the Post-Revolutionary Mind*. New Haven, CT: Yale University Press, 1991.

———. "Les deux faces du despotisme: gloire, ambition et personnalisation de la politique chez Germaine de Staël." In *Despotes et despotismes dans les oeuvres du Groupe de Coppet. Cahiers Staëliens*, no. 65 (November 2015).

———. *Du boudoir à la Révolution, Laclos et les Liaisons dangereuses dans leur siècle*. Marseilles: Agone, 2013.

———, ed. *The invention of the Modern Republic*. Cambridge: Cambridge University Press, 1994.

———. "Madame de Staël, le gouvernement des passions et la Révolution française." In *Actes du IV Colloque de Coppet*, pp. 175–81. Lausanne: Jean Touzot, 1988.

———. *Montaigne's Politics: Authority and Governance in the "Essais"*. Princeton, NJ: Princeton University Press, 2008.

———. "Mon triste écrit sur la Reine: Germaine de Staël et le fantôme de la révolution." *CahiersStaëliens*, n.s., no. 61 (2010–11): 197–208.

———. "The Political Passions of Other Nations, National Choices and the European Order in the Writings of Germaine de Staël." In *The Political Culture of the Sister Republics, 1794–1806: France, the Netherlands, Switzerland and Italy*, ed. J. Oddens, M. Rutjes, and E. Jacobs, pp. 33–40. Amsterdam: Amsterdam University Press, 2015.

Fouché, Joseph. *Mémoires*. 1824. Ed. Louis Madelin, 1945. Paris: Perrin, 2015.

Frayssinet, Marc. *Les idées politiques des Girondins*. Toulouse: Vialelle et Perry, 1903.

Fumaroli, Marc. *L'Etat culturel, une religion moderne*. Paris: Editions de Fallois, 1995.

Furet, François. *Penser la Révolution française*. Paris: Gallimard, 1977.

———. *La Révolution française, de Turgot à Jules Ferry (1770–1880)*. Paris: Gallimard, 2007.

———, ed. *Terminer la Révolution: Mounier et Barnave dans la révolution française*. Grenoble: Presses de l'Université de Grenoble, 1990.

Furet, François, and Ran Halévi. *La Monarchie républicaine, La Constitution de 1791*. Paris: Fayard, 1996.

————, eds. *Orateurs de la Révolution française.* Vol. 1, *Les Constituants.* Paris: Gallimard, 1989.

Furet, François, Jacques Julliard, and Pierre Rosanvallon. *La république du centre, la fin de l'exception française.* Paris: Calmann-Levy, 1988.

Furet, François, and Mona Ozouf, eds. *A Critical Dictionary of the French Revolution.* Cambridge, MA: Harvard University Press, 1989.

————. *Dictionnaire critique de la Révolution française.* Paris: Flammarion, 1988.

————. *La Gironde et les Girondins.* Paris: Payot, 1991.

Gautherot, Gustave. *Les relations franco-helvétiques de 1789 à 1792.* Paris: Champion, 1908.

Gildea, Robert. *Children of the Revolution: The French 1799–1914.* London: Penguin, 2009.

Girault de Coursac, Paul and Pierrette. *Le Sécret de la Reine: La politique personnelle de Marie-Antoinette pendant la Révolution.* Paris: François-Xavier de Guibert, 1996.

Godechot, Jacques. *Les constitutions de la France depuis 1789.* Paris: Flammarion, 1979.

————. *La grande nation.* Paris: Flammarion, 1983.

Goetz-Bernstein, H.-A. *La politique extérieure de Brissot et des Girondins.* Paris: Hachette, 1912.

Goodden, Angelica. *Madame de Staël: The Dangerous Exile.* Oxford: Oxford University Press, 2008.

Goodman, Dena, and Kathleen Wellman, eds. *The Enlightenment.* Problems in European Civilization. Boston: Wadsworth, Cengage Learning, 2004.

Grange, Henri. *Benjamin Constant amoureux et républicain, 1795–1799.* Paris: Les Belles Lettres, 2004.

————. *Les idées de Necker.* Paris: Klincksieck, 1974.

Grunberg, Gérard. *Napoléon Bonaparte, le noir génie.* Paris: Editions du CNRS, 2015.

Gueniffey, Patrice. *Bonaparte: (1769–1802).* Paris: Gallimard, 2013.

————. *Le dix-huit brumaire: l'épilogue de la révolution française, 9–10 novembre 1799.* Paris: Gallimard, 2008.

————. *Le nombre et la raison: la Révolution française et les élections.* Preface by François Furet. Paris: Ecole des hautes études en sciences sociales, 1993.

Guillemin, Henri. *Benjamin Constant muscadin: 1795–1798.* Paris: Gallimard, 1958.

————. *Mme de Staël et Napoléon, ou Germaine et le caïd ingrat.* 1966. Paris: Seuil, 1987.

Gusdorf, Georges. *La conscience révolutionnaire: les idéologues.* Paris: Payot, 1978.

Gwynne, G. E. *Madame de Staël et la révolution française: politique, philosophie, littérature*. Paris: Nizet, 1969.

Hague, William. *William Pitt the Younger, a Biography*. London: Harper, 2005.

Hamilton, Paul. *Realpoetik: European Romanticism and Literary Politics*. Oxford: Oxford University Press, 2013.

Hampson, Norman. *Prelude to Terror*. Oxford: Oxford University Press, 1988.

Harris, Robert D. *Necker: Reform Statesman of the Ancien Régime*. Berkeley: University of California Press, 1979.

Haussonville, comte Othenin de, ed. *Madame de Staël et Monsieur Necker, d'après leur correspondance inédite*. Paris: Calmann-Lévy, 1925.

Hawkins, Richmond Laurin. *Mme de Staël and the United States*. 1930. New York: Kraus Reprints, 1966.

Haydon, Colin, and William Doyle, eds. *Robespierre*. Cambridge: Cambridge University Press, 2006.

Hennessy, Peter. *The Prime Minister: The Office and Its Holders since 1945*. London: Palgrave Macmillan, 2001.

Henning, Ian Allan. *L'Allemagne de Mme de Staël et la polémique romantique: première fortune de l'ouvrage en France et en Allemagne, 1814–1830*. Geneva: Slatkine, 1975.

Herold, J. Christopher. *Mistress to an Age: A Life of Mme de Staël*. New York: Bobbs-Merrill, 1958.

Hippeau C., and Bernard Jolibet, eds. *L'instruction publique en France pendant la révolution: discours et rapports de Mirabeau, Talleyrand-Perigord, Condorcet, Lanthenas, Romme, Le Peletier de Saint-Fargeau, Cales, Lakanal, Daunou et Fourcroy*. Paris: Klincksieck, 1990.

Hofmann, Etienne. *Les Principes de Politique de Benjamin Constant, la genèse d'une oeuvre*. 2 vols. Geneva: Droz, 1980.

Holmes, Stephen. *Benjamin Constant and the Making of Modern Liberalism*. New Haven, CT: Yale University Press, 1984.

Hont, Istvan. *Jealousy of Trade: International Competition and the Nation-State in Historical Perspective*. Cambridge, MA: Belknap Press of Harvard University Press, 2005.

Hume, David. *Essays, Moral, Political and Literary*. Ed. Eugene F. Miller. Indianapolis, IN: Liberty Classics, 1985.

Hunt, Lynn. *Politics, Culture and Class in the French Revolution*. Berkeley: University of California Press, 1984.

Isbell, John. "Madame de Staël, Ministre de la Guerre? Les discours de Narbonne devant l'Assemblée législative." *Annales Historiques de la Révolution française* 307, no. 1 (1997): 93–104.

d'Ivernois, Francis. *Reflections on the War. In Response to the Reflections on Peace addressed to Mr Pitt and the French Nation*. Trans. from the original French. London, June 1795.

Jainchill, Andrew. *Reimagining Politics after Terror: The Republican Origins of French Liberalism.* Ithaca, NY: Cornell University Press, 2008.

Jasinski, Béatrice W. "Constant et le cercle constitutionnel." In *Benjamin Constant et la révolution française, 1789–1799,* ed. Dominique Verray and Anne-Lise Delacrétaz, pp. 119–49. Geneva: Droz, 1989.

———. *L'engagement de Benjamin Constant, amour et politique (1794–1796).* Paris: Minard, 1971.

———. "Madame de Staël, l'Angleterre de 1813–1814 et les 'Considérations sur la Révolution française.'" *Revue d'Histoire littéraire de la France,* no. 1 (January–March 1966):12–24.

Jaume, Lucien, ed. *Coppet, Creuset de l'esprit libéral.* Colloque 1998., Aix: Presses Universitaires d'Aix-Marseille, 2000.

———. *Le discours Jacobin et la démocratie.* Paris: Fayard, 1989.

Jefferson, Ann. *Genius in France: An Idea and Its Uses.* Princeton, NJ:, Princeton University Press, 2014.

Jenkins, Jeremy. *Revolution and the Republic: A History of Political Thought in France since the Eighteenth Century.* Oxford: Oxford University Press, 2011.

Jordan, David P. *The King's Trial: The French Revolution vs. Louis XVI.* Berkeley: University of California Press, 1979.

Jupp, Peter. *Lord Grenville: 1759–1834.* Oxford: Clarendon Press, 1985.

Kale, Steven. *French Salons: High Society and Political Sociability from the Old Regime to the Revolution of 1848.* Baltimore: Johns Hopkins University Press, 2004.

Karmin, Otto, ed. "Une lettre inédite de Sir Francis d'Ivernois sur Mme de Staël." *Bulletin de l'Institut national genevois* 42 (1914).

———. *Sir Francis d'Ivernois: 1757–1842: sa vie, son oeuvre et son temps.* Geneva: Revue historique de la révolution française et de l'Empire, 1820.

Kates, Gary. *The Cercle Social, the Girondins, and the French Revolution.* Princeton, NJ: Princeton University Press, 1985.

Kelly, Linda. *Juniper Hall, an English Refuge from the French Revolution.* London: Weidenfeld and Nicolson, 1991.

Kerchove, Arnold de. *Une amie de Benjamin Constant: Belle de Charrière.* Paris: Editions de la nouvelle revue critique, 1937.

Kloocke, Kurt. *Benjamin Constant, une biographie intellectuelle.* Geneva: Droz, 1984.

Knott, Sarah, and Barbara Taylor, eds. *Women, Gender and Enlightenment.* Houndmills, Basingstoke, Hampshire: Palgrave Macmillan, 2005.

Kondratieva, Tamara. *Bolcheviks et jacobins: itinéraire des analogies.* Paris: Payot, 1989.

Koselleck, Reinhart. *Critique and Crisis: Enlightenment and the Pathogenesis of Modern Society.* Cambridge, MA: MIT Press, 1988.

Koyré, Alexandre. *Etudes newtoniennes.* Paris: Gallimard, 1968.

Lacretelle, Charles de. *Dix années d'épreuves pendant la Révolution, mémoires*. Paris: Tallandier, 2011.

Lamartine, Alphonse de. *Histoire des Girondins*. 1847–48. Ed. Mona Ozouf. 2 vols. Paris: Bouquins, 2014.

Larg, David Glass. *Madame de Staël, la seconde vie (1800–1807)*. Paris: Champion, 1928.

Laros, Katherine Elisabeth. *Madame de Staël as a Critic of Goethe and Schiller*. Whitefish, MT: Kessinger Publishing, 2008.

La Tour du Pin, Madame de. *Mémoires, 1778–1815*. Paris: Mercure de France, 1979.

Latreille, Albert. *L'oeuvre militaire de la révolution, l'armée et la nation à la fin de l'ancien régime: les derniers ministres de la guerre de la monarchie*. Paris: Chapelot, 1914.

Le Brun, Annie. *Les Châteaux de la subversion*. Paris: Gallimard, 1982.

Leclercq, Henri. *Feuillants et Girondins (août 1791–20 avril 1792)*. Paris: Librairie Letouzey, 1940.

Lefebvre, Georges. *La France sous le Directoire, (1795–1799)*. Edition intégrale du cours "Le Directoire," ed. Jean René Suratteau. Paris: Editions sociales, 1977.

Lemay, Edna H., and Alison Patrick, eds. *Revolutionaries at Work: The Constituent Assembly 1789–1791*. Oxford: Voltaire Foundation, 1996.

Lemay, Edna H., and Mona Ozouf, eds. *Dictionnaire des législateurs, 1791–1792*. Ferney-Voltaire: Centre international d'études du XVIIIème siècle, 2007.

Lenôtre, Georges. *La captivité et la mort de Marie-Antoinette: les Feuillants, le Temple, la conciergerie: d'après des relations des témoins oculaires et des documents inédits*. Paris: Perrin, 1928.

Lentz, Thierry. *Le congrès de Vienne, une refondation de l'Europe 1814–1815*. Paris: Perrin, 2013.

———. *Le 18 brumaire: les coups d'état de Napoléon Bonaparte (novembre–décembre 1799)*. Paris: Picollec, 1997.

———. *Napoléon et l'Europe: regards sur une politique*. Paris: Fayard, 2005.

Lévy, Maurice. *Le roman 'gothique' anglais, 1764–1824*. Paris: Albin Michel, 1995.

Lezay-Marnesia, Adrien. *Lettre à un suisse sur la nouvelle constitution helvétique: précédée de cette constitution*. Paris: Impr. Roederer, an VI (1798).

Lilti, Antoine. *Figures publiques: l'invention de la célébrité, 1750–1850*. Paris: Fayard, 2014.

———. *Le monde des salons, sociabilité et mondanité à Paris au XVIIIème siècle*. Paris: Fayard, 2005.

Linton, Marisa. *Choosing Terror: Virtue, Friendship and Authenticity in the French Revolution*. Oxford: Oxford University Press, 2013.

Lotterie, Florence, and Georges Poisson, eds. *Jean-Jacques Rousseau devant Coppet*. Geneva: Slatkine, 2012.

Lucas, Colin, ed. *The French Revolution and the Formation of Modern Political Culture*. Vol. 2, *The Political Culture of the French Revolution*. Oxford: Pergamon Press, 1988.

Luttrell, Barbara. *Mirabeau*. New York: Harvester Press, 1990.

Mackintosh, James. *Vindiciae Gallicae: defence of the French Revolution*. 1791. Critical edition. London: Palgrave/MacMillan, 2008.

Manin, Bernard. "Saint-Just, la logique de la terreur." *Libre*, no. 6 (1979): 165–233.

Martucci, Roberto. *L'Ossessione costituente: forma di governo e costituzione nella rivoluzione francese*. Bologna: Il Mulino, 2001.

Mascelli Migliorini, Luigi. *Napoléon*. Paris: Perrin, 2001.

Mathiez, Albert. *Girondins et Montagnards*. Paris: Firmin Didot, 1930.

Matucci, Mario, ed. *Gli 'idéologues' e la rivoluzione: Atti del Colloquio Internazionale di Grosseto*, 1989. Pisa:, Pacini, 1991.

Mauduit, Xavier. *L'Homme qui voulait tout: Napoléon, le faste et la propagande*. Paris: Editions Autrement, 2015.

Mauzi, Robert. *L'idée du bonheur dans la littérature et la pensée française au XVIIIème siècle*. 1979. Paris: Albin Michel, 1994.

Melchior-Bonnet, Bernardine. *Les Girondins*. Paris: Tallandier, 1989.

Meyer, Michel. *Le philosophe et les passions*. Paris: Livre de poche, 1991.

Michelet, Jules. *Histoire de la révolution française*. 2 vols. Paris: Robert Laffont, 1979.

Michon, Georges. *Histoire du parti feuillant: Adrien Duport*. Paris: Payot, 1924.

Minois, Georges. *Histoire de la célébrité, les trompettes de la renommée*. Paris: Perrin, 2012.

Mitchell, C. J. *The French Legislative Assembly of 1791*. Leiden: E. J. Brill, 1988.

———. "Political Divisions within the Legislative Assembly of 1791." *French Historical Studies* 13, no. 3 (Spring 1984): 356–89.

Mitchell, Leslie G. *Charles James Fox and the Disintegration of the Whig Party:1782–1794*. London: Oxford University Press, 1971.

———. *The Whig World, 1760–1837*. London: Hambeldon Continuum, 2005.

Montesquieu, Charles-Louis de Secondat de. *The Spirit of the Laws*. Ed. A. Cohler, B. Miller, and H. Stone. Cambridge: Cambridge University Press, 1989.

Moravia, Sergio. *Il pensiero degli idéologues (1780–1815)*. Florence: La Nuova Italia, 1974.

———. *Il tramonto dell'Illuminismo*. Bari: Laterza, 1968. Reprint, 1986.

Mori, Jennifer. *William Pitt and the French Revolution, 1785–1795*. Edinburgh: Keele University Press, 1997.

Morris, Gouverneur. *Journal (1789–1792)*. Ed. Anne Cary-Morris and Ernest Pariset. Paris: Mercure de France, 2002.

Morrissey, Robert. *Napoléon et l'heritage de la gloire*. Paris: PUF, 2010.

Mousnier, Roland. *Les Institutions de la France sous la monarchie absolue, 1598–1789*. 2 vols. Paris: PUF, 2005.

Mousson-Lestang, Jean-Pierre. *Histoire de la Suède*. Paris: Hatier, 1995.

Munteano, Basil. *Les idées politiques de Madame de Staël et la constitution de l'an III*. Paris: Les Belles Lettres, 1931.

Naya, Emmanuel, and Anne-Pascale Pouey, eds. *Eloge de la médiocrité: le juste milieu à la Renaissance*. Paris: Editions Rue d'Ulm, 2005.

Necker, Jacques. *Compte rendu au roy*. 1781. Preface by Léonard Burnand. Geneva: Slatkine Reprints, 2005.

———. *De la révolution française*. 4 vols. Paris: J. Drisonnier, 1796.

———. *Dernières vues de politique et de finance offertes à la nation française*. Paris: An X (1802).

———. *Du pouvoir exécutif dans les grands états*. 2 vols. Paris, 1792. English translation: *On Executive Power in Large States*. 2 vols. London, 1792.

———. *Réflexions philosophiques sur l'égalité*. Ed. Jean-Fabien Spitz. Paris: Les Belles Lettres, 2005.

Nicolson, Harold. *Benjamin Constant*. London: Constable, 1948.

Nordmann, Claude J. *Gustave III, un démocrate couronné*. Lille: Presses Universitaires de Lille, 1986.

O'Gorman, Francis. *The Whig Party and the French Revolution*. London: Macmillan, 1967.

"Oraison funèbre de M. de Mirabeau, prononcée par M. l'abbé Serutti," suivi du discours de M. l'évêque d'Autun, 4 avril 1791. Paris: Imprimerie Labarre, 1791.

Ozouf, Mona. "De Thermidor à Brumaire: le discours de la Révolution sur elle même." *Revue historique*, no. 243 (1970): 31–66.

———. *L'Homme régénéré: essais sur la Révolution française*. Paris: Gallimard, 1989.

———. *Les mots des femmes: essai sur la singularité française*. Paris: Fayard, 1995.

———. "Le Panthéon." In *Les lieux de mémoire*, ed. Pierre Nora, 1:139–66. Paris: Gallimard, 1984.

———. *Varennes, la mort de la royauté*. Paris: Gallimard, 2005.

Pallain, Georges, ed. *Correspondance diplomatique de Talleyrand*. 4 vols. Paris: Plon; London: Bentley; Leipzig: Brockhouse, 1889–91.

Palmer, R .R. *Twelve Who Ruled: The Year of the Terror*. 1941. Introd. by Isser Woloch. Princeton, NJ: Princeton University Press, 2005.

Pange, comtesse Jean de. *Auguste-Guillaume Schlegel et Madame de Staël*. Paris: Editions Albert, 1938.

———. *Monsieur de Staël*. Paris: Editions des portiques, 1931.

Pasquino, Pasquale. *Sieyès et l'invention de la constitution en France.* Paris: O. Jacob, 1998.

Patrick, Alison. *The Men of the First French Republic: Political Arguments in the National Convention of 1792.* Baltimore: Johns Hopkins University Press, 1972.

Perrochon, Henri. *Les sources suisses de la religion de Madame de Staël.* Paris: Klincksieck, 1970.

Petitau, Natalie. *Napoléon Bonaparte, la nation incarnée.* Paris: Colin, 2015.

Pettit, Philip. *Republicanism: A Theory of Freedom and Government.* Oxford: Oxford University Press, 1999.

Picavet, François. *Les idéologues: essai sur l'histoire des idées et des théories scientifiques, philosophiques, religieuses etc. en France depuis 1789.* Paris: Alcan, 1891.

Pitt, William. *The War Speeches of William Pitt the Younger.* Ed. R.Coupland. Oxford: Clarendon Press, 1940.

Poniatowski, Michel. *Talleyrand et le Directoire 1796–1800.* Paris: Perrin, 1982.

Popkin, Jeremy D. *The Right Wing Press in France, 1792–1800.* Chapel Hill: University of North Carolina Press, 1980.

Poulet, Georges. "Madame de Staël." In *Etudes sur le temps humain/4,* pp. 193–212. Paris: Plon, 1964.

Price, Munro. *The Fall of the French Monarchy: Louis XVI, Marie Antoinette and the Baron de Breteuil.* London: Macmillan, 2002.

Proschwitz, Gunnar von, ed. *Gustav III par ses lettres.* Stockholm: Touzot, 1986.

Quinet, Edgar. *La révolution.* Preface by Claude Lefort. 2 vols. Paris: Belin, 1987.

Reddy, William M. *The Navigation of Feeling: A Framework for the History of Emotions.* Cambridge: Cambridge University Press, 2001.

Reeder, John, ed. *On Moral Sentiments: Contemporary Responses to Adam Smith.* Bristol: Thoemmes Press, 1997.

Roberts, Michael. *The Whig Party, 1807–1812.* London: Cass, 1965.

Robespierre, Maximilien de. *Discours et rapports à la Convention.* Ed. Marc Bouloiseau. Paris: Union générale d'éditions, 1988.

Roland, Manon. *Mémoires de Mme Roland.* Ed. Paul de Roux. Paris: Mercure de France, 1966. Reprint, 1986.

Rosanvallon, Pierre. *La Monarchie impossible: Les Chartes de 1814 et 1830.* Paris: Fayard, 1994.

Rose, Robert Barrie. *Gracchus Babeuf: The First Revolutionary Communist.* London: Arnold, 1978.

Rosenblatt, Helena. *Liberal Values, Benjamin Constant and the Politics of Religion.* Cambridge: Cambridge University Press, 2008.

Schroeder, Paul W. *The Transformation of European Politics, 1763–1848.* Oxford: Clarendon Press, 1994.

Scott, Samuel. *The Response of the Royal Army to the French Revolution.* Oxford: Clarendon Press, 1978.

Scurr, Ruth. *Fatal Purity: Robespierre and the French Revolution.* New York: Henry Holt, 2006.

Serna, Pierre. *La République des girouettes, 1789–1815 et au delà: une anomalie politique, la France de l'extrême centre.* Seyssel: Champ Vallon, 2005.

———. "Le retour du refoulé, ou l'histoire de la révolution anglaise à l'ordre du jour de la crise du Directoire." In *La Révolution, 1789–1871,* ed. Philippe Bourdin, pp. 213–40. Clermont Ferrant: Université Blaise Pascal, 2008.

Seth, Catriona, ed. *Imaginaires gothiques, aux sources du roman noir français.* Paris: Desjonquères, 2010.

Skinner, Quentin. *Liberty before Liberalism.* Cambridge: Cambridge University Press, 1998.

Smith, Adam. *The Theory of Moral Sentiments.* 1759. Ed. D. D. Raphael and A. L. Macfie. Oxford: Clarendon Press, 1991.

Soboul, Albert, ed. *Le procès de Louis XVI.* Collection archives. Paris: Gallimard-Julliard, 1973.

Söderhjelm, Alma. *Marie Antionette et Barnave, Correspondance secrete (juillet 1791–janvier 1792).* Paris: Colin, 1934.

Sonenscher, Michael. *Before the Deluge: Public Debt, Inequality, and the Intellectual Origins of the French Revolution.* Princeton, NJ: Princeton University Press, 2007.

———. *Sans-Culottes: An Eighteenth-Century Emblem in the French Revolution.* Princeton, NJ: Princeton University Press, 2008.

Souriau, Maurice. *Les idées morales de Madame de Staël.* Paris, Bloud, 1910.

Staël-Holstein, Erik-Magnus de. *Correspondance diplomatique.* 1783–99. Ed. L. Leouzon Le Duc. Paris: Hachette, 1881.

Staum, Martin S. *Minerva's Message: Stabilizing the French Revolution.* Montreal: McGill-Queen's University Press, 1996.

Szmurlo, Karyna, ed. *Germaine de Staël: Forging a Politics of Mediation.* Oxford: Voltaire Foundation 2011.

Tackett, Timothy. *Becoming a Revolutionary: The Deputies of the French National Assembly and the Emergence of Revolutionary Culture (1789–1790).* Princeton, NJ: Princeton University Press, 1996.

———. *Religion, Revolution, and Regional Culture in Eighteenth-Century France: The Ecclesiastical Oath of 1791.* Princeton, NJ: Princeton University Press, 1986.

———. *When the King Took Flight.* Cambridge, MA: Harvard University Press, 2003.

Takeda, Chinatsu, ed. *Les idéologues et le groupe de Coppet.* Paris: Picard, 2003.

Tardieu de Maleissye, Aristarque-Marie. *Observations sur l'ouvrage de Mme de Staël intitulé: Considérations sur la Révolution.* Paris: Fonvielle, 1822.

Thompson, Eric. *Popular Sovereignty and the French Constituent Assembly, 1789–1791.* Manchester: Manchester University Press, 1952.

Tierchant, Hélène. *Hommes de la Gironde, ou la liberté éclairée.* Bordeaux: Dossiers d'Aquitaine, 1993.

Tillier, Anton von. *Histoire de la république helvétique: depuis sa fondation en 1798 jusqu'à sa dissolution en 1803.* Trans. from the German. Paris: A. Cherbuliez, 1846.

Tombs, Robert. *France, 1814–1914.* London: Longman, 1996.

Travers, Emeric. *Benjamin Constant, les principes et l'histoire.* Preface by Philippe Raynaud. Paris: Champion, 2005.

Troper, Michel. *La séparation des pouvoirs dans l'histoire constitutionnelle française.* Preface by Charles Eisenmann, Paris: Librairie générale de droit et de jurisprudence, 1973.

———. *Terminer la Révolution: la Constitution de 1795.* Paris: Fayard, 2006.

Tulard, Jean, ed. *La Contre-révolution, origines, histoire, postérité.* Paris: Perrin, 1990.

———. *Le 18 Brumaire. Comment Terminer la Révolution.* Paris: Perrin, 1999.

———. *Le grand empire, 1804–1815.* 1982. Paris: Albin Michel, 2009.

———. *Les Thermidoriens.* Paris: Fayard, 2005.

Vandal, Albert. *L'avènement de Bonaparte.* 2 vols. Paris: Plon-Nourrit, 1902.

Vovelle, Michel. *La chute de la monarchie (1787–1792).* Nouvelle histoire de la France contemporaine, vol. 1. Paris: Seuil, 1972.

Walton, Charles. *Policing Public Opinion in the French Revolution: The Culture of Calumny and the Problem of Free Speech.* Oxford: Oxford University Press, 2009.

Walzer Michael, ed. *Regicide and Revolution: Speeches at the Trial of Louis XVI.* Cambridge: Cambridge University Press, 1974.

Waresquiel, Emmanuel de. *Talleyrand, le prince immobile.* Paris: Fayard, 2003.

Welch, Cheryl B. *Liberty and Utility: The French Ideologues and the Transformation of Liberalism.* New York: Columbia University Press, 1984.

Wick, Daniel L. *A Conspiracy of Well-Intentioned Men: The Society of Thirty and the French Revolution.* New York: Garland Publishing, 1987.

Wilson, Robert McNair. *Germaine de Staël, the Woman of Affairs.* London: Eyre & Spottiswoode, 1931.

Winegarten, Renée. *Germaine de Staël & Benjamin Constant: A Dual Biography.* New Haven, CT: Yale University Press, 2008.

Winock, Michel. *L'échec au roi (1791–1792)*. Paris: Olivier Orban, 1990.
———. *Madame de Staël*. Paris: Fayard, 2010.
Wood, Dennis. *Benjamin Constant: A Biography*. London, Routledge, 1993.
Woolf, Stuart. *Napoleon's Integration of Europe*. London, Routledge, 1991.

Index